Working Memory and Human Cognition

JOHN T. E. RICHARDSON

RANDALL W. ENGLE

LYNN HASHER

ROBERT H. LOGIE

ELLEN R. STOLTZFUS

ROSE T. ZACKS

New York   Oxford

OXFORD UNIVERSITY PRESS

1996

Oxford University Press

Oxford New York
Athens Auckland Bangkok Bombay
Calcutta Cape Town Dar es Salaam Delhi
Florence Hong Kong Istanbul Karachi
Kuala Lumpur Madras Madrid Melbourne
Mexico City Nairobi Paris Singapore
Taipei Tokyo Toronto

and associated companies in
Berlin Ibadan

Copyright © 1996 by Oxford University Press, Inc.

Published by Oxford University Press, Inc.,
198 Madison Avenue, New York, New York 10016

Library of Congress Cataloging-in-Publication Data
Working memory and human cognition / John T. E. Richardson . . . [et. al.].
p. cm. — (Counterpoints)
Includes bibliographical references and index.
ISBN 0-19-510099-9; 0-19-510100-6 (pbk)
1. Memory. 2. Memory—Age factors. 3. Cognition—Age factors.
I. Richardson, John T. E. II. Series: Counterpoints (Oxford University Press)
BF371.W67 1996
153.1'3—dc20   95-23830

2 4 6 8 9 7 5 3 1

Printed in the United States of America
on acid-free paper

Preface

The purpose of this contribution to the "Counterpoints" series is to compare and contrast different conceptions of working memory. This is one of the most important notions to have informed cognitive psychology over the last 20 years or so, and yet it has been used in a wide variety of ways. This, in part, is undoubtedly because contemporary usage of the phrase "working memory" encapsulates various themes that have appeared at different points in the history of research into human memory and cognition. In Chapter 2, Robert Logie describes in detail these different "ages" of working memory, which he summarizes in the following way:

> working memory as contemplation
> working memory as primary memory
> working memory as short-term memory
> working memory as processor
> working memory as a constraint on language comprehension
> working memory as activation, attention, and expertise
> working memory as multiple components.

In part, however, this is also because the concept of working memory has been taken on board by theorists with different agendas and different objectives in their research. This is well illustrated by the three major contributions to the present volume. Robert Logie devotes the bulk of his chapter to an extended argument that is firmly within the tradition of his seventh "age": that is, the conception of working memory as consisting of a number of discrete components, each of which has a characteristic set of functions. This conception was first articulated by Baddeley and Hitch in

1974, but their original account has undergone significant modification in the intervening years, and Logie himself has been closely involved in this process. Logie postulates the existence of three particular components that are thought to be responsible for temporary verbal storage, for temporary visuospatial storage, and for the central coordination of both processing and storage, including the retrieval of information from long-term memory. Logie is explicit that this formulation contradicts many other accounts of working memory—including those described in the two subsequent chapters—that conceptualize working memory as a single processing system.

The research that is described in Chapter 3 by Ellen Stoltzfus, Lynn Hasher, and Rose Zacks is based upon somewhat different aims and methods. It originated in previous attempts by these researchers to understand the apparent decline in mental resources with advancing age. This motivated a program of experiments on inference formation and semantic priming in old and young adults, and the results led in turn to a focus on the inhibitory processes that control the entrance of information into working memory and that function to up-date the contents of working memory by deleting information no longer relevant to the task in hand. The resulting account is presented by Stoltzfus and her colleagues as a fairly general theoretical framework for understanding how working memory affects performance across a broad range of cognitive tasks and a variety of subject populations.

A different account is presented in Chapter 4 by Randall Engle. This research was originally predicated upon the assumption that working memory constituted a general processing resource whose capacity varied from one individual to another. However, in Engle's account working memory is simply equated with the set of units in long-term memory whose activation exceeds a particular threshold, and it does not constitute a functionally separate component or buffer store. The theory originated in correlational studies of performance in complex memory-span tasks and was then developed through experimental research on the speeded recognition of sentences. Engle's present account investigates individual differences in a broader range of tasks that demand the retrieval of information from both long-term and short-term memory. Results indicate that working-memory capacity affects retrieval based upon controlled effortful search but not retrieval based upon automatic activation. Engle's conclusion (which converges both with that of Logie and with that of Stoltzfus and her colleagues) is that individual differences in working memory are tantamount to differences in attentional resources and lead to differences in the ability to inhibit or suppress irrelevant information in cognitive tasks.

This volume was originally conceived by Marc Marschark and developed through a symposium that he organized at the University of North Carolina at Greensboro, involving Patricia Carpenter, Randall Engle, Lynn Hasher, and Robert Logie. Because of other commitments, Patricia

Carpenter was unable to contribute to this volume, but we have tried to give a full and accurate account of the work carried out by her and her colleagues. I am grateful to Marc Marschark for inviting me to edit this volume and to the other contributors for their cooperation and support, and especially for their advice in preparing the introductory and concluding chapters.

Brunel University   J.T.E.R.
March 1995

Contents

CONTRIBUTORS, xi

1. Evolving Concepts of Working Memory, 3
John T. E. Richardson

   Early Concepts of Working Memory, 3
   Production-System Models, 6
   Associative-Network Models, 7
   Working Memory and Reading Comprehension, 9
   A General Resource or a Domain-Specific Resource?, 11
   Reading Comprehension and Working-Memory Capacity, 13
   The Role of Inhibitory Processes, 15
   Multicomponent Models of Working Memory, 17
   Conclusion, 23

2. The Seven Ages of Working Memory, 31
Robert H. Logie

   Age I: Working Memory as Contemplation, 32
   Age II: Working Memory as Primary Memory, 32
   Age III: Working Memory as Short-Term Memory, 33
   Age IV: Working Memory as Processor, 34
   Age V: Working Memory as a Constraint on Language
      Comprehension, 34
   Age VI: Working Memory as Activation, Attention, and
      Expertise, 37
   Age VII: Working Memory as Multiple Components, 40

Multiple Components and Dual-Task Performance, 41
The Model of Baddeley and Hitch, 48
The Multiple-Component Model: Gateway or Workspace?, 50
Working Memory as a Workspace, Not a Gateway, 55
Conclusion, 59

3. **Working Memory and Aging: Current Status of the Inhibitory View, 66**
Ellen R. Stoltzfus, Lynn Hasher, and Rose T. Zacks

Working Memory and the Limited-Capacity Assumption, 67
Individual Differences in Working-Memory Capacity, 68
Group Differences in Working-Memory Capacity Associated
    with Aging, 69
An Alternative View to Capacity, 70
Further Considerations and Future Directions, 77

4. **Working Memory and Retrieval: An Inhibition-Resource Approach, 89**
Randall W. Engle

Free Retrieval from Natural Categories, 92
Speeded Recognition of Simple Facts, 98
Issues in Explaining Individual Differences in Working-
    Memory Capacity, 108
An Inhibition-Resource Hypothesis of Working-Memory
    Capacity, 109
Conclusion, 116

5. **Evolving Issues in Working Memory, 120**
John T. E. Richardson

Working Memory and Long-Term Memory, 120
The Capacity of Working Memory, 122
Inhibitory Processes in Working Memory, 124
The Gateway Hypothesis, 127
A Single Component or a Complex System, 129
Reading Span and Memory Span, 131
A General Resource or a Domain-Specific Resource?, 134
Verbal and Visuospatial Working Memory, 136
The Phonological Loop, 137
The Visuospatial Scratchpad, 141
The Central Executive, 143
Conclusion, 147

AUTHOR INDEX, 155

SUBJECT INDEX, 161

Contributors

Randall W. Engle, Department of Psychology, University of South Carolina.

Lynn Hasher, Department of Psychology, Social and Health Sciences, Duke University, North Carolina.

Robert H. Logie, Department of Psychology, University of Aberdeen, UK.

John T. E. Richardson, Department of Human Sciences, Brunel University, UK.

Ellen R. Stoltzfus, Department of Psychology, Kenyon College, Ohio.

Rose T. Zacks, Department of Psychology, Michigan State University.

WORKING MEMORY AND HUMAN COGNITION

1

Evolving Concepts
of Working Memory

John T. E. Richardson

The expression "working memory" has come to denote a complex collection or family of theoretical constructs that overlap in various interesting ways but that lack any obvious defining thread or "core." To help readers to locate these various constructs within contemporary cognitive psychology, this introductory chapter describes the evolving applications of the term "working memory" in recent experimental research. This will help them to appreciate the broader historical perspective provided by Robert Logie in Chapter 2, and the different research paradigms and theoretical viewpoints adopted by Logie (Chapter 2), by Ellen Stoltzfus, Lynn Hasher, and Rose Zacks in Chapter 3, and by Randall Engle in Chapter 4. Each of these contributions to this book has a different starting point and a different research agenda, yet readers will identify a broad consensus emerging from their different analyses. In Chapter 5, I shall summarize the main issues that have divided researchers in this field and give an integrated account of what we have learned about working memory.

Early Concepts of Working Memory

As far as I have been able to ascertain, the expression "working memory" was first employed by Miller, Galanter, and Pribram (1960) in their book *Plans and the Structure of Behavior*. Their analysis of the organization and control of human actions is widely acknowledged to be a milestone in the early development of cognitive psychology, and it is interesting that working memory was assigned a central role in this account:

> We should not lose sight of the fact that something important does
> happen to a Plan when the decision is made to execute it. It is taken out
> of dead storage and placed in control of a segment of our information-
> processing capacity. . . . The parts of a Plan . . . being executed have
> special access to consciousness and special ways of being remembered
> that are necessary for coordinating parts of different Plans and for coor-
> dinating with the Plans of other people. When we have decided to exe-
> cute some particular Plan, it is probably put into some special state or
> place where it can be remembered while it is being executed. Particularly
> if it is a transient, temporary kind of Plan that will be used today and
> never again, we need some special place to store it. The special place may
> be on a sheet of paper. Or (who knows?) it may be somewhere in the
> frontal lobes of the brain. Without committing ourselves to any specific
> machinery, therefore, we should like to speak of the memory we use for
> the execution of our Plans as a kind of quick-access, "working memory."
> (p. 65)

In short, Miller and colleagues had in mind one particular component of the
human information-processing system that was implicated in the executive
control of cognition and behavior and also served as a form of short-term
storage. Its contents were assumed to be directly available to conscious
awareness. This conception is broadly consistent with the theoretical interpretations of working memory that are to be found in contemporary
research.

Moreover, although it could be augmented by external devices such as
notepads, Miller et al. (1960) were clearly seeking to characterize a part of
the cerebral apparatus responsible for intentional behavior. Much later on
in the book, it became clear that their somewhat flippant rhetorical question ("who knows?") had been merely an artful literary device. On the
basis of the findings of recent neurophysiological investigations, they put
forward an explicit proposal concerning the neuroanatomical locus of this
system:

> The frontal "association areas," sometimes referred to as "the organ of
> civilization," are intimately connected with the limbic systems to form
> the internal core of the forebrain. This most forward portion of the
> primate frontal lobe appears to us to serve as a "working memory" where
> Plans can be retained temporarily when they are being formed, or trans-
> formed, or executed. (p. 207; see also p. 200)

This proposal anticipated contemporary neuropsychological accounts of
the executive function of the frontal lobes to a quite remarkable extent
(see, e.g., Shallice, 1988, chap. 14; Shimamura, Janowsky, & Squire,
1991).

Nowadays, however, the early theorizing of Miller and colleagues is
mentioned rarely if at all in discussions of working memory. Most trace
the origins of the concept to a later publication by Atkinson and Shiffrin
(1968) that contained a detailed analysis concerning the structure and
functioning of human memory. This analysis postulated three major struc-

tural components, a sensory register, a short-term store, and a long-term store, and each of these had access to control processes such as coding procedures, rehearsal operations, and search strategies. Atkinson and Shiffrin speculated that the short-term store could be regarded as a "working memory" that received selected inputs from the sensory register and the long-term store (pp. 90, 92). They proposed that information could be maintained within this store by a control process that consisted of systematically rehearsing the last few items presented. This process was described as a "rehearsal buffer," although the maximal size of the buffer depended upon the extent to which the available capacity of the short-term store had to be shared with other control processes such as coding procedures or search strategies.

In their paper, Atkinson and Shiffrin did not appear to attach special importance to the working-memory component of the system, and they did not consider its possible contribution to tasks beyond the domain of learning and memory. Nevertheless, in a subsequent article, Atkinson and Shiffrin (1971) proposed that the flow of information through the short-term store and the subject's control of that flow of information were central to the system underlying human memory. They articulated their concept of working memory in the following manner:

> In our thinking we tend to equate the short-term store with "consciousness," that is, the thoughts and information of which we are currently aware can be considered part of the contents of the short-term store. . . . Because consciousness is equated with the short-term store and because control processes are centered in and act through it, the short-term store is considered a working memory: a system in which decisions are made, problems are solved and information flow is directed. (p. 83)

In short, Atkinson and Shiffrin regarded the operations of working memory not merely as being essential to the encoding, storage, and retrieval of information, but as being intrinsic to human cognition in all its forms.

Both the original account presented by Miller et al. (1960) and that offered by Atkinson and Shiffrin (1971) exemplified what Baddeley (1986) later defined as "the general concept of working memory": in other words, "the temporary storage of information that is being processed in any of a range of cognitive tasks" (p. 34). Within a further ten years, as Klapp, Marshburn, and Lester (1983) observed, Atkinson and Shiffrin's account of working memory based on conventional laboratory-based research into human learning and remembering became virtually taken for granted as a basis for textbook treatments of short-term memory in North America. Nevertheless, in the intervening period, the general concept of working memory had been elaborated by researchers with rather different traditions and objectives. Some were concerned with developing a general account of human knowledge representation based on production systems or associative networks; others were exploring individual differences in cognitive tasks such as reading.

Production-System Models

The interest in production rules as a formalism for representing knowledge stems from automata theory and the development of formal grammars. It has dominated research on expert systems, where these are sometimes described as "condition-action rules." Each rule consists of a set of conditions or premises, together with a set of actions or conclusions to be implemented or inferred if the relevant conditions hold. A production system contains a collection of rules, an interpreter that decides when and how to apply the rules, and a working memory that holds data, goals, and intermediate results (see Jackson, 1986, chap. 3).

Newell and Simon (1972) employed the broad architecture of production systems to develop an account of human problem solving. They postulated a short-term memory whose capacity was relatively limited, which served as a dynamic working memory for the production system, and whose contents were immediately available to the processes of the system. They commented that this conception was entirely consistent with the functional definition of short-term memory as the collection of information of which a subject was aware at any particular moment in time (p. 804; see also pp. 20, 30, 795). Elsewhere, Newell (1972, 1973a) proposed that this framework would provide a general analysis of the control processes responsible for the coding and storage of information in human memory. In this case, he claimed that the short-term memory served as a mental scratchpad that could essentially be identified with the notion of short-term memory prevalent within cognitive psychology. Nevertheless, he explicitly criticized the model presented by Atkinson and Shiffrin (1968) for failing to give a specific representation of the control processes that allowed the subjects to perform according to different mnemonic strategies. Newell (1973b) argued that this failure to specify the control structure underlying a specific task would inhibit the resolution of theoretical issues, and that production systems provided (at that point, at least) the only available model of human control processes.

Simple production-system models of human cognition employed a working memory containing a fixed number of "slots," each of which was capable of holding a single stimulus element. This was partly motivated by the early arguments of Miller (1956), who in his classic paper entitled "The Magical Number Seven, Plus or Minus Two" postulated that the capacity of immediate memory was limited to a particular number of items. Critics of production systems objected that they were only capable of simulating human behavior in a convincing way if the total number of "slots" available was increased far beyond any reasonable estimate of the immediate memory span (Anderson, 1983a, p. 14; Rumelhart & Norman, 1983). For instance, Ohlsson (1987) advanced a production-system model of logical reasoning that incorporated a working memory with a total capacity of about 75 elements. Nevertheless, Neches, Langley, and Klahr (1987) argued that a modest working memory was pragmatically well motivated because it reduced the problems involved in selecting the productions to be executed and in resolving conflicts among them. Conversely, storage demands can be reduced by incorporating devices for efficient conflict resolution, such as allowing productions to be executed in parallel (see Carpenter, Just, & Shell, 1990; Neches, 1987).

Newell (1972, 1973a) himself assumed that short-term memory contained a small number of symbolic expressions or "chunks," each of which could be a complex configuration of elements. Once again, this was prompted by the work of Miller (1956), who showed that in human beings the apparent memory span could be increased by grouping the items to be remembered into units or "chunks," attaching new names to these chunks, and then remembering the new names rather than the original items. Subsequent research suggested, however, that chunking and other devices for enhancing memory performance act to enrich the organizational structure of long-term memory rather than that of short-term memory (see Ericsson & Pennington, 1993). In addition, Anderson (1976, p. 99) attacked Newell's use of chunking as unprincipled and unrestricted and objected that his theory was essentially tantamount to allowing arbitrarily many slots in short-term memory. In fact, Newell (1972) even entertained the notion that short-term memory was indefinitely large but unreliable, so that with longer sequences of items there would be an increasing probability that elements would be lost, which would lead to an effective limit on storage capacity as opposed to an absolute limit.

Associative-Network Models

Another formalism for representing human knowledge is that of associative networks, which originated in graph theory. In the most general terms, a graph consists of a set of nodes, together with a set of links connecting them. A network is a graph in which the links are directed and labeled. In the case of "associative" or "semantic" networks, the nodes stand for concepts and the links stand for relationships among them (Findler, 1979). The earliest application of this approach to knowledge representation was the work of Quillian (1967, 1968), who simulated language understanding using a network that was based on dictionary-like definitions of English words. This system compared the meanings of arbitrary pairs of words by simultaneously searching along all possible paths from each of the nodes corresponding to the original words until a common node was reached. By analogy with the functioning of neural systems, this sort of process was characterized in terms of "activation" gradually spreading outwards from each concept through the network of associations. This notion was later elaborated by Collins and Loftus (1975) and by Anderson (1983b).

Quillian's model incorporated some interesting assumptions about the structural relationships among concepts and the process of memory search. The general formalism offered by associative networks is both perspicuous and flexible and permits the efficient retrieval of relevant information through the mechanism of spreading activation. Quillian himself proposed that the latter mechanism provided a plausible account of context effects and the resolution of ambiguities in the reading of narrative. Anderson (1972) and Rumelhart, Lindsay, and Norman (1972) subsequently put forward models of free recall consisting of an associative network among the list items and a short-term store containing a fixed number of words, as in the more general theory of memory advanced by Atkinson and Shiffrin (1968). In Anderson's account, the short-term store, though structurally distinct, consisted of the area or partition of long-term memory that was currently activated. Similarly, Rumelhart et al. (1972) proposed that the short-term store contained the associative links upon which the interpretative processes of long-term memory were working at any one time (see also Lindsay & Norman, 1972, pp. 426–429).

Quillian's associative network did provide a reasonable analysis of dictionary-like definitions, but it did not provide a convenient format in which to make explicit the constituent structure or the abstract content of the full range of declarative statements. Such a format is provided by the predicate calculus, in which sentences are represented as propositions consisting of a property (a "predicate" or "relation") that applies to one or more objects (or "arguments"). A particularly influential application of this approach was the "case grammar" developed by the linguist C. J. Fillmore (1968). In itself, however, this analysis does not specify the structural relations between the resulting representations. In a variety of theories developed during the early 1970s (e.g., Kintsch, 1972, 1974; Rumelhart et al., 1972; Schank, 1972), therefore, this problem was handled by embedding the propositional representations of individual statements as subgraphs in an associative network, thus employing the advantages of both formalisms.

One such theory was put forward as a model of memory for sentences by Anderson and Bower (1973). Like Anderson's (1972) account of free recall, the Anderson and Bower model incorporated a long-term store consisting of an associative network, together with a short-term store or working memory consisting of the area or partition of long-term memory that was currently activated. However, a distinctive feature of this account was that the working memory was not structurally separate from the long-term store, but was identified with the activated partition of that store. Moreover, on this account the storage capacity of working memory was limited, not by any specific number of "slots," but by the number of nodes within long-term memory that could be held in an active state at any one time (Anderson & Bower, p. 216). Similar proposals on the nature of short-term memory or working memory were presented by Cowan (1988, 1993) and by Cantor and Engle (1993), and these are discussed by Robert Logie in Chapter 2 and by Randall Engle in Chapter 4, respectively.

Anderson (1976) considered that an associative network provided the appropriate formalism for representing declarative knowledge about events and objects in the world, but that a different formalism was necessary to represent procedural knowledge about how to carry out skilled activities. For instance, the representation of information in his model of sentence memory depended upon the operation of a natural language parser containing syntactic rules that were not amenable to propositional analysis because they did not possess the constituent structure of propositions. Anderson argued that such procedures were best captured by production rules, and he presented a more complex theory concerned with Adaptive Control of Thought (ACT) that combined an associative-network model of declarative knowledge and a production-system model of procedural knowledge. However, these two models were integrated, insofar as the working memory whose contents were to be processed by the production rules was explicitly identified with the currently activated partition of the associative network.

The original theory of ACT was subsequently developed into a general analysis of cognitive architecture and a general theory of the acquisition of cognitive skills (Anderson, 1983a). More recently, it was augmented by procedures for the analysis of particular problem domains, based upon the assumption that cognition is adapted to the properties of the environment (Anderson, 1993). Nevertheless, each of these variants exploited the same general framework, in which working memory provided the means by which the production system operated as the interpreter of the associative network. The contents of working memory consisted of declarative knowledge that had been retrieved from the associative network or else deposited by encoding processes or by the action of production rules. New information encoded within working memory could activate associated facts in the associative network, or it could trigger procedural representations in the production system by matching their conditions (see Anderson, 1983a, pp. 19–20).

Working Memory and Reading Comprehension

One area in which these ideas proved especially influential was the study of reading. For instance, Kintsch and van Dijk (1978) set forth a model of text comprehension and production that included an associative-network theory of declarative knowledge, a working memory for building up semantic structures, and a set of semantic mapping rules for deriving the structure of a text. Kintsch and van Dijk had assumed that the working memory was a limited-capacity buffer akin to Atkinson and Shiffrin's (1968) short-term store, but they acknowledged that it could be regarded as the distribution of activation in the associative network, as in Anderson's (1976) account. Just and Carpenter (1980) commented that the semantic mapping rules could also be construed as production rules integrating the contents of working memory.

Just and Carpenter themselves gave an analysis of the reading process whereby both declarative knowledge and procedural knowledge (including the structure of the material being read) were represented as production rules operating upon the contents of a limited-capacity working memory, although semantic relationships among individual concepts were represented in an associative network. Some production rules operated in a relatively slow, serial fashion to alter the contents of working memory, whereas other rules operated in a relatively fast, parallel, and automatic fashion to produce spreading activation among the concepts associated with the target words. Whenever a concept was activated by perceptual encoding, by the operation of a production rule, or by spreading activation, a pointer to its meaning was inserted into working memory. This would then decay over time unless reactivated by a subsequent process or displaced by other information.

These accounts proposed that a limited-capacity working memory was an essential component of the processes underlying normal reading. From this it follows that individuals with a larger working memory should be able to hold more items for processing during reading and achieve better semantic integration of the text as a whole. Both Kintsch and van Dijk (1978) and Just and Carpenter (1980) drew the general implication that working-memory capacity should predict individual differences in reading performance. A fundamental difficulty with this sort of account, however, is that reading comprehension often turns out to be unrelated to performance in tests of short-term serial recall. For example, Perfetti and Goldman (1976) found no difference between skilled and less skilled readers in performance on a probe digit task, and Perfetti and Lesgold (1977) inferred from other work that no relationship existed between digit span and reading skill.

Nevertheless, Perfetti and Goldman did find that skilled readers were better than less skilled readers in performance on a probe discourse task, which was only weakly correlated with performance on the probe digit task. They concluded that skilled and less skilled readers differed not in terms of the capacity of working memory, but in terms of the effectiveness with which they could make use of its limited capacity in processing discourse. Perfetti and Lesgold incorporated this proposal into a detailed account of comprehension, which involved a limited-capacity working memory containing an executive processor that generated segmented sentence representations. They suggested that good readers differed from poor readers in terms of the speed or the efficiency of their encoding processes, and that this would leave a larger residual capacity in short-term memory to be devoted to storing the results of those encoding processes during reading itself.

Daneman and Carpenter (1980) similarly suggested that differences in reading comprehension reflected differences in the trade-off between the processing functions and the storage functions of working memory. Although good and poor readers might not differ in their performance on short-term memory tasks whose processing demands were minimal, Daneman and Carpenter predicted that good and poor readers would differ in their performance in tasks that made significant demands upon both the processing functions and the storage functions of working memory. They devised a test of "reading span," in which subjects read aloud a series of unrelated sentences and attempted to recall the last word from each of the sentences in the order in which they had occurred. This measure was found to be correlated with verbal scores from the Scholastic Aptitude Test (SAT) and especially with reading comprehension measures relating to fact retention and pronominal reference, but a conventional measure of word span was not. Subsequent research found that reading span was also correlated with performance in general tests of reading comprehension (Baddeley, Logie, Nimmo-Smith, & Brereton, 1985; Masson & Miller, 1983) as well as in more specific tests requiring the resolution of apparent inconsistencies in simple "garden path" passages (Daneman & Carpenter, 1983), the integration of information from different parts of a passage (Masson & Miller, 1983), or learning the meaning of a novel word from its context (Daneman & Green, 1986).

A General Resource or a Domain-Specific Resource?

Perfetti and Goldman (1976) had found that good readers manifested better retention of narrative discourse than did poor readers even when they listened to text being read aloud. They inferred that these individual differences resulted from coding processes that were typical of language comprehension more generally (see also Perfetti & Lesgold, 1977). Daneman and Carpenter (1980) developed a modified test of memory span in which subjects assessed whether each of a series of unrelated sentences was true or false and then attempted to recall the last word from each of the sentences. Measures of both reading comprehension and listening comprehension proved to be highly correlated with the resulting index of memory span, regardless of whether the sentences to be assessed had been read silently by the subjects, read aloud, or heard. Daneman and Carpenter interpreted these findings to mean that individual differences in reading comprehension resulted from general comprehension processes that taxed working memory rather than specifically visual processes that were peculiar to reading.

Baddeley et al. (1985) evaluated the predictive capacity of a similar test of reading span in which subjects judged whether each of a series of unrelated sentences made sense and attempted to recall either the agent or the object of each sentence. They compared this with a counting-span task in which subjects counted and subsequently recalled the number of dots in each of a series of displays. (The tasks are described in more detail by Robert Logie in Chapter 2.) The reading span was highly correlated with a general measure of reading comprehension, but the counting span was less strongly associated with reading comprehension, and the latter correlation was not at all significant when the effect of reading span was controlled. Baddeley et al. (1985) acknowledged that this finding was strictly inconsistent with the idea of a single working-memory system, but they proposed instead that the counting span was not a good measure of working-memory capacity in adults, a suggestion made previously by Daneman and Carpenter (1980).

Daneman and Green (1986) similarly compared the original reading-span task devised by Daneman and Carpenter (1980) with a "speaking-span" task in which subjects were presented with a series of unrelated words and then used each word in turn to generate aloud a sentence containing that word. The reading span and the speaking span were highly correlated with each other, but the latter showed the stronger association with performance in a contextual vocabulary-production task in which subjects had to generate synonyms of target words that were appropriate to given sentence contexts. Indeed, the correlation between reading span and vocabulary production was not at all significant when the effects of speaking span were controlled. Daneman and Green (1986) concluded that "working memory is not a general system with a unitary capacity. Rather, the capacity of working memory will vary as a function of how efficient the individual is at the specific processes demanded by the task to which working memory is being applied" (p. 17).

Daneman and Tardif (1987) noted that indices of reading span provided only an indirect assessment of the efficiency of working-memory processes. They devised another variation of the reading-span task in which subjects had to construct a single word by combining the letters of two words from a series of four, and then attempted to recall the solutions from several series in the order in which they had been presented. This verbal-span task was supplemented by nonverbal tasks involving analogous mathematical or spatial processes: One task required subjects to combine the digits in two numbers from a series of three so that the result was divisible by three, while the other task required subjects to identify a winning line in three square matrices representing the horizontal planes of a three-dimensional tic-tac-toe game. From each of these three tasks, Daneman and Tardif were able to obtain a direct process measure of the capacity of working memory from performance in the criterion task, as well as an indirect measure of the residual storage capacity from the recall of the respective solutions.

The researchers found that reading comprehension was highly correlated with both measures of the reading or verbal span, that it was less highly correlated with the measures of the mathematical span, and that it showed no sign of any correlation with the measures of the spatial span. Daneman and Tardif concluded that reading comprehension was determined by a language-specific system that was specialized for the representation or processing of verbal or symbolic information rather than by a general or central working-memory system that was also responsible for spatial processing. In other words, they hypothesized the existence of at least two separate working memories, a processor for representing and manipulating verbal-symbolic information and a processor for representing and manipulating spatial information.

In the Daneman and Tardif (1987) study, the direct and indirect measures of span produced very similar correlations with reading comprehension, which was interpreted as confirming the notion that the residual storage capacity of working memory was determined by the efficiency of cognitive processing. (Unfortunately, correlations *between* the direct and indirect measures were not reported.) However, Daneman and Tardif also obtained memory-free process measures of the capacity of working memory by repeating the same three tasks without a requirement to recall the solutions. They found that the predictive power of each of the three process measures was essentially the same, regardless of whether subjects had been required to recall the respective solutions. They therefore concluded that the additional memory requirement during the execution of such tasks was dispensable and that indirect storage measures of working-memory capacity were redundant (and arguably inappropriate) for assessing individual differences in processing efficiency.

However, Engle, Cantor, and Carullo (1992) offered several major criticisms of Daneman and Tardif's study. First, as had been acknowledged by Daneman and Tardif themselves, performance in the spatial-span task was close to a ceiling, and for this reason alone the spatial span would have been expected to have little predictive value in a correlational analysis. Moreover, as will be mentioned in a moment, Turner and Engle (1989) found that the difficulty of the processing task was an important determinant of whether or not a complex-span measure would predict reading comprehension. Third, Daneman and Tardif did not test whether the storage-free processing measures accounted for the same variance in reading comprehension as those obtained when storage was required. Finally, the verbal-processing task used by Daneman and Tardif placed heavy emphasis on word knowledge, which Engle, Nations, and Cantor (1990) found to be an important determinant of reading comprehension separate from working-memory capacity. Engle et al. (1992) did acknowledge that there might be separate verbal and nonverbal working memories, but they concluded that this view could not be supported by the data obtained in Daneman and Tardif's study.

Reading Comprehension and Working-Memory Capacity

Nevertheless, Turner and Engle (1989) insisted that the various findings obtained by Daneman and Carpenter (1980, 1983) were still consistent with the idea that good readers had a larger working-memory capacity than did poor readers regardless of the task being performed. On this assumption, good readers just have more capacity available for both processing and storage. Turner and Engle claimed that the task which had originally been developed by Daneman and Carpenter to measure the reading span could be regarded as the combination of a primary storage task involving the retention of a series of words and a secondary processing task involving the reading of sentences. They devised a sentence–word-span task in which subjects judged whether each of a series of sentences made sense and attempted to recall the last word in each sentence, and an analogous operations–digit-span task in which subjects judged whether each of a series of arithmetic equations was correct and attempted to recall the number on the right-hand side of each equation. Finally, they also constructed sentence–digit and operations–word-span tasks by presenting random combinations of sentences and digits and random combinations of arithmetic equations and words.

When the effects of quantitative SAT scores had been statistically controlled, Turner and Engle found that measures of reading comprehension were predicted by the sentence–word and operations–word spans, but not by the sentence–digit or the operations–digit spans. This suggested that the residual capacity of working memory (as measured by the primary storage task of remembering a series of words) was independent of the particular skills (reading or arithmetic) involved in the secondary processing task. This was taken in turn to support the view that individuals might be good or poor reading comprehenders because of a large or small working-memory capacity and not because of more or less efficient reading skills. This does of course ignore the fact that even arithmetic equations have to be parsed and encoded using processes that are presumably based upon those underlying normal reading. As Turner and Engle themselves remarked, "The operations task, while not 'reading' as we normally think of it, certainly makes use of a verbal code for the numbers and operations" (1989, p. 150; see also Logie, 1995, p. 23).

Turner and Engle also showed that measures of reading comprehension were not associated with simple measures of word span or digit span, thus replicating findings obtained earlier by Daneman and Carpenter (1980) and also by Masson and Miller (1983). They argued that in these latter tasks subjects were able to use a variety of memory strategies such as chunking, recoding, or elaboration, whereas complex-span tasks provided a relatively "pure" measure of the number of items that could be held in working memory without the aid of rehearsal, since the secondary task would make it more difficult to use these strategies. Consistent with this proposal, Turner and Engle found that reading span was less highly associated with reading comprehension when the sentences to be read aloud were relatively simple ones (and thus presumably permitted the limited use of memory strategies). However, these correlations were also attenuated when the sentences to be read aloud were relatively demanding. Turner and Engle attributed this to restriction of range or to subjects' allocating all their resources to the retention component of their task, but neither explanation is supported by the results that they described. Moreover, in subsequent work, Engle and his colleagues found a consistent positive association between simple word span and reading comprehension (Cantor, Engle, & Hamilton, 1991; Engle et al., 1990; Engle, Carullo, & Collins, 1991; La Pointe & Engle, 1990).

Just and Carpenter (1992) cited additional evidence that performance differences related to reading span were much more apparent if the reading comprehension task was relatively demanding. They suggested that this was difficult to explain in terms of individual differences in the efficiency of specific processes, because any efficiency differences should manifest themselves regardless of the total cognitive demand. However, they argued that it was easily explained in terms of individual differences in total processing capacity, because capacity limitations would affect performance only when the resource demands of the task exceeded the available supply. Accordingly, Just and Carpenter modified their earlier (1980) theory to propose that the total processing capacity was determined by the total amount of activation available for maintaining elements in working memory and for propagating activation to associated elements in the course of processing. A similar account of the relationship between working memory and comprehension, the General Capacity Theory, was given by Engle et al. (1992; see also Cantor & Engle, 1993), and this account is critically discussed by Randall Engle in Chapter 4.

The Role of Inhibitory Processes

A somewhat different approach to conceptualizing individual differences in cognitive function was adopted by Hasher and Zacks (1979), who proposed that encoding processes varied in terms of their attentional requirements from those that were largely automatic, demanded minimal contribution from attentional resources, and did not interfere with concurrent processing to those that were effortful, required considerable attentional capacity, and would interfere with other effortful cognitive activities. They argued that attentional capacity also varied both within and between individuals. Following Kahneman (1973), this was used to explain the effects of arousal and effort upon cognitive processing, but it was also used to explore the detailed pattern of age-related changes in learning and remembering.

Hasher and Zacks (1988) endeavored to apply this "general capacity" view of individual differences to the concept of working memory that had evolved in the research on individual differences in discourse processing. They described five experiments that assessed retrieval from memory in old and young adults by means of inference formation or semantic priming. Results showed that older adults were impaired in comparison with younger adults, especially when they were unable to control the presentation rate or else when they were required to retrieve information from memory. This pattern was broadly consistent with the assumption that older adults had a reduced working-memory capacity, and Hasher and Zacks had interpreted the initial findings from their research in just this way (see Zacks, Hasher, Doren, Hamm, & Attig, 1987).

Nevertheless, they acknowledged that a number of commentators had put forward serious conceptual or empirical criticisms of the limited-capacity assumption and its specific application to accounts of age-related changes in cognition. The findings of an additional study (subsequently published by Hamm & Hasher, 1992) implied that the underlying difficulty confronting older people was not an impairment in their working-memory capacity at all but an impairment in the efficiency of the inhibitory processes in working memory that controlled the access of relevant information and the removal of irrelevant information. Hasher and Zacks (1988) summarized their position in the following manner:

> The central assumption is that under some circumstances (most notably here, aging), the efficiency of the inhibitory processes that underlie selective attention is reduced. This decrement in inhibition allows more irrelevant information to enter working memory, and once entered, it allows the irrelevant information to receive sustained attention. This then sets the stage for subsequent reduced rates of success in accessing required information from memory. (p. 219)

Hasher, Stoltzfus, Zacks, and Rypma (1991) went on to test this idea by using the attentional phenomenon of negative priming, in which the time taken to identify a target is longer if it was used as a distractor on the previous trial (see Tipper, 1985). This phenomenon appears to reflect the active suppression or inhibition of responses that would otherwise compete with the (correct) response to the target (Neill, Valdes, & Terry, 1995; Tipper & Cranston, 1985). Hasher et al. (1991) confirmed the phenomenon in the case of young adult subjects, but they found no negative priming in older adults, even though there was indirect evidence that they had previously processed the distractor items. They concluded that the mechanisms of selective attention were responsible for age-related impairments in the encoding, maintenance, and retrieval of task-relevant information.

The subsequent elaboration of this account is described in Chapter 3 by Ellen Stoltzfus, Lynn Hasher, and Rose Zacks. The distinctive feature of their position is that it focuses upon the contents of working memory rather than upon its capacity per se. They put forward the specific view that cognitive performance depends upon the extent to which the contents of working memory (that is, the currently activated information) reflect the subject's current task goals. Deficient inhibitory control over the contents of working memory will lead to that system being preoccupied by task-irrelevant information, with consequent difficulties in accessing and retrieving task-relevant information. This account appears to explain the pattern of cognitive deficits in older adults, and it may well be relevant to the study of individual differences in performance more generally.

Cantor and Engle (1993) presented data obtained from college students concerning the relationship between working-memory capacity (assessed from the operations–word span) and the speeded recognition of sentences. They interpreted their findings as support for the General Capacity Theory of working memory that had been advanced by Engle et al. (1992), but they pointed out that these findings would also be broadly consistent with an inhibition model of the sort described by Hasher and Zacks (1988) if it were applied to the analysis of individual differences in younger adults. Conway and Engle (1994) showed that the same sort of model was needed to explain individual differences in the retrieval of information from both long-term and short-term memory: More specifically, the findings showed that differences in working-memory capacity were important only when the task involved conflict or interference between competing information, and this could not be explained simply in terms of differences in capacity or in the overall level of activation available to the system.

In Chapter 4, Randall Engle describes additional research to suggest that these individual differences pertain to the controlled or intentional aspects of memory rather than to its automatic aspects. These experiments serve to integrate the earlier General Capacity Theory with the inhibition theory devised by Hasher and Zacks, but Engle now claims that the control of inhibition in working memory is itself a process constrained by the available attentional resources. Consequently, individual differences in cognitive performance will represent differences in executive control rather than differences in the automatic activation of representations in long-term memory.

Multicomponent Models of Working Memory

In opposition to the general concept of working memory, there has evolved over the last 20 years or so a family of more specific models that reject the assumption of a single unitary device and postulate instead a complex system of working memory with its own internal structures and processes. This research has been carried out predominantly in Europe rather than in North America and began with a seminal paper by Baddeley and Hitch (1974). Indeed, recent accounts of working memory in British textbooks have tended to be devoted exclusively to the specific models developed by Baddeley and his colleagues (for example, Baddeley, 1994; Eysenck, 1990; Parkin, 1993). In Chapter 2, Robert Logie will describe in some detail the current status of this approach to working memory, but it will nevertheless be helpful to provide a brief description here of its historical development since 1974.

Baddeley and Hitch (1974) focused upon the one attribute of working memory about which there would at the time have been very little dispute: its apparently limited capacity, as evidenced in the limited span of immediate memory. They investigated the effects of a concurrent serial-recall task on performance in reasoning, comprehension, and free recall. They argued: "Such a concurrent memory load might reasonably be expected to absorb some of the storage capacity of a limited capacity working memory system" (p. 50). It would therefore disrupt performance in any criterion task that relied on such a system. They found that a concurrent memory load of six items impaired performance in all three sorts of task. They also showed that phonemic similarity among the stimulus items impaired both reasoning and comprehension, and that suppressing any relevant articulatory activity by requiring subjects to produce irrelevant vocalizations ("articulatory suppression") impaired performance in free recall and, to a lesser extent, in reasoning. These results were taken to support the notion of working memory as a short-term store that had access to phonemic coding.

Contrary to this notion, however, Baddeley and Hitch observed that a concurrent memory load of up to three items had little or no effect on the ability to carry out reasoning, comprehension, or free recall. To explain this unexpected finding, they suggested that the maintenance of items from the concurrent serial-recall task could be carried out by a separate slave component, hence releasing the central core of the system for performance of the criterion task. Impaired performance would accordingly be obtained in a task that demanded central processing capacity only when a concurrent memory load exceeded the capacity of this slave component and required the support of the general-purpose work space. Baddeley and Hitch (1974) described the slave component as "a phonemic response buffer which is able to store a limited amount of speech-like material in the appropriate serial order" (p. 77). In other words, the characteristic form of encoding employed by this component was assumed to be "speech-like" or phonemic in nature; and the characteristic form of organization that it employed was assumed to be temporal and serial. In addition, the characteristic function of this component was to serve as a buffer store that was responsible for holding verbal responses until they could be emitted; Baddeley and Hitch (1974) described it as a "phonemic rehearsal buffer" (p. 86) and a "phonemic loop" (p. 78) through which stimulus items could be recycled and maintained in memory.

In a subsequent study, Baddeley, Thomson, and Buchanan (1975b) found that performance in short-term serial recall with a specific vocabulary of stimulus material was negatively correlated with the average time taken to articulate that material, even when the number of syllables and the number of phonemes that the material contained were held constant. This effect of word length was obtained even when the material was presented visually, but not when subjects engaged in articulatory suppression. These results seemed to rule out an explanation of the word-length effect in terms of an auditory memory system. Baddeley et al. (1975b) interpreted their findings using the multicomponent model of working memory put forward by Baddeley and Hitch (1974), except that the phonemic re-

sponse buffer was described as an "articulatory rehearsal loop" or an "articulatory loop system" (p. 587), linked to the mechanisms underlying
speech production. This system was taken to be sufficient to explain the
effects of articulatory suppression, phonemic similarity and word length in
recall, as well as the existence of neurological patients with selective deficits of verbal short-term memory.

Nevertheless, Colle and Welsh (1976) demonstrated that the immediate serial recall of visually presented items was impaired if subjects were
exposed to irrelevant speech sounds that they were instructed to ignore.
This impairment was specific to sequences of phonemically distinct items,
and as a result the phonemic similarity effect was essentially abolished.
Salamé and Baddeley (1982) found that the magnitude of the impairment
was also related to the degree of phonemic similarity between the unattended speech sounds and the material to be remembered. However, long
words were no more disruptive than were short words as unattended
speech, which suggested that they themselves were probably not being
articulated. Moreover, the effect of unattended speech was eliminated
when subjects were required to engage in articulatory suppression. Salamé
and Baddeley explained these results by suggesting that the articulatory
loop itself consisted of two components, a phonological memory store and
a control process involving articulatory rehearsal. They proposed that under auditory presentation stimuli would gain obligatory access to the phonological store, whereas under visual presentation access could be provided by subvocal rehearsal.

In addition, using auditory presentation, Baddeley, Lewis, and Vallar
(1984) found that requiring subjects to engage in articulatory suppression
during both the presentation and the recall of the items to be remembered
abolished the word-length effect but not the phonemic similarity effect.
These findings imply that the storage capability of the articulatory loop is
based on an abstract phonological code that is neither articulatory in
nature nor contingent on the process of articulatory rehearsal. Baddeley
et al. (1984) concluded that the word-length effect reflected the operation
of an articulatory rehearsal mechanism, but that the phonemic similarity
effect and the effect of unattended speech both reflected the contribution
of a short-term phonological store to which spoken material would gain
direct access without the mediation of articulatory rehearsal (see also Baddeley, 1986, pp. 84–85). This "fractionation" of the articulatory loop was
also supported by detailed analysis of the performance of neurological
patients with defective short-term memory (e.g., Vallar & Baddeley,
1984).

The contents of this short-term phonological store were assumed to
be vulnerable to rapid decay over the course of 1 to 2 seconds, unless they
could be "refreshed" by means of the control process of articulatory rehearsal (see Baddeley, 1986, pp. 92–96; 1990, p. 72). Hence, an important function of covert articulation is to maintain the contents of the
phonological store. However, articulatory suppression eliminates the ef-

fects of both phonemic similarity and unattended speech under conditions of visual presentation, though not under conditions of auditory presentation (Hanley & Broadbent, 1987; Richardson, Greaves, & Smith, 1980). These results indicate that a second major function of covert articulation is to translate orthographic information into a phonological trace to be stored within working memory. Monsell (1987) suggested that the two functions of articulatory rehearsal and articulatory translation might be subserved by different mechanisms. Evidence on this question has come from research on patients with acquired anarthria, who as a result of brain damage lack the capacity to articulate speech sounds but have fairly intact auditory and visual comprehension.

Various studies have found that anarthric patients may sometimes not show effects of phonemic similarity or word length in immediate serial recall (Baddeley & Wilson, 1985; Cubelli & Nichelli, 1992; Vallar & Cappa, 1987). Nevertheless, Cubelli and Nichelli (1992) suggested that anarthric patients showed two qualitatively different patterns of memory impairment. Cases of the "locked-in" syndrome associated with bilateral lesions of the anterior pons showed effects of phonemic similarity with both auditory and visual presentation, but did not produce effects of word length in either modality; this suggests a selective impairment of the mechanism underlying articulatory rehearsal. In contrast, cases of anarthria due to cortical damage in the pars opercularis of the left frontal lobe showed effects of both phonemic similarity and word length with auditory presentation but not with visual presentation; this suggests a selective impairment of the mechanism underlying articulatory translation. In other words, these two functions of covert articulation appear to be distinct and dissociable.

It is not especially surprising that patients with acquired anarthria should exhibit some residual capability for using articulatory processing, despite their complete inability to produce intelligible vocalizations, as they may well have retained some capacity for making subvocal articulatory gestures. However, this outcome would indeed be surprising in individuals with congenital anarthria, because they would never have produced a single intelligible utterance, and it would be implausible to ascribe to them any capacity for covert articulation. In fact, Bishop and Robson (1989) found that children with congenital anarthria associated with cerebral palsy had normal memory spans and showed normal word-length and phonemic similarity effects when they were compared with cerebral-palsied children with normal speech. Baddeley (1990) concluded: "It appears then that inner speech is not dependent on outer speech for either its development or its operation. This suggests that the term 'phonological loop' is perhaps preferable to 'articulatory loop,' since the latter seems to imply a direct involvement of articulation" (p. 87).

Baddeley and Hitch (1974) noted that the idea of a phonemic response buffer had been put forward to explain patterns of performance in verbal tasks, and they suggested that there might be other systems whose role was to support a single common central processor. In particular, they raised the idea of a peripheral memory component based upon the visual system and described a number of tasks using visual perception or visual imagery that might be used to study the operation of such a component. Subsequent work by Baddeley, Grant, Wight, and Thomson (1975a) and Baddeley and Lieberman (1980) tended to confirm the existence of this store, which was described as a visuospatial "scratchpad" or "sketchpad." The findings obtained by Baddeley and Lieberman tended to imply that this component was sensitive to disruption by concurrent movement and not by a concurrent visual task, which led them to conclude that this system was spatial in nature. Other researchers confirmed that visual short-term memory could be disrupted by irrelevant movement (Morris, 1987; Quinn & Ralston, 1986; Smyth, Pearson, & Pendleton, 1988), but disruption by irrelevant visual material was also obtained (Beech, 1984; Logie, 1986; Quinn, 1988). These results suggested that the visuospatial scratchpad involves a short-term visual store that has a direct link with the processes underlying visual perception, but that can be refreshed by a form of spatial rehearsal that can be blocked or suppressed by irrelevant movements. The evidence subsequently obtained in both experimental and neuropsychological studies was broadly consistent with this account (see Logie, 1995).

In contrast, the operating characteristics of the central component of the working-memory system have been much less clearly defined and have thus proved to be more difficult to investigate experimentally. This was described as "the more flexible and executive component of the system" or simply as "the central executive" (Baddeley & Hitch, 1974, p. 77). Levy (1978) observed that functions had been ascribed to the central executive without any detailed specification of how they might be performed, while Baddeley (1981) himself acknowledged that this component represented "the area of our residual ignorance" about working memory (p. 21). Indeed, he elegantly defined the task facing future research aimed at reducing this area of ignorance:

> An adequate theory of the Central Executive would probably include not only a specification of its method of manipulating control processes and integrating the growing number of peripheral systems, but would also require an understanding of selective attention and probably of the role and function of consciousness. (p. 21)

One of the reasons for equivocation over the operating characteristics of the central executive is that its functions were apparently highly task specific. Thus, Hitch (1978) was able to give a very detailed account of the operations to be attributed to the central executive when subjects were required to carry out mental arithmetic.

As was mentioned previously, Baddeley and Hitch (1974) proposed that performance in reasoning, comprehension, and free recall was impaired by a concurrent memory load of six items because it exceeded the capacity of the phonemic response buffer and thus called upon the storage capability of the central executive. Similarly, Baddeley et al. (1975b) argued that, when access to the articulatory rehearsal loop was prevented by means of articulatory suppression, "memory depends entirely on the capacity of the executive working memory system" (p. 587). They added that the latter "is not phonemically based, and does not have the same temporal limitation as the articulatory loop" (p. 587), although this of course leaves the type of coding that was used by the central executive wholly mysterious. Other early versions of the multicomponent model of working memory concurred that the central executive might itself serve as an information store (Baddeley, 1976, p. 179; 1979; Hitch & Baddeley, 1977).

This implies that two tasks carried out concurrently should manifest a direct trade-off in the form of a negative correlation between the levels of performance achieved (cf. Navon & Gopher, 1979; Norman & Bobrow, 1975). Baddeley (1981) referred to the findings of an unpublished experiment suggesting a positive correlation across different subjects between verbal reasoning and immediate serial recall. Richardson (1984) objected to the logic of Baddeley's (1981) argument and presented results which showed that under appropriate circumstances a negative correlation would indeed be obtained. Nevertheless, Baddeley interpreted his findings to mean that there existed two separate but related systems, a verbal memory system and an executive controller. He remarked that on this interpretation the central executive was "becoming increasing like a pure attentional system" (p. 22).

Subsequently, Baddeley (1986, chap. 10) adopted an existing account of the control of action that had been developed by Norman and Shallice (1982; Shallice, 1982). This incorporated a limited-capacity supervisory attentional system that served as the locus of conscious control in tasks involving planning or decision making or in problematic situations. Consequently, the processing capacity of this system could be occupied by an irrelevant task that demanded organized planning of behavior, of which the main example cited by Baddeley was the generation of random sequences of letters. Shallice (1982) proposed that impairment of this system would generate the classic pattern of behavioral deficits associated with damage to the frontal lobes, a pattern that Baddeley (1986, p. 238) described as the "dysexecutive syndrome" (see also Shimamura et al., 1991).

One consequence of adopting this account of the central executive was that it became explicitly regarded as a general attentional resource that coordinated the contributions of different storage subsystems and not as a general work space that itself had both processing and storage properties (e.g., Baddeley, 1986, chap. 10; 1990, chap. 6). Indeed, Baddeley (1993) recently restated his position that the central executive component of the working memory system "does not itself involve storage" (p. 167) and even considered the suggestion that the system might more accurately be termed "working attention" rather than "working memory." He acknowledged that it was possible to devise experimental tasks in which working memory could be assumed to be operative and yet in which there was no obvious requirement for storage, that memory storage was only one component of working memory, and that on his account its most crucial component, the central executive, was concerned with attention and coordination rather than with storage. However, Baddeley suggested that the temporary storage of information was "an absolutely essential feature of the working-memory system as a whole" (1993, p. 168), and that this warranted the retention of the term "working memory."

Conclusion

Insofar as there is a core to the general concept of working memory, it is the assumption that there is some mechanism responsible for the temporary storage and processing of information and that the resources available to this mechanism are limited. As Engle et al. (1992) pointed out, the idea that there are limitations upon attentional resources or immediate memory capacity has a long history in psychology and can also be found in other areas of the discipline. For Piaget, for instance, the capacity of the "field of attention" (also termed the "field of assimilation," the "field of centration," and the "field of equilibrium") determined the mechanisms of constructive operations and hence the process of cognitive development (see Chapman, 1987). This was elaborated by neo-Piagetian researchers in terms of the limitations of central processing capacity at various stages of intellectual development (e.g., Case, 1974, 1978, 1985; Halford, 1982; McLaughlin, 1963; Pascual-Leone, 1970, 1984), and some of these went on to identify this notion explicitly with the general concept of working memory (Morra, Moizo, & Scopesi, 1988; Pascual-Leone, 1987; and cf. Case, 1987).

The general concept of working memory is clearly a central ingredient in models based on production systems, but the application of these models to human cognition in their classical form has proved rather problematic. In experimental research, this concept has been articulated as a distinct cognitive structure but also as the currently active portion of long-term memory. Indeed, all of the contributors to this text agree that working memory has an important role in the retrieval of knowledge represented in long-term memory. The concept has proved most valuable in analyzing the cognitive processes responsible for comprehension, and it is a sign of the importance of the work by Daneman, Carpenter, and their colleagues that it is discussed in each of the chapters that follow. Research on this topic has tended to move away from traditional methods for studying learning and memory toward a variety of new paradigms involving dual-task methodology, inference formation, and semantic priming, although one recent analysis of serial recall clearly belongs to this class of theories with its emphasis on working memory as a single workspace or "blackboard" (Jones, 1993).

In contrast to theories that regard working memory as an essentially unitary mechanism, Baddeley and his colleagues (principally in the United Kingdom, but also in Italy) have developed a framework based on a complex system of components. The exact characterization of these components has fluctuated over the years, but they are currently described as a "central executive," a "phonological loop," and a "visuospatial scratchpad." The focus of this research has been predominantly on the operations of the two latter components as buffer stores, and most of the experimental evidence has accordingly been concerned with short-term memory. Nevertheless, the different operations that are taken to define these theoretical components can in principle be applied to a wide range of cognitive tasks. The model has, for example, been applied to the investigation of reading and reading development (Gathercole & Baddeley, 1993). Moreover, some neo-Piagetian researchers have argued that attentional capacity should be elaborated in terms of a central processing component that should be distinguished from any short-term memory store (e.g., Chapman, 1987; Halford, 1987).

Acknowledgments

I am grateful to Randall Engle, Lynn Hasher, and Robert Logie for their comments on a previous version of this chapter, and to Leslie Smith for his advice on Paigetian and neo-Piagetian precursors of working memory.

References

Anderson, J. R. (1972). FRAN: A simulation model of free recall. In G. H. Bower (Ed.), *The psychology of learning and motivation: Advances in research and theory* (Vol. 5, pp. 315–378). New York: Academic Press.

Anderson, J. R. (1976). *Language, memory, and thought*. Hillsdale, NJ: Erlbaum.

Anderson, J. R. (1983a). *The architecture of cognition*. Cambridge, MA: Harvard University Press.

Anderson, J. R. (1983b). A spreading activation theory of memory. *Journal of Verbal Learning and Verbal Behavior, 22*, 261–295.

Anderson, J. R. (1993). *Rules of the mind*. Hillsdale, NJ: Erlbaum.

Anderson, J. R., & Bower, G. H. (1973). *Human associative memory*. Washington, DC: Winston.

Atkinson, R. C., & Shiffrin, R. M. (1968). Human memory: A proposed system and its control processes. In K. W. Spence & J. T. Spence (Eds.), *The psychology of learning and motivation: Advances in research and theory* (Vol. 2, pp. 89–195). New York: Academic Press.

Atkinson, R. C., & Shiffrin, R. M. (1971). The control of short-term memory. *Scientific American, 225*(2), 82–90.

Baddeley, A. D. (1976). *The psychology of memory*. New York: Basic Books.

Baddeley, A. D. (1979). Working memory and reading. In P. A. Kolers, M. E. Wrolstad, & H. Bouma (Eds.), *Processing of visible language* (Vol. 1, pp. 355–370). New York: Plenum Press.

Baddeley, A. (1981). The concept of working memory: A view of its current state and probable future development. *Cognition, 10,* 17–23.

Baddeley, A. (1986). *Working memory.* Oxford: Oxford University Press.

Baddeley, A. (1990). *Human memory: Theory and practice.* Hove, UK: Erlbaum.

Baddeley, A. (1993). Working memory or working attention? In A. Baddeley & L. Weiskrantz (Eds.), *Attention: Selection, awareness, and control. A tribute to Donald Broadbent* (pp. 152–170). Oxford: Oxford University Press.

Baddeley, A. (1994). Memory. In A. M. Colman (Ed.), *Companion encyclopedia of psychology* (Vol. 1, pp. 281–301). London: Routledge.

Baddeley, A. D., Grant, S., Wight, E., & Thomson, N. (1975a). Imagery and visual working memory. In P.M.A. Rabbitt & S. Dornic (Eds.), *Attention and performance V* (pp. 205–217). London: Academic Press.

Baddeley, A. D., & Hitch, G. (1974). Working memory. In G. H. Bower (Ed.), *The psychology of learning and motivation: Advances in research and theory* (Vol. 8, pp. 47–89). New York: Academic Press.

Baddeley, A., Lewis, V. J., & Vallar, G. (1984). Exploring the articulatory loop. *Quarterly Journal of Experimental Psychology, 36A,* 233–252.

Baddeley, A. D., & Lieberman, K. (1980). Spatial working memory. In R. S. Nickerson (Ed.), *Attention and performance VIII* (pp. 521–539). Hillsdale, NJ: Erlbaum.

Baddeley, A., Logie, R., Nimmo-Smith, I., & Brereton, N. (1985). Components of fluent reading. *Journal of Memory and Language, 24,* 119–131.

Baddeley, A. D., Thomson, N., & Buchanan, M. (1975b). Word length and the structure of short-term memory. *Journal of Verbal Learning and Verbal Behavior, 14,* 575–589.

Baddeley, A., & Wilson, B. (1985). Phonological coding and short-term memory in patients without speech. *Journal of Memory and Language, 24,* 490–502.

Beech, J. R. (1984). The effects of visual and spatial interference on spatial working memory. *Journal of General Psychology, 110,* 141–149.

Bishop, D.V.M., & Robson, J. (1989). Unimpaired short-term memory and rhyme judgement in congenitally speechless individuals: Implications for the notion of "articulatory coding." *Quarterly Journal of Experimental Psychology, 41A,* 123–140.

Cantor, J., & Engle, R. W. (1993). Working-memory capacity as long-term memory activation: An individual-differences approach. *Journal of Experimental Psychology: Learning, Memory, and Cognition, 19,* 1101–1114.

Cantor, J., Engle, R. W., & Hamilton, G. (1991). Short-term memory, working memory, and verbal abilities: How do they relate? *Intelligence, 15,* 229–246.

Carpenter, P. A., Just, M. A., & Shell, P. (1990). What one intelligence test measures: A theoretical account of the processing in the Raven Progressive Matrices Test. *Psychological Review, 97,* 404–431.

Case, R. (1974). Structures and strictures: Some functional limitations on the course of cognitive growth. *Cognitive Psychology, 6,* 544–573.

Case, R. (1978). Intellectual development from birth to adulthood: A neo-Piagetian interpretation. In R. S. Siegler (Ed.), *Children's thinking: What develops?* (pp. 37–72). Hillsdale, NJ: Erlbaum.

Case, R. (1985). *Intellectual development: Birth to adulthood.* Orlando, FL: Academic Press.

Case, R. (1987). The structure and process of intellectual development. *International Journal of Psychology, 22,* 571–607.

Chapman, M. (1987). Piaget, attentional capacity, and the functional implications of formal structure. In H. W. Reese (Ed.), *Advances in child development and behavior* (Vol. 20, pp. 289–334). Orlando, FL: Academic Press.

Colle, H. A., & Welsh, A. (1976). Acoustic masking in primary memory. *Journal of Verbal Learning and Verbal Behavior, 15,* 17–31.

Collins, A. M., & Loftus, E. F. (1975). A spreading-activation theory of semantic processing. *Psychological Review, 82,* 407–428.

Conway, A.R.A., & Engle, R. W. (1994). Working memory and retrieval: A resource-dependent inhibition model. *Journal of Experimental Psychology: General, 123,* 354–373.

Cowan, N. (1988). Evolving conceptions of memory storage, selective attention, and their mutual constraints within the human information-processing system. *Psychological Review, 104,* 163–191.

Cowan, N. (1993). Activation, attention, and short-term memory. *Memory & Cognition, 21,* 162–167.

Cubelli, R., & Nichelli, P. (1992). Inner speech in anarthria: Neuropsychological evidence of differential effects of cerebral lesions on subvocal articulation. *Journal of Clinical and Experimental Neuropsychology, 14,* 499–517.

Daneman, M., & Carpenter, P. A. (1980). Individual differences in working memory and reading. *Journal of Verbal Learning and Verbal Behavior, 19,* 450–466.

Daneman, M., & Carpenter, P. A. (1983). Individual differences in integrating information between and within sentences. *Journal of Experimental Psychology: Learning, Memory, and Cognition, 9,* 561–584.

Daneman, M., & Green, I. (1986). Individual differences in comprehending and producing words in context. *Journal of Memory and Language, 25,* 1–18.

Daneman, M., & Tardif, T. (1987). Working memory and reading skill reexamined. In M. Coltheart (Ed.), *Attention and performance XII: The psychology of reading* (pp. 491–508). Hove, UK: Erlbaum.

Engle, R. W., Cantor, J., & Carullo, J. J. (1992). Individual differences in working memory and comprehension: A test of four hypotheses. *Journal of Experimental Psychology: Learning, Memory, and Cognition, 18,* 972–992.

Engle, R. W., Carullo, J. J., & Collins, K. W. (1991). Individual differences in working memory for comprehension and following directions. *Journal of Educational Research, 84,* 253–262.

Engle, R. W., Nations, J. K., & Cantor, J. (1990). Is "working memory capacity" just another name for word knowledge? *Journal of Educational Psychology, 82,* 799–804.

Ericsson, K. A., & Pennington, N. (1993). The structure of memory performance in experts: Implications for memory in everyday life. In G. M. Davies & R. H. Logie (Ed.), *Memory in everyday life* (pp. 241–272). Amsterdam: North-Holland.

Eysenck, M. W. (1990). Working memory. In M. W. Eysenck (Ed.), *The Blackwell dictionary of cognitive psychology* (pp. 372–375). Oxford: Basil Blackwell.

Fillmore, C. J. (1968). The case for case. In E. Bach & R. T. Harms (Eds.), *Universals in linguistic theory* (pp. 1–88). New York: Holt, Rinehart, & Winston.

Findler, N. V. (Ed.) (1979). *Associative networks: Representation and use of knowledge by computers.* New York: Academic Press.

Gathercole, S. E., & Baddeley, A. (1993). *Working memory and language.* Hove, UK: Erlbaum.

Halford, G. S. (1982). *The development of thought.* Hillsdale, NJ: Erlbaum.

Halford, G. S. (1987). A structure-mapping approach to cognitive development. *International Journal of Psychology, 22,* 609–642.

Hamm, V. P., & Hasher, L. (1992). Age and the availability of inferences. *Psychology and Aging, 7,* 56–64.

Hanley, J. R., & Broadbent, C. (1987). The effect of unattended speech on serial recall following auditory presentation. *British Journal of Psychology, 78,* 287–297.

Hasher, L., Stoltzfus, E. R., Zacks, R. T., & Rypma, B. (1991). Age and inhibition. *Journal of Experimental Psychology: Learning, Memory, and Cognition, 17,* 163–169.

Hasher, L., & Zacks, R. T. (1979). Automatic and effortful processes in memory. *Journal of Experimental Psychology: General, 108,* 356–388.

Hasher, L., & Zacks, R. T. (1988). Working memory, comprehension, and aging: A review and a new view. In G. H. Bower (Ed.), *The psychology of learning and motivation: Advances in research and theory* (Vol. 22, pp. 193–225). San Diego, CA: Academic Press.

Hitch, G. J. (1978). The role of short-term working memory in mental arithmetic. *Cognitive Psychology, 10,* 302–323.

Hitch, G. J., & Baddeley, A. D. (1977). Working memory. In *Cognitive psychology: A third-level course* (Unit 15). Milton Keynes, UK: Open University Press.

Jackson, P. (1986). *Introduction to expert systems.* Wokingham, UK: Addison-Wesley.

Jones, D. (1993). Objects, streams, and threads of auditory attention. In A. Baddeley & L. Weiskrantz (Eds.), *Attention: Selection, awareness, and control. A tribute to Donald Broadbent* (pp. 87–104). Oxford: Oxford University Press.

Just, M. A., & Carpenter, P. A. (1980). A theory of reading: From eye fixations to comprehension. *Psychological Review, 87,* 329–354.

Just, M. A., & Carpenter, P. A. (1992). A capacity theory of comprehension: Individual differences in working memory. *Psychological Review, 99,* 122–149.

Kahneman, D. (1973). *Attention and effort.* Englewood Cliffs, NJ: Prentice-Hall.

Kintsch, W. (1972). Notes on the structure of semantic memory. In E. Tulving & W. Donaldson (Eds.), *Organization of memory* (pp. 247–308). New York: Academic Press.

Kintsch, W. (1974). *The representation of meaning in memory.* Hillsdale, NJ: Erlbaum.

Kintsch, W., & van Dijk, T. A. (1978). Toward a model of text comprehension and production. *Psychological Review, 85,* 363–394.

Klapp, S. T., Marshburn, E. A., & Lester, P. T. (1983). Short-term memory does not involve the "working memory" of information processing: The demise of a common assumption. *Journal of Experimental Psychology: General, 112,* 240–264.

La Pointe, L. B., & Engle, R. W. (1990). Simple and complex word spans as measures of working memory capacity. *Journal of Experimental Psychology: Learning, Memory, and Cognition, 16,* 1118–1133.

Levy, B. A. (1978). Speech analysis during sentence processing: Reading versus listening. *Visible Language, 12,* 81–101.

Lindsay, P. H., & Norman, D. A. (1972). *Human information processing: An introduction to psychology.* New York: Academic Press.

Logie, R. H. (1986). Visuo-spatial processes in working memory. *Quarterly Journal of Experimental Psychology, 38A*, 229–247.

Logie, R. H. (1995). *Visuo-spatial working memory*. Hove, UK: Erlbaum.

Masson, M.E.J., & Miller, J. A. (1983). Working memory and individual differences in comprehension and memory of text. *Journal of Educational Psychology, 75*, 314–318.

McLaughlin, G. H. (1963). Psycho-logic: A possible alternative to Piaget's formulation. *British Journal of Educational Psychology, 33*, 61–67.

Miller, G. A. (1956). The magical number seven, plus or minus two: Some limits on our capacity for processing information. *Psychological Review, 63*, 81–97.

Miller, G. A., Galanter, E., & Pribram, K. H. (1960). *Plans and the structure of behavior*. New York: Holt.

Monsell, S. (1987). On the relation between lexical input and output pathways for speech. In A. Allport, D. G. MacKay, W. Prinz, & E. Scheerer (Eds.), *Language perception and production: Relationships between listening, speaking, reading and writing* (pp. 273–311). London: Academic Press.

Morra, S., Moizo, C., & Scopesi, A. (1988). Working memory (or the M operator) and the planning of children's drawings. *Journal of Experimental Child Psychology, 46*, 41–73.

Morris, N. (1987). Exploring the visuo-spatial scratch pad. *Quarterly Journal of Experimental Psychology, 39A*, 409–430.

Navon, D., & Gopher, D. (1979). On the economy of the human processing system. *Psychological Review, 86*, 214–255.

Neches, R. (1987). Learning through in incremental refinement of procedures. In D. Klahr, P. Langley, & R. Neches (Eds.), *Production system models of learning and development* (pp. 163–219). Cambridge, MA: MIT Press.

Neches, R., Langley, P., & Klahr, D. (1987). Learning, development, and production systems. In D. Klahr, P. Langley, & R. Neches (Eds.), *Production system models of learning and development* (pp. 1–53). Cambridge, MA: MIT Press.

Neill, W. T., Valdes, L. A., & Terry, K. M. (1995). Selective attention and the inhibitory control of cognition. In F. N. Dempster & C. J. Brainerd (Eds.), *Interference and inhibition in cognition* (pp. 207–261). San Diego, CA: Academic Press.

Newell, A. (1972). A theoretical exploration of mechanisms for encoding the stimulus. In A. W. Melton & E. Martin (Eds.), *Coding processes in human memory* (pp. 373–434). Washington, DC: Winston.

Newell, A. (1973a). Production systems: Models of control structures. In W. G. Chase (Ed.), *Visual information processing* (pp. 463–526). New York: Academic Press.

Newell, A. (1973b). You can't play 20 questions with nature and win: Projective comments on the papers of this symposium. In W. G. Chase (Ed.), *Visual information processing* (pp. 283–308). New York: Academic Press.

Newell, A., & Simon, H. A. (1972). *Human problem solving*. Englewood Cliffs, NJ: Prentice-Hall.

Norman, D. A., & Bobrow, D. G. (1975). On data-limited and resource-limited processes. *Cognitive Psychology, 7*, 44–64.

Norman, D. A., & Shallice, T. (1982). *Attention to action: Willed and automatic control of behavior* (CHIP Technical Report No. 99). La Jolla, CA: University of California, San Diego, Center for Human Information Processing. Published (1986) in R. J. Davidson, G. E. Schwarts, & D. Shapiro (Eds.), *Con-

sciousness and self-regulation: Advances in research and theory (Vol. 4, pp. 1–18). New York: Plenum Press.

Ohlsson, S. (1987). Truth versus appropriateness: Relating declarative to procedural knowledge. In D. Klahr, P. Langley, & R. Neches (Eds.), *Production system models of learning and development* (pp. 287–327). Cambridge, MA: MIT Press.

Parkin, A. J. (1993). *Memory: Phenomena, experiment and theory.* Oxford: Basil Blackwell.

Pascual-Leone, J. (1970). A mathematical model for the transition rule in Piaget's developmental stages. *Acta Psychologica, 32*, 301–345.

Pascual-Leone, J. (1984). Attention, dialectic, and mental effort: Toward an organismic theory of life stages. In M. L. Commons, F. A. Richards, & C. Armon (Eds.), *Beyond formal operations: Late adolescent and adult cognitive development* (pp. 182–215). New York: Praeger.

Pascual-Leone, J. (1987). Organismic processes for neo-Piagetian theories: A dialectical causal account of cognitive development. *International Journal of Psychology, 22*, 531–570.

Perfetti, C. A., & Goldman, S. R. (1976). Discourse memory and reading comprehension skill. *Journal of Verbal Learning and Verbal Behavior, 14*, 33–42.

Perfetti, C. A., & Lesgold, A. M. (1977). Discourse comprehension and sources of individual differences. In M. A. Just & P. A. Carpenter (Eds.), *Cognitive processes in comprehension* (pp. 141–183). Hillsdale, NJ: Erlbaum.

Quillian, M. R. (1967). Word concepts: A theory and simulation of some basic semantic capabilities. *Behavioral Science, 12*, 410–430.

Quillian, M. R. (1968). Semantic memory. In M. Minsky (Ed.), *Semantic information processing* (pp. 227–270). Cambridge, MA: MIT Press.

Quinn, J. G. (1988). Interference effects in the visuo-spatial sketchpad. In M. Denis, J. Engelkamp, & J.T.E. Richardson (Eds.), *Cognitive and neuropsychological approaches to mental imagery* (pp. 181–189). Dordrecht: Martinus Nijhoff.

Quinn, J. G., & Ralston, G. E. (1986). Movement and attention in visual working memory. *Quarterly Journal of Experimental Psychology, 38A*, 689–703.

Richardson, J.T.E. (1984). Developing the theory of working memory. *Memory & Cognition, 12*, 71–83.

Richardson, J.T.E., Greaves, D. E., & Smith, M.M.C. (1980). Does articulatory suppression eliminate the phonemic similarity effect in short-term recall? *Bulletin of the Psychonomic Society, 16*, 417–420.

Rumelhart, D. E., Lindsay, P. H., & Norman, D. A. (1972). A process model for long-term memory. In E. Tulving & W. Donaldson (Eds.), *Organization of memory* (pp. 197–246). New York: Academic Press.

Rumelhart, D. E., & Norman, D. A. (1983). *Representation in memory* (CHIP Technical Report No. 116). La Jolla, CA: University of California, San Diego, Center for Human Information Processing. Abridged version published (1985) as: Representation of knowledge. In A. M. Aitkenhead & J. M. Slack (Eds.), *Issues in cognitive modeling* (pp. 15–62). London: Erlbaum. Original version published (1988) in R. C. Atkinson, R. J. Herrnstein, G. Lindzey, & R. D. Luce (Eds.), *Stevens' handbook of experimental psychology: Vol. 2. Learning and cognition* (2nd ed., pp. 511–587). New York: Wiley.

Salamé, P., & Baddeley, A. (1982). Disruption of short-term memory by unattended speech: Implications for the structure of working memory. *Journal of Verbal Learning and Verbal Behavior, 21*, 150–164.

Schank, R. C. (1972). Conceptual dependency: A theory of natural language understanding. *Cognitive Psychology, 3*, 552–631.

Shallice, T. (1982). Specific impairments of planning. *Philosophical Transactions of the Royal Society London B, 298*, 199–209.

Shallice, T. (1988). *From neuropsychology to mental structure.* Cambridge: Cambridge University Press.

Shimamura, A. P., Janowsky, J. S., & Squire, L. R. (1991). What is the role of frontal lobe damage in memory disorders? In H. S. Levin, H. M. Eisenberg, & A. L. Benton (Eds.), *Frontal lobe function and dysfunction* (pp. 173–195). New York: Oxford University Press.

Smyth, M. M., Pearson, N. A., & Pendleton, L. R. (1988). Movement and working memory: Patterns and positions in space. *Quarterly Journal of Experimental Psychology, 40A*, 497–514.

Tipper, S. P. (1985). The negative priming effect: Inhibitory priming by ignored objects. *Quarterly Journal of Experimental Psychology, 37A*, 571–590.

Tipper, S. P., & Cranston, M. (1985). Selective attention and priming: Inhibitory and facilitatory effects of ignored primes. *Quarterly Journal of Experimental Psychology, 37A*, 591–611.

Turner, M. L., & Engle, R. W. (1989). Is working memory capacity task dependent? *Journal of Memory and Language, 28*, 127–154.

Vallar, G., & Baddeley, A. D. (1984). Fractionation of working memory: Neuropsychological evidence for a phonological short-term store. *Journal of Verbal Learning and Verbal Behavior, 23*, 151–161.

Vallar, G., & Cappa, S. F. (1987). Articulation and verbal short-term memory: Evidence from anarthria. *Cognitive Neuropsychology, 4*, 55–77.

Zacks, R. T., Hasher, L., Doren, B., Hamm, V., & Attig, M. S. (1987). Encoding and memory of explicit and implicit information. *Journal of Gerontology, 42*, 418–422.

2

The Seven Ages
of Working Memory

Robert H. Logie

Ever since George Miller's classic paper on short-term memory was published in 1956, the "magical number seven" has retained its appeal as an estimate of the capacity of short-term memory (i.e., seven "chunks" of information). The appeal comes in part from the suggestion that the limit on the capacity of short-term memory places a constraint on some aspects of human information processing. The appeal also comes from the extensive reference to the number seven in other major aspects of human endeavor, such as the "Seven Ages of Man" from Shakespeare's play *As You Like It*, the T. E. Lawrence novel *The Seven Pillars of Wisdom*, the "Seven Deadly Sins," or the Seven Wonders of the World. Less well known but found in any good encyclopedia are the Seven Liberal Arts, the Seven Sages of Rome, and the Seven Types of Ambiguity. Within cognitive psychology, it turns out that there are also seven different identifiable ways in which philosophers and psychologists have thought of the functional cognition underlying processing and temporary storage of information, with labels ranging from "contemplation" and "primary memory" to "short-term memory." The contemporary term for this cognitive function is "working memory." However, even this expression is associated with a range of different theoretical assumptions.

The itinerary for the chapter is that I shall first briefly describe each of the seven instantiations of what is nowadays generally referred to as "working memory." A number of the more historical versions of working memory are already well known and are ably covered in general textbooks on cognitive psychology. As such, I shall make only transitory references to these in order to set the context for the remainder of the chapter. There are at least three contemporary "ages" of working memory that are still developing concurrently, and I shall give more detailed attention to these current uses of the term. I shall then discuss which view of working memory fits best with the voluminous corpus of empirical data that has now accumulated on the topic. I shall go on to argue that working memory is best thought of as a number of separable components, each of which has a characteristic set of functions, and which can be brought to bear singly or in concert in an attempt to match task demands in the laboratory and in aspects of everyday cognition. The chapter will end with a discussion of the idea that working memory acts as a "gateway" to long-term memory. I will argue that the multicomponent working memory operates as a workspace that is involved only after representations in long-term memory have been activated.

Age I: Working Memory as Contemplation

One of the earliest recorded references to a concept akin to working memory is found in the writings of the seventeenth-century British philosopher John Locke (1690):

> The next faculty of mind . . . is that which I call *retention*. . . . This is done in two ways.
> First by keeping the idea which is brought into it, for some time actually in view, which is called *contemplation*.
> The other way of retention is, the power to revive again in our minds those ideas which, after imprinting, have disappeared, or have been as it were laid aside out of sight. . . . This is *memory* which is as it were the storehouse of our ideas. (Book II, chap. X, paras. 1–2)

Notably, Locke explicitly distinguishes between a temporary workspace for the "idea in view" and a more permanent "storehouse of ideas." Three centuries later, this is roughly equivalent to the distinction between short-term memory (or working memory) and long-term memory (or permanent memory). That there is such a distinction is held by the majority of cognitive psychologists, although the exact nature of each of the systems involved and just how independent they are is still the subject of debate. Cognitive psychology has now, of course, accumulated a considerable body of data that speaks to the organization of the "storehouse of ideas." The nature of "contemplation" and what might comprise and constrain the "idea in view" are, at least in spirit, the topic of this and the other chapters in this book.

Age II: Working Memory as Primary Memory

The concept appeared again in the writings of William James (1905), who referred to "the specious present," for which he coined the expression "primary memory," as distinct from the storehouse of "secondary memory" (pp. 643–650). These terms were revived in an influential paper by Waugh and Norman (1965), who specified more detailed characteristics of primary memory. It was a system that was limited in its capacity, and information in primary memory could be displaced by new material unless it was maintained by verbal rehearsal. Rehearsal was also a mechanism for copying information from primary memory to secondary memory.

Age III: Working Memory as Short-Term Memory

The ideas behind Waugh and Norman's primary memory were considerably extended and revised by Atkinson and Shiffrin (1968), who referred to short-term memory as a combination of storage and control processes. Unlike their predecessors, Atkinson and Shiffrin recognized the need to incorporate a range of control processes in addition to verbal rehearsal, such as alternative strategies for coding and for retrieval. In their article, Atkinson and Shiffrin briefly introduced the term "working memory," but their discussion focused on the concept of a short-term buffer for storage and processing of auditory-verbal-linguistic (a-v-l) information. They also suggested explicitly that subjects had complete discretion as to the use of control processes, and that increased effort devoted toward control processes would reduce the storage capacity of the buffer and vice versa. In other words, the suggestion was of a flexible system of limited capacity that could function for storage or processing, and the capacity limitation entailed a trade-off between these two functions.

Evidence for the model was derived from studies of both normal adult subjects and brain-damaged patients. Examples of the evidence from normal subjects were the coding differences in long-term and short-term storage (e.g., Baddeley, 1966a, 1966b; Conrad, 1964) and the different components of the serial-position curve in verbal free recall (see Glanzer & Cunitz, 1966). The brain-damaged patients described had severe difficulty in learning new information but could recall information that they had learned prior to their injury. Their short-term buffer also appeared to be unimpaired in that they could store sequences of digits and maintain the sequence by verbal rehearsal. However, as soon as rehearsal stopped or was prevented, the sequence was forgotten. In other words, their short-term buffer appeared to be intact but their long-term storage was grossly impaired (e.g., Milner, 1959; Teuber, Milner, & Vaughan, 1968).

Atkinson and Shiffrin did raise the possibility that there was a separate visual buffer to complement their concept of an a-v-l buffer, which also might have a rehearsal capability. At the time their article was written, however, there was only limited evidence for this view (e.g., Posner, 1966), and the notion of a number of temporary buffers was laid to one side, pending further data. As a result, the theory put forward by Atkinson and Shiffrin has been widely interpreted as a model comprising a single, flexible system for processing and storage.

Age IV: Working Memory as Processor

An alternative view was provided by Craik and Lockhart (1972), who attempted to emphasize processing rather than structure in memory. The nature or level of initial processing was thought to determine the ease with which information could later be recalled. Thus, memory was seen as a by-product of cognitive processing rather than as a separate entity. There is, however, a widespread misconception that the Levels-of-Processing approach advocated a unitary theory of memory, with no distinction, for example, between a short-term and a long-term memory system. In fact, in Craik and Lockhart's paper they made this distinction quite explicit. The primary-memory system was conceived of as the vehicle for processing, to include not only maintenance rehearsal but also semantic judgments, lexical judgments, and phonological or graphemic decisions. Within the Levels-of-Processing model, deep levels of processing such as semantic judgments should lead to better retention than shallow levels of processing such as maintenance rehearsal. The model ran into a number of difficulties, not least in providing an adequate measure of "depth" that was independent of the experimental outcome (Baddeley, 1978). Moreover, rehearsal does result in long-term learning, even though it was considered by Craik and Lockhart to operate at a shallow level of processing. Thus, Levels of Processing had a number of shortcomings as a model of long-term learning.

The nature of the primary-memory system responsible for carrying out the processing was never developed in any great detail, although in many respects Levels of Processing constituted an attempt to specify more clearly the nature and function of the control processes alluded to by Atkinson and Shiffrin (1968). One explicit feature of Atkinson and Shiffrin's model was that the short-term buffer acted as a way-station between a short-lived sensory store and long-term memory. The control processes were therefore responsible for transfer of information from the short-term buffer to long-term memory. The latter was also a feature of Levels of Processing. Moreover, even though Craik and Lockhart's view emphasized processing rather than cognitive architecture, the model did include the means to store information on a temporary basis by maintenance rehearsal (e.g., subvocal repetition) as well as by elaborative processing (e.g., through forming semantic associations or visual images).

Age V: Working Memory as a Constraint on Language Comprehension

Atkinson and Shiffrin's (1968) view of short-term memory was subsequently very influential, and a number of features of their model appear in the contemporary literature on working memory. One of these features was a common theme underlying the views of primary memory, short-term memory, and working memory: the assumption, implicit or explicit, that a single system was responsible for temporary storage and processing. This theme is particularly salient in recent approaches to capacity limitations in language comprehension (see Daneman & Carpenter, 1980; Just & Carpenter, 1992). This is one of the major current ages of working memory, and I shall discuss it in a little more depth, although Randall Engle provides further details in Chapter 4 of this volume.

As John Richardson mentioned in Chapter 1, Daneman and Carpenter (1980) devised a task that they described as a measure of working-memory span. This task incorporated both processing and storage components, and the assumption was that these tapped the processing and storage capacity of working memory. The task involves presenting subjects with a series of sentences that they are required to read. After a complete sequence of sentences has been presented, subjects then have to recall the last word from each sentence in the order of presentation. For example, the subjects might be asked to read "When at last his eyes opened, there was no gleam of triumph, no shade of anger," followed by another sentence, "The taxi turned up Michigan Avenue where they had a clear view of the lake." They would then have to recall the words "anger" and "lake." If successful, subjects would then be given a sequence of three sentences, and so on until they were no longer able to recall correctly all of the final words. The longest sequence of sentences for which all of the final words could be recalled was taken as each subject's "reading span." This is thought to reflect capacity limitations for that subject when processing visually presented text, and the capacity-limited system is referred to as a "working memory" that is involved in processing language.

Just and Carpenter (1992) and their colleagues subsequently developed this model in an elegant series of studies on the relationship between reading span and reading times. For example, King and Just (1991) measured word-by-word reading times for relatively simple sentences, such as "the reporter that attacked the senator admitted the error," and for syntactically complex sentences, such as "the reporter that the senator attacked admitted the error." Subjects with poorer reading spans took longer to read the complex sentences than did those with higher spans. These individual differences in reading times were even greater for words that were pivotal to the meaning of the sentence. Thus, in the complex example, low-span subjects spent more time reading the word "admitted" than reading other words in the sentence, and more time reading that word than did high-span subjects. Moreover, when given a concurrent memory load, the comprehension performance of the high-span subjects was less disrupted than was the performance of the low-span subjects. These and similar data were taken to suggest that subjects with a high score on the reading-span test have a larger working memory. As such, they have extra processing capacity to deal with the extra processing demands of syntactically complex sentences, and this is reflected in their faster reading times.

Just and Carpenter (1992) described a theory of capacity limitation in language processing that was offered as an account of these individual differences in comprehension ability and reading span. Their notion is of a cognitive capacity limited by an available budget of activation. Within this budget, activation can be allocated flexibly, but once all of the available activation has been allocated, any new processing or storage can be accomplished only by reducing the level of activation somewhere else. In ongoing comprehension of text, the representations of segments early in the text stream are deactivated to allow the activation of representations of later segments. Thus, high-capacity individuals enjoy a larger budget of activation, and they can therefore handle complex syntax and additional memory loads more effectively than can individuals with a more modest activation budget. The reading-span task is thought to provide a measure of the budget allocation in relation to language processing, and this explains the relationship between individual differences in reading span and in reading comprehension. At least one core component of cognitive capacity is a working memory that is thought to comprise the orchestration of all representations that are currently activated above some threshold. As the level of activation is lowered for those representations activated previously, these segments are less readily available in working memory, while fresh activations take their place.

In Just and Carpenter's theory, the general approach to reading span is that it measures the capacity of a working memory that specializes in language processing (Daneman & Tardif, 1987). However, reading span seems to be related to performance on tasks that also require the processing and temporary storage of other sorts of material. Baddeley, Logie, Nimmo-Smith, and Brereton (1985) devised a modified version of the reading-span task that involved greater demands on both processing and temporary memory. Subjects were given sequences of sentences that were rather simpler than those used by Daneman and Carpenter (1980). The sentences either made sense (for example, "The policeman ate the apple") or were nonsense (for example, "The scientist knitted the film"). As each sentence was presented, subjects had to judge whether the sentence made sense. After the sequence of sentences was completed, experimental participants were required to recall either the grammatical objects of the sentences or the grammatical subjects of the sentences in the order in which they had been presented. Thus, for the two sentences presented above, if the objects were requested, the correct responses would be "apple" and "film." If the subjects were requested, the correct responses would be "policeman" and "scientist." Participants were not informed whether the subjects or the objects would be required until all of the sentences had been presented, and this was intended to place a heavy storage load on working memory. Moreover, because the semantic content of each sentence had to be assessed, this ensured that there was also a processing requirement. As in Daneman and Carpenter's task, the number of sentences was successively incremented over trials until participants could no longer accurately recall the required items.

In these experiments, we found that this form of reading span was highly correlated with measures of reading comprehension, thus replicating Daneman and Carpenter's results. However, we also looked at relationships with another measure of processing and storage that we called "counting span." This was based on a task described by Case, Kurland, and Goldberg (1982) and involved presenting the subjects with a series of colored dot patterns. For each pattern, subjects had to count up the number of dots shown in a particular color, after which a further pattern would be presented. After all of the patterns had been seen, subjects were then asked to recall the sequence of totals that they had counted for the patterns. As in the case of reading span, this task had a processing component (i.e., counting the dots) and a storage component (i.e., retaining the totals counted). We found a clear correlation between the two tasks, and both were correlated with reading comprehension. This suggests that the mental capacity that is measured by the two span tasks and described by Just and Carpenter (1992) as "working memory" can be applied to language processing but is most likely a general-purpose system for processing and temporary storage. The generality of this system has also been shown by Yuille, Oakhill, and Parkin (1989), who reported significant correlations in young children between reading comprehension and a task involving the reading of short digit strings with later recall of the final digits in each string. Randall Engle has described analogous correlations between comprehension and performance with a procedure involving sequences of simple arithmetic equations (Engle, Cantor, & Carullo, 1992; Turner & Engle, 1989; see also Chapter 4 in this volume by Randall Engle).

Age VI: Working Memory as Activation, Attention, and Expertise

The general theme of a single, flexible working memory being the host to activated representations and activated procedures from long-term memory is a key feature of other areas of research such as cognitive changes and limitations in older adults (e.g., Hasher & Zacks, 1988; Salthouse, 1991; Salthouse & Babcock, 1991; see Chapter 3 in this volume by Ellen Stoltzfus, Lynn Hasher, and Rose Zacks). It is also an assumption underlying certain contemporary models of short-term memory (e.g., Cowan, 1993). In Cowan's model, two levels of activation are associated, respectively, with the current focus of attention and a corpus of readily available information. The highest levels of activation are associated with the current contents of working memory. A moderate level of activation is associated with the information that either has recently been in working memory or is closely associated with its contents. Thus, for example, I am writing this text while sitting on a train, and it is the current focus of my attention. I could readily call to mind information about trains, tickets, stations, and my planned destination, all of which are at activation levels st below the threshold for inclusion in my current working memory. Other information about an airplane journey later in the day is also bubbling about in the background, and it too is readily available. The rest of my knowledge base is at a much lower level of activation. Therefore, the information, say, about a particular castle in Scotland takes longer to retrieve than does information about airplanes and trains, but, after it has been retrieved, other things that I know about Scottish castles become available just below the working-memory activation threshold and replace information related to the current external context of the train.

Cowan has extended his approach to provide an account of some interesting data from studies of memory span. Serial recall of sequences of randomly ordered digits, letters, or words has long been taken as one measure of verbal short-term memory span. However, there are some reasons to believe that not only short-term memory capacity contributes to span. For example, Wetherick (1975, 1976; Wetherick and Alexander, 1977) showed that a subject's ability to recall word sequences where the words are all drawn from the same semantic category is better than a subject's recall of sequences of words drawn from several different semantic categories. Besner and Davelaar (1982) reported that nonwords that sound like words (e.g., *brane*) are recalled more easily than are nonwords without this property. More recently, Hulme, Maughan, and Brown (1991) reported the related finding that recall of word sequences is better than recall of sequences of nonsense syllables. These findings suggest that lexical or semantic information (or both) may be contributing to memory span. Thus, when a word or even a word-like item is presented, its stored entry in semantic memory or in the mental lexicon is activated, and this activation makes the word more readily available in working memory for later recall.

The idea of having information readily available but not actually in working memory is also central to a model of extended working memory being developed by Ericsson, Kintsch, and their colleagues (Ericsson & Kintsch, 1991; Ericsson & Pennington, 1993). Their model is derived from research on the development and employment of cognitive expertise. They suggest that information pertaining to an individual's area or areas of expertise is readily available, giving the impression that working memory has a much larger capacity when it operates within those domains of expertise. One especially pertinent study on this topic was that of an athlete who was trained to become expert at retaining lengthy random sequences of digits (Ericsson & Chase, 1982). After extensive training he was able to repeat back sequences of 80 digits that he had heard only a few moments before. Apparently he was using his knowledge of athletics to encode the numbers in meaningful chunks, such as record times for the 100-meter sprint or record heights for the high jump. There are numerous other examples of impressive memory performance associated with expertise, ranging from the recall of chess positions by expert chess players (e.g., Charness, 1976; De Groot, 1965; Saariluoma, 1992), through expert memory for meal orders in a restaurant (Ericsson & Polson, 1988), to the recall of the physical features of houses by expert burglars (Logie, Wright, & Decker, 1992).

Ericsson and Pennington (1993) argue that information in the domain of expertise is at a generally higher base level of activation, giving it privileged access to working memory over domains that are outside the individual's areas of expertise. According to this view, the capacity constraints on working memory that are reflected in Miller's "magical number seven" give a rather simple-minded notion of how working memory functions. According to Ericsson and Pennington, working-memory capacity for our areas of expertise is much larger than working-memory capacity for other things. However, it is worth noting that most of us have not spent inordinate amounts of time practicing the retention of sequences of random numbers, although various strategies such as chunking are available to most people as a way of inducing modest improvements in their digit span. Despite the effects of expertise and of mnemonic strategies, there remains some value in retaining the notion of a theoretical basic capacity for working memory, but in allowing also for exceptions that might account for variability in the capacity of individual subjects.

The utility of having general rules of thumb with exceptions in some particular cases is an approach echoed in other domains of science. For example, Newton's laws of motion were useful theories of the behavior of physical masses in space but were subject to a number of qualifications arising from the effects of other forces such as gravity, friction, and collision with other physical masses. So, too, psychologists' ideas about limited working-memory capacity provide a useful theory to which we can add qualifications about the effects of expertise. I am referring here to expertise in its broadest sense, of cognitive skills that allow for the application of learned procedures and strategies for task performance. For example, chunking digits in groups of three can be thought of as an easily acquired form of expertise that leads to better memory performance. Working memory then can be viewed as a capacity-constrained system acting as a workspace for information processing and temporary storage, but whose operation can be supplemented by contributions from long-term memory.

Indeed, it could be argued that the limited-capacity model of working memory has greater practical value than at least some aspects of Newton's laws of motion because the limited capacity of working memory can at least be demonstrated under laboratory conditions: It is not very difficult to reproduce digit spans of seven, plus or minus two, in practical classes with students. Moreover, there is a very large literature showing how readily an experimenter can explore the characteristics of working memory by manipulating the conditions under which verbal memory span is tested. For example, the experiments by Wetherick (1975, 1976) and by Hulme et al. (1991) described above show how the contribution of long-term memory to verbal memory span can be manipulated directly. Digit span and word span are also extremely useful as simple diagnostic and investigative tools for cognitive impairment following brain damage, both for clinical and for theoretical purposes. With all due respect to Newton and his successors, it is extremely difficult to set up an experiment where we could observe a moving mass that was *not* subject to the effects of gravity, not to mention the theoretical complexities that were added later.

The arguments in favor of a limited-capacity working-memory system are compelling, and the notion that it is a single flexible system seems to offer a simple model that makes relatively few assumptions. However, it is important to balance the seduction of simplicity with explanatory adequacy in the light of the available data. On these grounds, I shall argue that the idea of a single, flexible system underlying cognitive capacity is too simple and that working memory is better thought of as a set of specialized mechanisms that act in concert according to the demands of the task in question. I shall also explore a number of difficulties with the view originally put forward by Atkinson and Shiffrin (1968) that working memory acts as a gateway between sensory input and long-term memory. This view is still prevalent as an assumption underlying contemporary thinking on the subject and commonly appears in textbooks.

Age VII: Working Memory as Multiple Components

The "gateway" view of working memory was significantly challenged by data from patients with impairments of short-term storage but with apparently normal long-term memory function. One of the best-known cases was reported by Warrington and Shallice (1969; Shallice & Warrington, 1970), who described a patient, K. F., with a severely impaired verbal short-term memory. Despite having a digit span of just two items, K. F. appeared to have normal long-term learning and retrieval. A number of such patients with specific short-term verbal memory deficits have been described in the literature (for a review, see Caplan & Waters, 1990). The point is that such patients can learn new information despite having a severe impairment in short-term memory. If we accept that it is reasonable to infer normal cognitive function from patterns of neuropsychological impairments, the data obtained from K. F. and other patients with short-term verbal-memory deficits force a rethinking of the idea of a single flexible system acting as a gateway into long-term memory. In other words, either (a) K. F. had an alternative route into long-term memory that did not involve working memory or (b) there are several working memory subsystems, not all of which are damaged in patients such as K. F.

In the remainder of the chapter I shall argue that these alternatives are not mutually incompatible, and that both could be true. In brief, I should like to argue, first, that it is more fruitful to consider working memory as comprising multiple components. This is an argument that has been rehearsed elsewhere but is worth reiterating and extending in the context of this book insofar as it contradicts contemporary theories, voiced by Just and Carpenter (1992), by Cowan (1993), by Ellen Stoltzfus, Lynn Hasher, and Rose Zacks (Chapter 3), and by Randall Engle (Chapter 4), which describe working memory as a single system. Second, I shall argue that working memory is better thought of as a system that operates after access to long-term memory has taken place, rather than acting as a means of transport for sensory input to long-term memory. On this view, working memory is seen as a workspace rather than a gateway, and sensory input reaches working memory via long-term memory, not the other way around.

Multiple Components and Dual-Task Performance

The idea that there might be multiple components of working memory gained considerable support from studies of normal subjects attempting to perform two or more tasks simultaneously. One implication of a limited-capacity, flexible system is that, if the task in hand demands all of the capacity, there should be no remaining capacity to cope with additional loads. Some very compelling evidence on this was reported by Allport, Antonis, and Reynolds (1972), who asked subjects to perform the ostensibly very demanding task of sight-reading music that they played on the piano. At the same time subjects had to attend to a text passage that was read to them through headphones. Skilled piano players could perform both tasks with little mutual interference. Numerous other studies have shown that normal adult subjects can simultaneously carry out two tasks, each of which would apparently place heavy demands on a single flexible working memory system (see, e.g., Baddeley, Bressi, Della Sala, Logie, & Spinnler, 1991; Baddeley, Logie, Bressi, Della Sala, & Spinnler, 1986; Farmer, Berman, & Fletcher, 1986; Klapp & Nettick, 1988). Also, several studies have shown that estimates of the difficulty of performing tasks are on their own poor predictors of how readily those tasks can be performed concurrently (Logie, Baddeley, Mane, Donchin, & Sheptak, 1989; Wickens & Liu, 1988).

In the studies by Baddeley et al. (1986, 1991), we looked first at the performance of normal subjects on two relatively demanding tasks. The first of these was standard digit span, which measures the maximum number of digits that can be recalled in the original order immediately following presentation. The second task involved the subject following a moving patch of light displayed on a computer screen. The target patch of light moved in a random fashion, and subjects were required to keep the tip of a light-sensitive pen on the target. The speed with which the target moved was gradually increased until the point at which the subject could stay on target about 40 percent to 60 percent of the time. Both digit-span and the "tracking-span" task reflected the maximum capacity of the cognitive system or systems responsible for task performance. Thus, digit span was taken to reflect the capacity for retention of a serially ordered verbal list.

Working Memory and Cognition

Tracking performance was taken to indicate the capacity for detecting the position of the target, continually updating working memory with information as to the changing location of the target and performing the required movements of the arm. Because the verbal string changed from trial to trial and the movement of the visual target was random, it is unlikely that performance would improve with practice over the relatively limited number of trials in this experiment. Thus, digit span could be thought of as a measure of the capacity of working memory to process and retain verbal information, whereas the tracking task might test working-memory capacity for dealing with visuospatial information and motor control.

If it were the case that a single, flexible working-memory system was involved in both tasks, we might expect that, when these two tasks were performed together, there would be a substantial disruption in the level of performance on both tasks. Alternatively, there might be no disruption of one task at the expense of a massive deterioration in performance on the other task. Data from this experiment are shown in Figure 2.1. In fact, when subjects perform the two tasks concurrently, there is very little drop in the performance of either. This finding is difficult to reconcile with the use of a single, flexible working-memory system, because either task performed on its own appeared to require the maximum capacity of whatever cognitive systems were responsible for task performance.

Such findings as these point toward the suggestion that there are at least two different cognitive systems involved, respectively responsible for

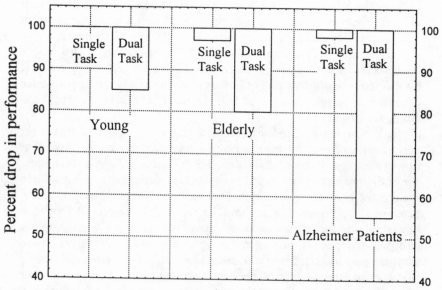

Fig. 2.1. Digit-span performance for groups of young and older subjects and a group of patients with Alzheimer-type dementia under single-task and dual-task conditions. (From Baddeley, Logie, Bressi, Della Sala, & Spinnler, 1986.)

each of the two tasks. Moreover, these two systems appeared to be able to work concurrently and more or less independently of one another. There was a small drop in the performance of both tasks under dual-task conditions, however, and this suggests that there was some cognitive cost or "processing overhead" of performing the two tasks simultaneously. Once we have made the assumption that there are two independent systems, it is then difficult to avoid making additional assumptions in order to account for this apparent dual-task overhead. One approach might be to suggest an extension of Just and Carpenter's (1992) theory in terms of the maximum amount of activation available. That is, there may be a maximum amount of energy in the system, and there may indeed be two cognitive systems that attempt to share the available energy, which is not quite sufficient to be spread across two independent systems working at maximum capacity. However, in this model, we have to assume further that each system on its own has a maximum allocation of activation, but that, when one system is operating on its own at its maximum capacity, this does not employ all of the activation potentially available to the cognitive system as a whole. Thus, the model becomes rather unwieldy and less attractive as a result.

An alternative model would be to suggest that the limitations on the performance of either or both of the tasks are not wholly determined by *cognitive* capacity. For example, the tracking task requires not only visual and spatial processing but also physical control of the muscles of the arm and hand. A limitation on performance could be set by a physical limitation on the speed of movement of the arm. This limitation could be reached before the task demands breached the capacity of the underlying cognitive mechanisms that were involved in task performance. It is more difficult to make this argument in the case of digit span, because this seems to rely more heavily on specifically cognitive resources. However, if the cognitive demands of tracking were minimal and largely at the level of an almost automated response to a visual stimulus, then the drop in digit-span performance under dual-task conditions could reflect the minimal cognitive load imposed by having to perform an additional task that itself made only limited demands on cognitive resources.

Indeed, the requirement to coordinate the performance of these two tasks simultaneously may be sufficient to account for the small observed decrement under dual-task conditions. That is, if digit span uses almost all of the activation capacity available to working memory, then some of that activation budget has to be allocated to coordinating digit span and the performance of a task that itself calls on little of the capacity of working memory. Conversely, the limited cognitive capacity that is allocated to performance of the tracking task may be further reduced by reallocating some of that budget to the coordinating function. The drop in both digit span and tracking when they are performed together may then signify a process of fiscal reallocation of activation.

This hybrid model incorporating both activation capacity and multiple specialized resources has some attractions, although in the form outlined here it begs a lot of questions as to how precisely the allocation occurs. It is also too powerful, in that there is no clear specification that would allow us to predict whether a task would be impaired under dual-task conditions. If there is no dual-task decrement, we can simply say that the systems were not using up all of their available allocation when they were performing each task on its own. If the performance of either or both tasks drops when they are performed together, we can invoke an explanation along the lines given above along with post hoc assumptions about the relative allocation of activation levels in each of the systems under single-task and dual-task conditions.

The experiments by Baddeley et al. (1986, 1991) provide additional evidence that is not consistent with this model. In addition to testing normal adults on digit span and tracking, we also tested a number of patients who had been diagnosed as suffering from the early stages of Alzheimer-type dementia. Like the normal subjects, the patients were first asked to perform the digit-span task on its own and the tracking task on its own. The Alzheimer group had lower digit spans and reached the 40 percent to 60 percent time-on-target when the target was moving rather more slowly than was the case for the normal adults. However, although the patients were performing at a relatively low level, they were able to perform each task on its own. The same criteria were used for assessing the span for each patient as had been used for the normal subjects. Therefore, the performance of each patient on each task was taken to indicate the maximum capacity of whatever system was responsible for task performance.

Previous studies have demonstrated that patients with mild forms of Alzheimer's disease can perform cognitive tasks, but at a somewhat reduced level compared to the healthy elderly (e.g., Morris, 1984, 1986). If we try to account for this pattern of data using the above model, it might suggest that Alzheimer's patients possess a smaller budget of available activation than neurologically intact adults. If the model is correct about the reallocation of activation to a coordinating function, then we should observe a modest impairment in both tasks when they are performed together, just as we found in the case of normal subjects. In fact, the Alzheimer's patients had considerable difficulty performing the two tasks simultaneously, and their data are also shown in Figure 2.1. Clearly, a model that is based upon the partial reallocation of available activation cannot readily account for these data.

One response could be that the brain damage suffered by Alzheimer's patients results in their cognitive functioning being organized in a fundamentally different way from that of intact people. However, without providing an account of the form that such reorganization might take, this approach simply finesses rather than answers the questions posed by these results. A more coherent account is to propose that the coordination of dual-task performance is accomplished by another cognitive resource that is independent of the resources required for digit span or for tracking and that is significantly impaired in patients with Alzheimer's disease.

If the revised model described earlier is wrong, this leaves open the question as to how we interpret the data obtained from normal adults. One approach would be to argue that in normal adults working memory comprises at least three systems. One of these systems provides temporary verbal storage and is used in digit span; another system provides perceptuo-motor control and is involved in tracking; and a third provides a coordinating function. To account for the data described here, let us assume that the coordinating function is also used to a certain extent in the performance of a single cognitive task. The coordinating function has its own "budget of activation," but little of that budget is required for the successful performance of a single task. However, when two tasks are required, the coordinating function is much more heavily loaded, and it may be unable to provide sufficient support for each of the two concurrent tasks, resulting in a small overall reduction in performance on each task. If we further assume that the coordinating function is impaired in Alzheimer's patients, this can account for the lower levels of single-task performance and also for the dramatic drop in performance associated with trying to perform two tasks at the same time.

Further evidence that is entirely consistent with this interpretation comes from experiments with normal adults performing somewhat different combinations of tasks. Logie, Zucco, and Baddeley (1990) investigated the effects of concurrent tasks on two forms of temporary memory span. In one task, the subject was briefly shown a square matrix pattern with half of the squares in the matrix filled in and half left blank. (An example is shown in Fig. 2.2.) After a short interval, the pattern was shown again but with one of the previously filled squares having been left blank. The subject's task was to identify the square that had been changed. The total number of squares in the pattern gradually increased until the subject was no longer able reliably to identify which square had been changed, and this was taken as an indication of the subject's span or maximum working-memory capacity for retaining visuospatial material. Performance on this task was compared with an equivalent verbal proce-

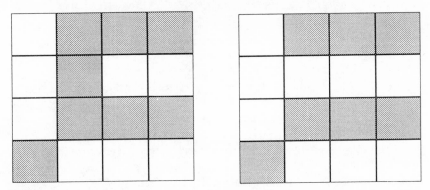

Fig. 2.2. Example of the square matrix patterns used by Logie, Zucco, and Baddeley (1990).

dure in which the subject was shown a sequence of letters that appeared one after another in the center of a computer screen. After the sequence had been completed, the same sequence was shown again but with one of the letters replaced by a new letter, and the subject had to identify the new letter in the sequence. The number of letters was gradually increased until the subject could no longer accurately identify the new letter.

These tasks were designed to measure working-memory capacity for visually presented patterns that are difficult to name and working-memory capacity for verbal sequences, respectively. Once the span for each task had been established, the subject was asked to perform each of the tasks concurrently with each of two secondary tasks. One of the secondary tasks involved simple mental arithmetic with auditory presentation. The other secondary task involved the auditory presentation of verbal instructions that required the subjects to generate the visual image of a number. An example of the number imaging task is shown in Figure 2.3.

Neither the primary span tasks nor the secondary tasks are readily open to the criticisms of the tracking task that was used in the studies by Baddeley et al. (1986, 1991). All of these tasks seem to involve both temporary storage and on-line cognitive processing, with few demands on perceptuo-motor control. In this sense, they all appear to place demands on working memory. This experiment thus provides a more rigorous test of the hypothesis of a single flexible system. If subjects are performing at the limits of their working-memory capacity on the visual-span task or the letter-span task, then the addition of a secondary task that also occupies working memory should result in a dramatic drop in performance. That is, performance on the visual-span task should be disrupted by both concurrent mental arithmetic and by the concurrent imagery task. Similarly, letter span should be affected by both of the secondary tasks.

Results of this experiment are depicted in Figure 2.4, which shows control levels of span as 100 percent, with the dual-task performance plotted as a proportion of that percentage. Figure 2.4 is striking in show-

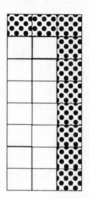

Fig. 2.3. Example of the number-imaging task used by Logie, Zucco, and Baddeley (1990).

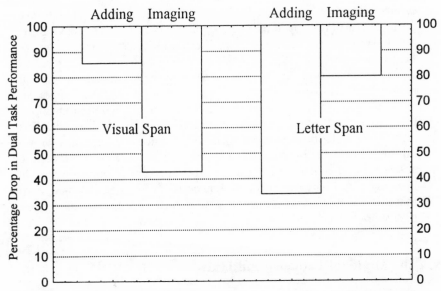

Fig. 2.4. Memory-span performance with matrix patterns and with letters with simultaneous adding or imaging. (Data from Logie, Zucco, and Baddeley, 1990.)

ing a clear double dissociation between the reduction found in the different dual-task conditions. Visual span is dramatically impaired by a concurrent imagery task but is only slightly affected by concurrent mental arithmetic. The converse is true in the case of letter span. Moreover, when we compared the performance of subjects on the secondary tasks we found an analogous pattern. Specifically, arithmetic performance was disrupted by concurrent letter span but not by concurrent visual span, while the converse was true of performance on the imagery task. Given the crossover interaction and the mirroring of the differential disruption in the secondary tasks, it would be very difficult to argue that the observed drop in performance was due to the extra demand of performing two tasks rather than one, since the interference is observed only for particular combinations of tasks. More crucially, the data are wholly inconsistent with a model of working memory as a single flexible system. Also, these data cannot be readily explained by a model that proposes a maximum activation budget for working-memory function without making further assumptions about how the activation might be allocated.

Although the crossover interaction is the most salient feature of the data in Figure 2.4, it is worth noting that there were small dual-task impairments found in the alternative task combinations. That is, mental arithmetic produced a small disruption in performance of the visual-span task, and the imagery task produced a small disruption in the verbal-span task. This result is readily explained if we incorporate the notion of a coordinating mechanism, discussed above, that is employed when performing more than one task at a time. This idea of a "cost of concurrence" or processing overhead is also found in other models of multiple cognitive resources, most notably in the attention literature (e.g., Navon & Gopher, 1979; Wickens, 1984; Wickens & Weingartner, 1985; Yee, Hunt, & Pellegrino, 1991).

The dissociations found in dual-task studies of normal adults and in studies of neurological patients strongly implicate a multiple-component working-memory system, with semi-independent specialized mechanisms that can act individually or in concert according to task demands. This form of modularity in working memory provides normal adults with a selection of mechanisms on which to draw, with flexibility of processing arising from the allocation of one or other specialist resource to provide processing and temporary storage functions. Conversely, it would seem that the model of working memory as a single flexible resource is difficult to sustain.

The Model of Baddeley and Hitch

A well-established model of a multicomponent working memory was originally proposed by Baddeley and Hitch (1974). Their model has been considerably modified and extended in recent years (e.g., Baddeley, 1986, 1990, 1992) and has had a dominant influence within Europe. The model comprises three components that respectively provide temporary verbal storage, temporary visuospatial storage, and a coordinating function. The verbal-storage component was originally named the "articulatory loop" but more recently has been referred to as the "phonological loop" (Baddeley & Logie, 1992). The visuospatial component is known as the "visuospatial scratchpad," whereas the coordinating mechanism is generally referred to as the "central executive." Extensive reviews of the evidence for the characteristics of each of these components have been published elsewhere (e.g., Baddeley, 1992; Baddeley & Logie, 1992; Logie, 1993, 1995; and see also Chapter 1 in this volume by John Richardson). Therefore, I shall discuss here some of this evidence for illustrative purposes only.

In brief, the phonological loop comprises a passive phonological store and an articulatory rehearsal process. Auditorily presented verbal information gains direct access to the passive store, which retains information in a phonological form. Information in the store is subject both to decay over time and to interference from new verbal material. Loss of information from the store can be prevented by means of subvocal rehearsal, and with continuing rehearsal the contents of the store could in principle be retained indefinitely. The operation of the store is impaired when it is subject to irrelevant speech (see Salamé & Baddeley, 1982). The disruptive effect is even greater when the irrelevant speech is phonologically similar to the material already in the passive store. The store also operates less efficiently when required to retain stimuli that are phonologically similar to one another (as in a sequence such as *man, mad, map, mat, mar*) compared with when the stimuli are phonologically distinct (for example, *bus, clock, spoon, fish, desk*: see Baddeley, 1966a, 1966b; Conrad, 1964). The phonological similarity effect supports the claim that the store is phonologically based.

According to the model, subvocal rehearsal is also responsible for translating visually presented verbal material into a phonological code for temporary retention in the phonological store. Evidence for this derives from studies showing that the phonemic similarity effect in the retention of visually presented words and letters is removed when the subjects are required to suppress subvocal rehearsal by repeating aloud an irrelevant word such as "the, the, the" or "hiya, hiya, hiya." In other words, when subjects are unable to rehearse visually presented items, they are not translated into a phonological code for retention in the store but may be retained using a visual or semantic code. Finally, the operation of the loop is limited by the length of time taken to pronounce the words for recall. For instance, words such as "cricket, wicket, bishop, parrot" take less time to say and are more difficult to recall than words such as "Friday, typhoon, vendor, practice." Likewise, words with five syllables such as "refrigerator, university, hippopotamus" take longer to say and are more difficult to recall than words of one syllable such as "salt, pen, cat, chair." Based on such findings, Baddeley, Thomson, and Buchanan (1975) argued that the capacity of the loop was limited by how much speech a subject could rehearse in around 2 seconds. This was thought to indicate the rate of decay of information from the phonological store.

The visuospatial scratchpad is thought to serve a similar function for visual or spatial material and to play a role in visual-imagery tasks. There is now an argument that the concept might be more useful if it were fractionated further into a system that provided passive storage for visual material and a companion system that retained movement sequences and might be used for some form of visuospatial rehearsal (Logie, 1995; Reisberg & Logie, 1993). Visual input is thought to have obligatory access to the passive visual system. The central executive component of the model provides the coordinating function for dual-task performance, and I discussed above some of the supporting evidence for this idea. It appears to play a role in reasoning and problem solving (Gilhooly, Logie, Wetherick, & Wynn, 1993; Logie, Gilhooly, & Wynn, 1994) and is thought to be involved in the allocation of attention (Baddeley, 1986, 1992).

Although the link between working memory and long-term memory has not been specified in detail, there is a general assumption that information can enter one or more subcomponents of working memory either from sensory input or from long-term memory. Working memory is also assumed to play an important role in transferring information from sensory input to long-term memory and in particular to be closely involved in the learning of novel information (Baddeley, Lewis, Eldridge, & Thomson, 1984). For example, as noted above, spoken verbal material is thought to have obligatory access to the phonological store, whereas visually pre-sented material is thought to have obligatory access to the visuospatial scratchpad. The model accounts for normal long-term learning in patients with verbal short-term memory deficits by arguing that only the phono-logical loop is impaired, thus permitting the central executive and the visuospatial scratch pad to effect long-term learning. This preserves the gateway hypothesis by means of additional assumptions about the nature of the various working-memory components. These assumptions are sup-ported by a large body of published data (for reviews, see Baddeley, 1986, 1992; Logie, 1993, 1995).

The Multiple Component Model: Gateway or Workspace?

I should like to put forward an alternative view that questions the status of working memory as comprising any kind of gateway between sensory input and long-term memory. The core of the argument is that access to acquired knowledge and prior learning occurs before information be-comes available to working memory. We know from the literature re-viewed above that stored semantic knowledge can play an important role in working-memory tasks. I should like to turn this around and question whether working memory can store and process information without pri-or access to stored knowledge and to the results of prior learning. On this view, working memory still plays an important role in long-term learning by processing the information it receives and returning it to long-term memory. To begin this discussion, let us examine the implications of a literal gateway hypothesis for the functioning of the phonological loop.

The Phonological Loop

If it were the case that information from auditory input were fed directly into the phonological store, we might expect that the acoustic properties of the auditory stimulus would be preserved as some form of echoic trace. It has become clear that the information in the phonological store is not simply a raw acoustic image. For example, the irrelevant speech effect referred to earlier appears to suggest preferential access by speech to the phonological store (Salamé & Baddeley, 1982, 1989). This indicates that access to stored representations of what are and what are not speech sounds seems to be a prerequisite for entry into the phonological store.[1]

In the case of visually presented material, access to the articulatory and phonological properties of printed text would similarly be required prior to phonological storage. In this respect, Besner and Davelaar (1982) ar-gued that the phonological codes used in reading were distinct from those used for temporary retention. It is also interesting that we can still access phonological codes for object names or in reading text even under articulatory suppression. For example, try saying "the, the, the" aloud and at the same time try mentally to name the objects around the room that you are in, or try mentally to generate the phonological codes for this printed text. These observations are entirely consistent with the view that the activation of stored phonological representations of words precedes the availability of phonological information within the phonological store of working memory. Whether other properties of text such as semantic information are accessed prior to their availability in working memory is a separate issue. For present purposes, it is simply sufficient to show that information regarding phonology and articulation is made available to the phonological loop. Thus, on logical grounds alone, access to stored knowledge must occur prior to the availability of phonological codes in working memory.

However, the issue is not so clear-cut. There has been some recent disquiet over the suggestion of a unique link between the phonological store and the articulatory aspects of speech. The rehearsal component of the phonological loop was originally thought to be based on articulatory codes and linked closely to the articulation of speech output (e.g., Baddeley, Lewis, & Vallar, 1984; Baddeley et al., 1975; Levy, 1971; Murray, 1965, 1968). I have already discussed the effects of word length, which indicate that articulation rate constrains the capacity of the loop (Baddeley et al., 1975; Ellis & Hennelly, 1980). A number of studies have shown that retention of a verbal sequence is impaired when subjects are required to recite an irrelevant word aloud (e.g., "the, the, the"), the technique known as articulatory suppression (Levy, 1971; Murray, 1965, 1968). These findings support the link with the speech system, but there is now an argument that subvocal rehearsal may be phonologically based rather than articulatory in nature (see Baddeley & Logie, 1992; Bishop & Robson, 1989; Martin, Blossom-Stach, Yaffee, & Wetzel, in press). In other words, we may be able mentally to rehearse a sequence of activated phonological codes, and nevertheless these codes do not depend on access to information concerning how the phonology is linked to the particular articulatory codes required for speech output.

For example, Bishop and Robson (1989) reported word-length effects in children who were congenitally anarthric. Because these youngsters had been unable to articulate from birth, it is unlikely that they could have developed any form of subvocal articulation. They did, however, possess good phonological skills, and the observed word-length effect may be based more on phonology than on articulation, at least in the case of these children. That is, the word-length effect in serial recall may be based on the time taken to rehearse the phonological codes underlying articulatory output. The effects of articulatory suppression could then be due to the repeated generation of the phonology of the irrelevant words, rather than to the overt articulation of those words.

A similar argument can be made in the case of the patient described by Martin et al. (in press), who appeared to have a severe impairment of the control mechanisms for articulation, but who showed evidence of rehearsal, albeit only for auditorily presented material. Consistent with the view of a phonologically based rehearsal mechanism, Baddeley and Logie (1992) argued that the phonological loop might in fact be capable of dealing with nonspeech sounds such as music, even if such sounds (e.g., the sound of a trumpet: Crowder, 1989; Crowder & Pitt, 1992) could not readily be produced by the articulators. The phonological loop might then be seen as the "seat of auditory imagery."

Whether or not the operation of the phonological loop is dedicated to speech-like material based on articulatory or on phonological codes, the information as to how to generate these codes has somehow to be extracted from the long-term knowledge base. Moreover, a reasonable amount of evidence shows that subvocal rehearsal is a learned strategy that subjects may or may not apply to serial-recall tasks. For example, Hitch, Woodin, and Baker (1989; see also Hitch, Halliday, Schaafstal, & Schraagen, 1988) have shown that subvocal rehearsal does not appear spontaneously in young children. Five-year-olds do not produce the effects of phonemic similarity or word length with visually presented material unless they are specifically taught to use subvocal rehearsal.

Indeed, some recent work with Sergio Della Sala and other colleagues (Della Sala & Logie, in press; Della Sala, Logie, Marchetti, & Wynn, 1991; Logie, Della Sala, Laiacona, Chalmers, & Wynn, in press) found that normal adults do not always spontaneously exhibit the effects of word length and phonemic similarity, and a major factor associated with the appearance of these effects is the strategy that subjects report using in these tasks. Subjects who report using verbal rehearsal show effects of phonemic similarity and word length; those who report using other strategies tend not to show these effects. Moreover, a number of our subjects reported changing strategies from one occasion to another and even from one trial to another within an experiment, with associated changes in the appearance or disappearance of the effects. This lack of test-retest reliability was true with both auditory and visual presentation, although under auditory presentation the phonemic similarity effect failed to appear in only 1 percent of the subject sample. The moral of this tale is that subvocal rehearsal and the use of the phonological store appear to be under strategic control and to involve a learned strategy. In other words, subvocal rehearsal can be thought of as a simple form of expertise that has been acquired by the majority of the normal adult population. The learned procedures for the serial recall of verbal sequences are retrieved from the knowledge base and are implemented as a strategy. Thus, access to long-term storage is required for the strategy, in addition to providing information as to the appropriate phonological and articulatory codes for the items that are to be retained and later recalled.

Having said this, the conceptual model of the phonological loop could still remain intact as a useful way of characterizing the component of the cognitive system that hosts the operation of articulatory rehearsal and of phonological storage. The major differences proposed in this account are that entry to the system is via access to knowledge of phonology stored in long-term memory, and that the use of the system is optional rather than obligatory in verbal serial-recall tasks.

Visuospatial Working Memory

Turning to the visuospatial scratchpad (VSSP), we can formulate an analogous argument. This component of working memory is thought to be involved in visual-imagery tasks and in temporary retention of visual and spatial information. As the phonological loop is linked to the speech system, so the VSSP has been linked to the control and production of physical movement. Evidence for this comes from studies in which subjects are required to generate and retain spatial images: for example, a series of movements between targets (Logie & Marchetti, 1991), body movements generated by the experimenter (Smyth & Pendleton, 1989), or an imaged matrix (Baddeley & Lieberman, 1980; Logie et al., 1990; Quinn & Ralston, 1986). Recall performance on such tasks is impaired by asking subjects concurrently to tap a series of keys laid out on a table or to move their arm to follow a moving target. The study by Logie et al. (1990) discussed above also provided evidence that visual-imagery processing and the processing and retention of visually presented information share cognitive resources. There is of course a large literature that attests to the overlap between visual imagery and visual perception (e.g., Finke, 1980; Kosslyn, 1980; Paivio, 1971). Although the exact nature and role of the VSSP is still a matter of debate (see, e.g., Logie, 1995; Reisberg & Logie, 1993), at least two sources of evidence suggest that visually presented information accesses stored knowledge in long-term memory without necessarily being processed first by working memory. The first of these sources is the literature on priming effects in both normal individuals and neurological patients. The second is the literature on visual perception, which has clearly established that the forms of visually presented stimuli are interpreted even in the very early stages of perception.

Dealing briefly with the perception literature, we know that visual patterns are processed in terms of edges, contours, grain, and patterns of light and shade. None of this initial analysis could be accomplished without reference to some form of representation concerning what edges and contours comprise. Moreover, visual scenes are processed differentially in terms of spatial frequency, with lower spatial frequencies processed first. This appears to allow rapid extraction of general shape, size, and gross identification of the object type. For example, identification of a visual stimulus as a human face can occur very rapidly (Fraser & Parker, 1988; Purcell & Stewart, 1986; Valentine & Bruce, 1986), with exposure durations as low as 40 to 50 milliseconds (ms). Clearly, processing may occur after the stimulus has disappeared, but it has been known for some time that even simple decisions about the nature of the stimulus typically take a minimum of 350 ms for an unpractised subject (Woodworth & Schlosberg, 1954). Insofar as the central-executive component of working memory is involved in decision making, this may reflect the time taken for the properties of the stimulus to be gleaned by reference to long-term knowledge about the stimulus and for that interpreted information to become available and be processed by working memory.

Evidence from various forms of priming, particularly preconscious priming, also seems to undermine the view that working memory functions as a gateway to long-term memory. In priming experiments, subjects are shown a series of objects or words that they have to identify or process in some way. There is an advantage in processing time for items that have been shown previously or preceded by a closely related item (Schacter, 1985, 1987). This occurs in the case of visually presented words and pictures and auditorily presented words (see Cooper, 1991; Graf & Schacter, 1985; Schacter, Cooper, & Delaney, 1990; Tulving & Schacter, 1990). Priming effects also arise even when the previous item was presented too rapidly to be consciously identified by the subject (e.g., Marcel, 1983a, 1983b). The references cited here represent only a small sample of the very large and rapidly growing literature on this topic. I shall not go into this literature in any more detail, but the clear message is that in normal adults sensory input can access previously stored representations without recourse to the bailiwick of working memory.

Data obtained from patients with visual neglect provide complementary evidence. These patients seem to ignore half (commonly, the left side) of their visual field, of visual objects, and of their body space. Thus, if asked to draw a clockface, they will tend to draw only the right-hand side of the face, although sometimes all 12 numbers are shown squashed into the right-hand side. When many visual-neglect patients are asked to describe a scene in front of them, they will omit objects on their left. However, although these patients appear to ignore information on their left-hand side, they are nonetheless affected by that information. For example, Halligan and Marshall (1991) showed visual-neglect patients pictures of two houses. In one of the pictures, the left half of the house was shown on fire. The patients denied that there was any difference between this picture and a picture of an identical house that was not on fire. That is, they ignored the left half of the picture. However, when asked which house they would prefer to live in, they chose the one that was not on fire.

One well-argued interpretation of these data is that, although the sensory information did not appear to be available in working memory, it was nevertheless activating semantic knowledge concerning fires and their unpleasant consequences (Bisiach, 1993). Thus, as in normal subjects, it would appear that sensory input can gain direct access to information in long-term memory without going through working memory first. Moreover, the results of accessing long-term semantic knowledge, in visual-neglect patients at least, may influence decisions without the individual being aware of why he or she is coming to particular decisions. One

possibility is that the activated information about unpleasant consequences can become available to working memory even though the information from sensory input does not.

There are other arguments that visually presented information is interpreted before it is available to working memory. For example, our visual
representation of a scene is not extracted from a raw visual input based on
retinal coordinates, but from a series of eye fixations, and it would be
impossible to have a coherent visual representation of a scene unless the
information from these fixations was subject to some form of organization, again requiring access to stored knowledge.

The Central Executive

The argument for the central executive is less contentious. It seems reasonably safe to assume that no one would argue that an executive processor
operates on anything other than information that has been touched by
stored knowledge and has been interpreted in the context of existing
knowledge. Indeed, the alternative models of working memory mentioned
earlier, such as those put forward by Hasher and Zacks (1988), by Just
and Carpenter (1992), and by Cowan (1993), all appear to refer to a
working memory consisting of a central executive that operates upon the
activation of long-term memory traces.

Working Memory as a Workspace, Not a Gateway

In this revised account, working memory operates not as a gateway but as
a workspace: a set of cognitive functions that can temporarily store information and run through procedures which process that information. A
schematic view of the "workspace" model of working memory is illustrated in Figure 2.5. In this scheme, the slave systems of working memory
are not input buffers in the strict sense. Rather, they function as "working
buffers." That is, they can serve as temporary buffers for information that
has yet to be processed or is about to be recalled overtly. Thus, information that has been recently presented to the senses may activate traces in
long-term memory, which then become available to components of working memory. Auditorily presented material activates long-term memory
traces for the properties of the material in question, and any activated
phonological or articulatory traces then become available for temporary
retention in the phonological loop. Any other information (such as visual
or semantic information) that happened to be activated at the same time
might then become available to other parts of the working-memory system, but not to the phonological loop.

In an analogous fashion, visually presented material activates long-

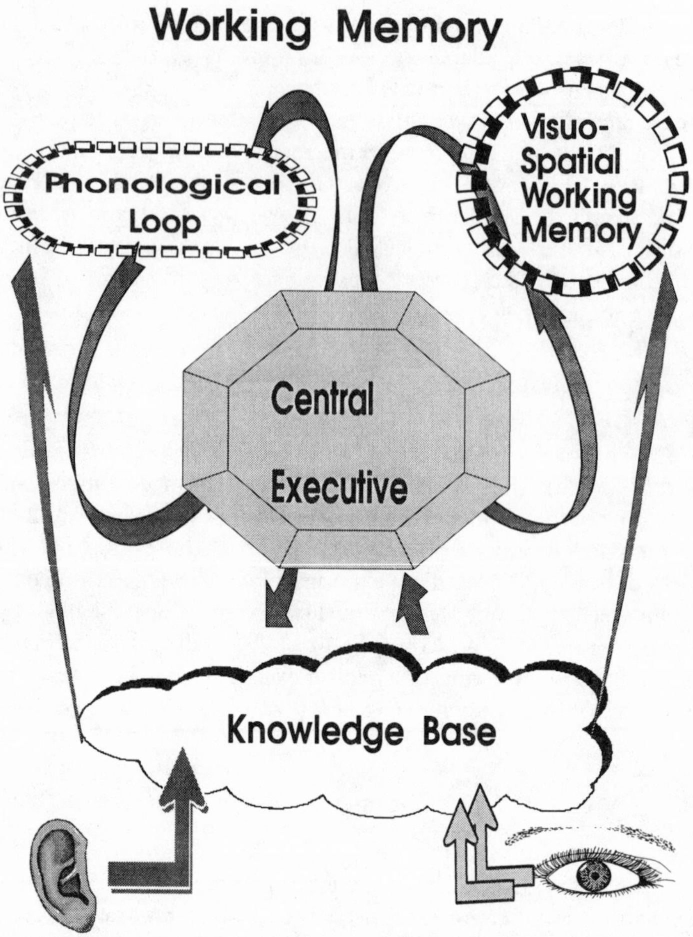

Working Memory

Fig. 2.5. A schematic view of working memory as a workspace rather than a gateway for cognition. (Adapted from Logie, 1995, p. 127.)

term memory traces for the properties of that material, and the visual and spatial information that is activated becomes available to the VSSP. Any additional information that becomes activated, such as semantic or phonological associates of the material, might be available to the central executive or the phonological loop.

This model has the advantage that it begins to specify the way that visually presented words can become available to the phonological loop, a feature that was somewhat underspecified in the original working-memory model. For example, if the word "book" is heard, the phonological representation of *book* and its articulatory codes can be used to store a phonological trace in the phonological loop, to rehearse the word, and to articulate it. On hearing the word, the visual and spatial properties of the word "book" become available to the VSSP, allowing generation of a temporary representation of the visual form of the word, which could then be written. Semantic information about books, such as what they are used for, could also be activated. This information would then be available to the central executive, allowing generation of an image of what a book looks like. The central executive could also draw upon information stored in the phonological loop and in the VSSP to carry out further processing on the properties of the visual or phonological form of the word to allow spelling, segmentation, rotation of an image of the word, and so on.

The other features of the model would then retain their original properties. Thus, for example, information in the phonological store would be subject to decay unless rehearsed. It would also be subject to interference or displacement by new auditory input, which would activate phonological long-term memory traces that in turn would become available to the phonological store, impinging on its previous contents. Overt production of speech would also activate the phonology associated with the articulatory sequence, and the activated phonology would become available to the phonological store. Articulatory suppression would have the effect of continually reactivating phonological traces that would enter the phonological store and disrupt its contents.

The model suggests an explanation for the effects of articulatory suppression that is slightly different from that currently offered. For example, the phonemic similarity effect is eliminated by articulatory suppression, but only if the material for recall is presented visually; auditory presentation results in a phonemic similarity effect whether or not the subject is simultaneously articulating an irrelevant word. Baddeley (1986, 1990) argues that subvocal articulation translates visually presented words into a phonological code, and repeating an irrelevant word prevents subvocal articulation, which in turn prevents phonological recoding. Within this same account, spoken material has direct access to the phonological store, and consequently articulatory suppression has no influence on the phonemic similarity effect.

In the revised version of the model outlined in this chapter, when a word is read, this activates the phonological information about that word, and this activated information becomes available to the phonological store. However, the act of repeatedly generating an irrelevant speech sound raises the level of activation for that speech sound to a level that is much higher than it would be for words that are read once or twice before the next word is presented or read from the list. Thus, the more highly activated trace for the "suppression" word (e.g., "the, the, the") would interfere with the entry into the phonological store of other, less highly activated phonological codes associated with the visually presented words.

This explanation also fits with the strategy-based account of the operation of the phonological loop that was discussed earlier. That is, because the phonological store is dominated by the highly activated trace of the suppression word, subjects use another component of working memory to store the word sequence, perhaps using visual or semantic codes. Hence, the phonemic similarity effect disappears when visual presentation of the words is accompanied by the repeated articulation of an irrelevant word. When the subjects hear the words to be recalled, the activation of the phonological trace is higher than it would be under visual presentation, and subjects therefore attempt to use the phonological store for retention with auditory presentation even under articulatory suppression. In this respect, it is notable that, although articulatory suppression does not un- dermine the phonemic similarity effect when presentation is auditory, nevertheless the overall levels of recall performance are poorer under artic- ulatory suppression, and this is consistent with the new account of these data presented here. Specifically, the higher level of activation for the suppression word competes with the lower levels of activation of the phonological codes for the heard material.

Although this explanation has still to be tested, some recent data reported by Longoni, Richardson, and Aiello (1993) are consistent with an activation-based model of the operation of the phonological loop. Longoni and co-workers examined the effects on the magnitude of the phonemic similarity effect of articulatory suppression during an interval between stimulus presentation and recall. In the articulatory-suppression condition, subjects were required to repeat the word "hiya" throughout presentation of an auditory list, as well as during a 10-second retention interval and during written recall. Longoni et al. (1993) found that the phonemic similarity effect was still present even after a 10-second delay that was occupied by articulatory suppression. Their results are shown in Table 2.1.

These data seem to be inconsistent with the existing assumption that the information in the store decays over a period of around 2 seconds unless it is rehearsed (Baddeley et al., 1975; see the discussion above). They are, however, consistent with a model that involves the activation of phonological information in long-term memory as well as the phonologi-

Table 2.1 Mean percentage correct responses in serial recall of phonemically distinct and similar items under silent learning and articulatory suppression with immediate and delayed recall

	Silent		Suppressed	
	Distinct	Similar	Distinct	Similar
Immediate	59.4	40.6	40.3	27.2
Delayed	79.4	50.3	57.8	38.1

Source: Longoni, A. M., Richardson, J. T. E., & Aiello A. (1993). Articulatory rehearsal and phonological storage in working memory. *Memory & Cognition, 21,* 11–22. Reproduced with permsission of the authors.

cal store. That is, information about the sequence of items may well be lost from the phonological store within a fairly short time without rehearsal. However, the model that is presented here allows for the possibility that activation of the phonological traces in long-term memory may not decay quite so rapidly, and after a 10-second delay the subjects may be relying on residual activation from this source rather than the phonological store.

Moreover, articulatory suppression is thought to affect the contents of the phonological store rather than the activation levels of long-term memory traces. Indeed, as the level of activation fades, the traces for the phonological codes may become even more difficult to discriminate from one another, and after a delay we might expect an even larger advantage for the phonologically distinct words. In the study by Longoni et al. (1993; see Table 2.1), it appeared that the phonemic similarity effect was in fact larger after a delay under suppression than it was for immediate recall under suppression. We might also expect less of an effect of articulatory suppression if recall were based upon access to activated phonological information in long-term memory, and it is notable that the levels of performance after a delay under suppression are only slightly lower than those for immediate recall in the silent condition.

The explanation for the word-length effect remains as before, namely that longer words take longer to say and can therefore be less readily rehearsed. Articulatory suppression prevents this rehearsal, and thus undermines the effects of word length. However, subjects may choose not to use subvocal rehearsal to retain the word sequence, relying upon visual or semantic information instead (see Della Sala et al., 1991). This would result in a reduction in the influence of word length in serial recall.

An additional feature of this model is that it provides an explicit way in which long-term memory could contribute to memory-span tasks if we assume that performance is based upon whatever information is available in working memory during recall. The subjects may use the contents of the articulatory loop, plus whatever information is available to the central executive and the VSSP when they attempt recall. Therefore, semantic and visual information can enhance recall performance over and above what can be achieved through the use of subvocal rehearsal and phonological coding (Hulme et al., 1991; Wetherick, 1975, 1976).

Conclusion

I began this chapter by going through one characterization of the ideas linked to human on-line cognitive processing and the temporary retention of information. These ideas have gone from a simple dichotomy between temporary and permanent storage mechanisms, through to the multiple fractionation of what Locke (1690) referred to as "contemplation." In following through these ideas I have tried to make a number of assumptions explicit and in particular to question the view that contemplation (i.e., working memory) arises directly from sensory input. The model that I have put forward is speculative, although I have pointed to ways in which it is consistent with a large body of published data, and ways in which aspects of the model might be tested. The spirit of this book is as a forum for debate, and what I have tried to do is show one way in which the debate as to the nature of working memory might move forward. The view of working memory outlined here is something of a hybrid drawn from currently parallel and more or less independent research tracks. The arguments in this chapter indicate that these tracks may not be wholly incompatible, and an exploration of the possible points of contact may prove to be of considerable mutual benefit.

Note

1. More recently, Jones (1994; Jones & Macken, 1993) has argued that an "irrelevant speech effect" in the serial recall of visually presented verbal sequences can be demonstrated with nonspeech material such as tones that vary from moment to moment. In contrast, invariant nonspeech stimuli do not result in any disruption of serial recall. Jones argues that the irrelevant speech effect can be explained by supposing that the recall of order information is disrupted by any auditory stream that changes state, and that it is not specifically a speech-based phenomenon. This raises a debate as to the precise interpretation of the irrelevant speech effect. Nevertheless, as is clear from the evidence reviewed in this chapter, the presumed nature of the components of working memory does not depend on the irrelevant speech effect alone, and the full implications of Jones's work for the multicomponent model of working memory remain to be explored.

References

Allport, D. A., Antonis, B., & Reynolds, P. (1972). On the division of attention: A disproof of the single channel hypothesis. *Quarterly Journal of Experimental Psychology, 24*, 225–235.

Atkinson, R. C., & Shiffrin, R. M. (1968). Human memory: A proposed system and its control processes. In K. W. Spence & J. T. Spence (Eds.), *The psychology of learning and motivation: Advances in research and theory* (Vol. 2, pp. 89–195). New York: Academic Press.

Baddeley, A. D. (1966a). Short-term memory for word sequences as a function of acoustic, semantic, and formal similarity. *Quarterly Journal of Experimental Psychology, 18*, 362–365.

Baddeley, A. D. (1966b). The influence of acoustic and semantic similarity on long-term memory for word sequences. *Quarterly Journal of Experimental Psychology, 18*, 302–309.

Baddeley, A. D. (1978). The trouble with levels: A reexamination of Craik and Lockhart's framework for memory research. *Psychological Review, 85*, 139–152.

Baddeley, A. (1986). *Working memory*. Oxford: Oxford University Press.

Baddeley, A. (1990). *Human memory: Theory and practice*. Hove, UK: Erlbaum.

Baddeley, A. (1992). Is working memory working? The fifteenth Bartlett Lecture. *Quarterly Journal of Experimental Psychology, 44*, 1–31.

Baddeley, A., Bressi, S., Della Sala, S., Logie, R. H., & Spinnler, H. (1991). The decline of working memory in Alzheimer's disease: A longitudinal study. *Brain, 114,* 2521–2542.

Baddeley, A. D., & Hitch, G. J. (1974). Working memory. In G. H. Bower (Ed.), *The psychology of learning and motivation: Advances in research and theory* (Vol. 8, pp. 47–90). New York: Academic Press.

Baddeley, A., Lewis, V. J., Eldridge, M., & Thomson, N. (1984). Attention and retrieval from long-term memory. *Journal of Experimental Psychology: General, 113,* 518–540.

Baddeley, A., Lewis, V. J., & Vallar, G. (1984). Exploring the articulatory loop. *Quarterly Journal of Experimental Psychology, 36,* 233–252.

Baddeley, A. D., & Lieberman, K. (1980). Spatial working memory. In R. S. Nickerson (Ed.), *Attention and performance VIII* (pp. 521–539). Hillsdale, NJ: Erlbaum.

Baddeley, A., & Logie, R. H. (1992). Auditory imagery and working memory. In D. Reisberg (Ed.), *Auditory imagery* (pp. 179–197). Hillsdale, NJ: Erlbaum.

Baddeley, A., Logie, R., Bressi, S., Della Sala, S., & Spinnler, H. (1986). Senile dementia and working memory. *Quarterly Journal of Experimental Psychology, 38A,* 603–618.

Baddeley, A., Logie, R. H., Nimmo-Smith, I., & Brereton, N. (1985). Components of fluent reading. *Journal of Memory and Language, 24,* 119–131.

Baddeley, A. D., Thomson, N., & Buchanan, M. (1975). Word length and the structure of short-term memory. *Journal of Verbal Learning and Verbal Behavior, 14,* 575–589.

Besner, D., & Davelaar, E. (1982). Basic processes in reading: Two phonological codes. *Canadian Journal of Psychology, 36,* 701–711.

Bishop, D.V.M., & Robson, J. (1989). Unimpaired short-term memory and rhyme judgement in congenitally speechless individuals: Implications for the notion of "articulatory coding." *Quarterly Journal of Experimental Psychology, 41A,* 123–141.

Bisiach, E. (1993). Mental representation in unilateral neglect and related disorders: The twentieth Bartlett memorial lecture. *Quarterly Journal of Experimental Psychology, 46A,* 435–461.

Caplan, D., & Waters, G. S. (1990). Short-term memory and language comprehension: A critical review of the neuropsychological literature. In G. Vallar & T. Shallice (Eds.), *Neuropsychological impairments of short-term memory* (pp. 337–389). Cambridge: Cambridge University Press.

Case, R. D., Kurland, D. M., & Goldberg, J. (1982). Operational efficiency and the growth of short-term memory span. *Journal of Experimental Child Psychology, 33,* 386–404.

Charness, N. (1976). Memory for chess positions: Resistance to interference. *Journal of Experimental Psychology: Human Learning and Memory, 2,* 641–653.

Conrad, R. (1964). Acoustic confusions in immediate memory. *British Journal of Psychology, 55,* 75–84.

Cooper, L. A. (1991). Dissociable aspects of the mental representation of visual objects. In R. H. Logie & M. Denis (Eds.), *Mental images in human cognition* (pp. 3–34). Amsterdam: Elsevier.

Cowan, N. (1993). Activation, attention, and short-term memory. *Memory & Cognition, 21,* 162–167.

Craik, F.I.M., & Lockhart, R. S. (1972). Levels of processing: A framework for memory research. *Journal of Verbal Learning and Verbal Behavior, 11,* 671–684.

Crowder, R. G. (1989). Imagery for musical timbre. *Journal of Experimental Psychology: Human Perception and Performance, 15,* 472–478.

Crowder, R. G., & Pitt, M. A. (1992). Research on memory/imagery for musical timbre. In D. Reisberg (Ed.), *Auditory imagery* (pp. 29–44). Hillsdale, NJ: Erlbaum.

Daneman, M., & Carpenter, P. A. (1980). Individual differences in working memory and reading. *Journal of Verbal Learning and Verbal Behavior, 19,* 450–466.

Daneman, M., & Tardif, T. (1987). Working memory and reading skill re-examined. In M. Coltheart (Ed.), *Attention and performance XII: The psychology of reading* (pp. 491–508). Hove, UK: Erlbaum.

De Groot, A. D. (1965). *Thought and choice in chess.* The Hague: Mouton.

Della Sala, S., & Logie, R. (in press). Impairments of methodology and theory in cognitive neuropsychology: A case for rehabilitation? *Neuropsychological Rehabilitation.*

Della Sala, S., Logie, R. H., Marchetti, C., & Wynn, V. (1991). Case studies in working memory: A case for single cases? *Cortex, 27,* 169–191.

Ellis, N. C., & Hennelly, R. A. (1980). A bilingual word-length effect: Implications for intelligence testing and the relative ease of mental calculation in Welsh and English. *British Journal of Psychology, 71,* 43–52.

Engle, R. W., Cantor, J., & Carullo, J. (1992). Individual differences in working memory and comprehension: A test of four hypotheses. *Journal of Experimental Psychology: Learning, Memory and Cognition, 18,* 972–992.

Ericsson, K. A., & Chase, W. G. (1982). Exceptional memory. *American Scientist, 70,* 607–615.

Ericsson, K. A., & Kintsch, W. (1991). *Memory in comprehension and problem solving: A long-term working memory* (Tech. Rep. No. 91–13). Boulder: University of Colorado, Institute of Cognitive Science.

Ericsson, K. A., & Pennington, N. (1993). The structure of memory performance in experts: Implications for memory in everyday life. In G. M. Davies & R. H. Logie (Eds.), *Memory in everyday life* (pp. 241–277). Amsterdam: Elsevier.

Ericsson, K. A., & Polson, P. G. (1988). An experimental analysis of a memory skill for dinner orders. *Journal of Experimental Psychology: Learning, Memory, and Cognition, 14,* 305–316.

Farmer, E. W., Berman, J.V.F., & Fletcher, Y. L. (1986). Evidence for a visuo-spatial scratch-pad in working memory. *Quarterly Journal of Experimental Psychology, 38A,* 675–688.

Finke, R. A. (1980). Levels of equivalence in imagery and perception. *Psychological Review, 87,* 113–132.

Fraser, I. H., & Parker, D. M. (1988) Visual parsing and priority effects in temporal order judgements of line drawn patterns. *Perception, 17,* 437–459.

Gilhooly, K. J., Logie, R. H., Wetherick, N. E., & Wynn, V. (1993). Working memory and strategies in syllogistic reasoning tasks. *Memory & Cognition, 21,* 115–124.

Glanzer, M., & Cunitz, A. R. (1966). Two storage mechanisms in free recall. *Journal of Verbal Learning and Verbal Behavior, 5,* 351–360.

Graf, P., & Schacter, D. L. (1985). Implicit and explicit memory for new associations in normal and amnesic patients. *Journal of Experimental Psychology: Learning, Memory, and Cognition, 11,* 501–518.

Halligan, P. W., & Marshall, J. C. (1991). Left neglect for near but not far space in man. *Nature, 350,* 498–500.

Hasher, L., & Zacks, R. T. (1988). Working memory, comprehension, and aging: A review and a new view. In G. H. Bower (Ed.), *The psychology of learning and motivation: Advances in research and theory* (Vol. 22, pp. 193–225). San Diego, CA: Academic Press.

Hitch, G. J., Halliday, M. S., Schaafstal, A. M., & Schraagen, J.M.C. (1988). Visual working memory in young children. *Memory & Cognition, 16,* 120–132.

Hitch, G. J., Woodin, M. E., & Baker, S. (1989). Visual and phonological components of working memory in children. *Memory & Cognition, 17,* 175–185.

Hulme, C., Maughan, S., & Brown, G.D.A. (1991). Memory for familiar and unfamiliar words: Evidence for a long-term memory contribution to short-term memory span. *Journal of Memory and Language, 30,* 685–701.

James, W. (1905). *Principles of psychology* (Vol. 1). London: Methuen.

Jones, D. M. (1994). Disruption of memory for lip-read lists by irrelevant speech: Further support for the changing state hypothesis. *Quarterly Journal of Experimental Psychology, 47A,* 143–160.

Jones, D. M., & Macken, W. J. (1993). Irrelevant tones produce an irrelevant speech effect: Implications for phonological coding in working memory. *Journal of Experimental Psychology: Learning, Memory, and Cognition, 19,* 369–381.

Just, M., & Carpenter, P. (1992). A capacity theory of comprehension: Individual differences in working memory. *Psychological Review, 99,* 122–149.

King, J., & Just, M. A. (1991). Individual differences in syntactic processing: The role of working memory. *Journal of Memory and Language, 30,* 580–602.

Klapp, S. T., & Nettick, A. (1988). Multiple resources for processing and storage in short-term working memory. *Human Factors, 30,* 617–632.

Kosslyn, S. M. (1980). *Image and mind.* Cambridge, MA: Harvard University Press.

Levy, B. A. (1971). The role of articulation in auditory and visual short-term memory. *Journal of Verbal Learning and Verbal Behavior, 10,* 123–132.

Locke, J. (1690). *An essay concerning humane understanding.* London: Thomas Bassett.

Logie, R. H. (1993). Working memory in everyday cognition. In G. M. Davies & R. H. Logie (Eds.), *Memory in everyday life* (pp 173–218). Amsterdam: Elsevier.

Logie, R. H. (1995). *Visuo-spatial working memory.* Hove, UK: Erlbaum.

Logie, R. H., Baddeley, A., Mane, A., Donchin, E., & Sheptak, R. (1989). Working memory and the analysis of a complex skill by secondary task methodology. *Acta Psychologica, 71,* 53–87.

Logie, R. H., Della Sala, S., Laiacona, M., Chalmers, P., & Wynn, V. (in press). Group effects, individual differences, and cognitive neuropsychology: The case of verbal short-term memory. *Memory & Cognition.*

Logie, R. H., Gilhooly, K. J., & Wynn, V. (1994). Counting on working memory in mental arithmetic. *Memory & Cognition, 22,* 395–410.

Logie, R. H., & Marchetti, C. (1991). Visuo-spatial working memory: Visual, spatial or central executive? In R. H. Logie & M. Denis (Eds.), *Mental images in human cognition* (pp. 105–115). Amsterdam: Elsevier.

Logie, R. H., Wright, R., & Decker, S. (1992). Recognition memory performance and residential burglary. *Applied Cognitive Psychology*, *6*, 109–123.

Logie, R. H., Zucco, G., & Baddeley, A. (1990). Interference with visual short-term memory. *Acta Psychologica*, *75*, 55–74.

Longoni, A. M., Richardson, J.T.E., & Aiello, A. (1993). Articulatory rehearsal and phonological storage in working memory. *Memory & Cognition*, *21*, 11–22.

Marcel, A. J. (1983a). Conscious and unconscious perception: Experiments on visual masking and word recognition. *Cognitive Psychology*, *15*, 197–237.

Marcel, A. J. (1983b). Conscious and unconscious perception: An approach to relations between phenomenal experience and perceptual processes. *Cognitive Psychology*, *15*, 238–300.

Martin, R. C., Blossom-Stach, C., Yaffee, L. S., & Wetzel, W. F. (in press). Consequences of a motor programming deficit for rehearsal and written sentence comprehension. *Quarterly Journal of Experimental Psychology*.

Miller, G. A. (1956). The magical number seven, plus or minus two: Some limits on our capacity for processing information. *Psychological Review*, *63*, 81–97.

Milner, B. (1959). The memory defect in bilateral hippocampal lesions. *Psychiatric Research Reports*, *11*, 43–58.

Morris, R. G. (1984). Dementia and the functioning of the articulatory loop system. *Cognitive Neuropsychology*, *1*, 143–158.

Morris, R. G. (1986). Short-term memory in senile dementia of the Alzheimer type. *Cognitive Neuropsychology*, *3*, 77–97.

Murray, D. (1965). Vocalization-at-presentation, with varying presentation rates. *Quarterly Journal of Experimental Psychology*, *17*, 47–56.

Murray, D. (1968). Articulation and acoustic confusability in short-term memory. *Journal of Experimental Psychology*, *78*, 679–684.

Navon, D., & Gopher, D. (1979). On the economy of the human processing system. *Psychological Review*, *86*, 214–255.

Paivio, A. (1971). *Imagery and verbal processes*. New York: Holt, Rinehart, & Winston.

Posner, M. (1966). Components of skilled performance. *Science*, *152*, 1712–1718.

Purcell, D. G., & Stewart, A. L. (1986). The face-detection effect. *Bulletin of the Psychonomic Society*, *24*, 118–120.

Quinn, J. G., & Ralston, G. E., (1986). Movement and attention in visual working memory. *Quarterly Journal of Experimental Psychology*, *38A*, 689–703.

Reisberg, D., & Logie, R. H. (1993). The ins and outs of visual working memory: Overcoming the limits on learning from imagery. In M. Intons-Peterson, B. Roskos-Ewoldsen, & R. Anderson (Eds.), *Imagery, creativity, and discovery: A cognitive approach* (pp. 39–76). Amsterdam: Elsevier.

Saariluoma, P. (1992). Visuo-spatial and articulatory interference in chess players' information intake. *Applied Cognitive Psychology*, *6*, 77–89.

Salamé, P., & Baddeley, A. (1982). Disruption of short-term memory by unattended speech: Implications for the structure of working memory. *Journal of Verbal Learning and Verbal Behavior*, *21*, 150–164.

Salamé, P., & Baddeley, A. (1989). Effects of background music on phonological short-term memory. *Quarterly Journal of Experimental Psychology*, *41A*, 107–122.

Salthouse, T. A. (1991). *Theoretical perspectives on cognitive aging*. Hillsdale, NJ: Erlbaum.

Salthouse, T. A., & Babcock, R. L. (1991). Decomposing adult age differences in working memory. *Developmental Psychology, 27*, 763–776.

Schacter, D. L. (1985). Priming of old and new knowledge in amnesic patients and normal subjects. *Annals of the New York Academy of Sciences, 444*, 41–53.

Schacter, D. L. (1987). Implicit memory: History and current status. *Journal of Experimental Psychology: Learning, Memory, and Cognition, 13*, 501–518.

Schacter, D. L., Cooper, L. A., & Delaney, S. M. (1990). Implicit memory for unfamiliar objects depends on access to structural descriptions. *Journal of Experimental Psychology: General, 119*, 5–24.

Shallice, T., & Warrington, E. K. (1970) Independent functioning of verbal memory stores: A neuropsychological study. *Quarterly Journal of Experimental Psychology, 22*, 261–273.

Smyth, M. M., & Pendleton, L. R. (1989). Working memory for movements. *Quarterly Journal of Experimental Psychology, 41A*, 235–250.

Teuber, H.-L., Milner, B., & Vaughan, H. G. (1968). Persistent anterograde amnesia after a stab wound in the basal brain. *Neuropsychologia, 6*, 267–282.

Tulving, E., & Schacter, D. L. (1990). Priming and human memory systems. *Science, 247*, 301–396.

Turner, M. L., & Engle, R. W. (1989). Is working memory capacity task dependent? *Journal of Memory and Language, 28*, 127–154.

Valentine, T., & Bruce, V. (1986). The effect of distinctiveness in recognising and classifying faces. *Perception, 15*, 525–536.

Warrington, E. K., & Shallice, T. (1969) The selective impairment of auditory verbal short-term memory. *Brain, 92*, 885–896.

Waugh, N. C., & Norman, D. A. (1965). Primary memory. *Psychological Review, 72*, 89–104.

Wetherick, N. E. (1975). The role of semantic information in short-term memory. *Journal of Verbal Learning and Verbal Behavior, 14*, 471–480.

Wetherick, N. E. (1976). Semantic information in short-term memory: Effects of presenting recall instructions after the list. *Bulletin of the Psychonomic Society, 8*, 79–81.

Wetherick, N., & Alexander, J. (1977). The role of semantic information in short-term memory in children aged 5 to 9 years. *British Journal of Psychology, 68*, 71–75.

Wickens, C. D. (1984). Processing resources in attention. In R. Parasuraman & R. Davies (Eds.), *Varieties of attention* (pp. 63–101). New York: Academic Press.

Wickens, C. D., & Liu, Y. (1988). Codes and modalities in multiple resources: A success and a qualification. *Human Factors, 30*, 599–616.

Wickens, C. D., & Weingartner, A. (1985). Process control monitoring: The effects of spatial and verbal ability and concurrent task demand. In R. E. Eberts & C. G. Eberts (Eds.), *Trends in ergonomics/human factors* (Vol. 2). Amsterdam: Elsevier.

Woodworth, R. S., & Schlosberg, H. (1954). *Experimental psychology*. London: Methuen.

Yee, P. L., Hunt, E., & Pellegrino, J. W. (1991). Coordinating cognitive information: Task effects and individual differences in integrating information from several sources. *Cognitive Psychology, 23*, 615–680.

Yuill, N., Oakhill, J., & Parkin, A. J. (1988). Working memory, comprehension ability and the resolution of text anomaly. *British Journal of Psychology, 80*, 351–361.

3

Working Memory and Aging: Current Status of the Inhibitory View

Ellen R. Stoltzfus, Lynn Hasher, and Rose T. Zacks

The construct of working memory has become a central component of many models of cognitive functioning, including those developed in the areas of thinking, problem solving, and memory, as well as in most aspects of language processing, such as comprehension, production, and reading. Generally, working memory is conceptualized as a mental workspace consisting of activated memory representations that are available in a temporary buffer for manipulation during cognitive processing. These activated representations may or may not be available to consciousness, but they are usually thought to be above some threshold of activation (Baddeley, 1986, 1992; cf. Cowan, 1988, 1993). Working memory has both storage and processing functions, enabling both the temporary maintenance of active representations in memory and also the manipulation of these representations in the service of current processing demands. In tasks such as language comprehension, in which complex processing of current information is ongoing but in which continuity with previous information must be preserved at all times, efficient operation of both the processing and storage components of working memory is critical. Demands placed on working memory at any given time will, of course, vary across situations and across individuals who differ in expertise or cognitive abilities.

Although there is considerable agreement that working memory plays a critical role in cognitive processing, a lack of consensus exists among cognitive theorists as to how best to conceptualize working memory and the role it plays in different cognitive activities. In this chapter we first consider conceptualizations of working memory that stress its purported limited capacity, and then we turn to an alternative (first proposed by

Hasher & Zacks, 1988) that focuses on the inhibitory control of the contents of working memory. Following a review of the evidence relevant to this alternative, particularly evidence stemming from studies exploring adult age differences in attention, memory, and language, we shall conclude with a discussion of issues that are in need of further clarification and investigation.

Working Memory and the Limited-Capacity Assumption

Almost all conceptions of working memory assume that there is a limit in the extent to which working memory is able to hold and process information. However, despite its apparent widespread appeal, significant problems exist with the limited-capacity assumption, some of which relate to limited-capacity notions in general, whereas others relate to working memory in particular. With regard to the former, Allport (1989) and Navon (1984) among others have provided excellent critiques of the general notion of capacity limitations on cognitive processing, and it is not our wish to reiterate here all of the arguments put forward by these authors. Suffice it to say that there are both conceptual and empirical shortcomings to limited-capacity views. These include the vagueness of the central constructs and the failures of findings (for instance, from dual-task situations) to conform to reasonable predictions derived from the assumption of a capacity limitation on some central resource.

With respect to working memory, one problem is that the locus of the proposed limitation in the ability to hold and process information has been hotly debated. Virtually every possible aspect of working memory has been pinpointed as the capacity limitation by one investigator or another; these include storage capacity, amount of available activation, processing capacity, and ability to allocate resources to both processing and storage components (see, e.g., Engle, Cantor, & Carullo, 1992). After many years of research, no consensus has been reached as to the particular source of the working-memory capacity limitation.

Other difficulties for the limited working-memory capacity notion have become apparent in the actual quest to measure working memory in terms of both its storage capacity and its processing capacity. Thus far, considerable effort has failed to yield any measure or group of measures that are agreed to measure the capacity of working memory in an accurate and reliable manner. Related to this is the existence of conflicting evidence regarding whether particular working-memory measures tap into a domain-specific resource or a general resource. For example, although Daneman and Tardif (1987) concluded in favor of the domain-specific view, Engle et al. (1992) concluded that working memory was a general resource that served a wide variety of verbal and nonverbal cognitive tasks.

Nonetheless, because of its face validity and intuitive appeal, and because it has served as a productive framework in a number of different contexts, the limited-capacity tradition has survived despite the problems discussed above. Here, we briefly review some of the work exploring the possibility that individual differences among adults and group differences among adults of varying ages might be attributed to variations in their working-memory capacity.

Individual Differences in Working-Memory Capacity

One main path for verifying specific hypotheses about the way in which limited capacity affects cognitive functioning is to compare individuals or groups that are presumed to differ in working-memory capacity. The research strategy is to use some measure of working-memory capacity and to correlate performance on that task with performance on other cognitive tasks that are of interest, such as language-comprehension. This sort of approach has been used to study individual differences in language processing and group differences among, for example, younger and older adults, children of various ages, and patients with Alzheimer's disease.

As John Richardson mentioned in Chapter 1, the first task used in the language-comprehension literature to measure working-memory capacity was the "reading-span" task (Daneman & Carpenter, 1980). In this task, subjects are asked to read sets of sentences of moderate complexity and then to do two things: to comprehend each sentence and to remember the last word of each sentence (thus tapping both the processing and the storage components of working memory). "Reading span" is then measured by the largest set of sentences in which a subject is able consistently to remember the last word of each sentence.

The early work by Daneman and colleagues showed that their index of working-memory capacity predicted several performance measures related to verbal ability, including the verbal score in the Scholastic Aptitude Test (SAT), the accuracy in determining the referent of a pronoun, the accuracy in determining novel word meanings by using the surrounding context, and scores on items testing comprehension (Daneman & Carpenter, 1980, 1983). Correlations between reading span and the various language-comprehension performance scores were in the .70 to .90 range, with correlations between reading span and verbal SAT generally above .50. Other investigators, however, have not been so successful at finding such strong correlations. For example, among a small (and possibly unrepresentative) sample of papers (Baddeley, Logie, Nimmo-Smith, & Brereton, 1985; Engle, Carullo, & Collins, 1991; Light & Anderson, 1985), the highest correlation between a version of the reading-span test and comprehension is about .54. In some instances (see Light & Anderson, 1985, Experiment 2), the correlations are not even statistically significant.

Another complication, which has arisen since the early research on working memory, involves conflicting findings on the predictive value of working-memory–span tasks (which involve both processing and storage components) versus simple span tasks (which mainly involve storage and are usually measured by digit or word span). Although Daneman (e.g., Daneman & Carpenter, 1980; Daneman & Tardif, 1987) has argued that simple span scores are not nearly as predictive as working-memory scores in a variety of tasks, others have more recently found that simple span scores can be as predictive as working-memory–span scores (see, for example, Engle et al., 1991).

Just, Carpenter, and their colleagues (e.g., Just & Carpenter, 1992; MacDonald, Just, & Carpenter, 1992) have recently correlated scores on the original working-memory–span tasks with performance on various language-processing tasks. The data are compelling in suggesting that the capacity of working memory accounts for much variance in the performance of young adults, at least in their population (undergraduates at Carnegie Mellon University). Despite this success in relating performance to the capacity of working memory, alternative explanations have been presented for these individual differences (see MacDonald & Perlmutter, 1993).

Group Differences in Working-Memory Capacity Associated with Aging

With regard to aging, the basic argument of capacity theories is that older adults exhibit poor performance across a wide variety of cognitive tasks because of the reduction in working memory that occurs with increasing age. This viewpoint predicts that older adults will have lower average scores on measures of working-memory capacity, and furthermore that the differences in working-memory capacity can account for age differences on the target cognitive tasks (so that, when working-memory capacity is partialed out, age will no longer exhibit a significant association with the level of performance). The support for the first of these predictions is fairly strong, but, even so, there are reports of failure to find age differences on tests of working-memory capacity (e.g., Hartley, 1986, 1993). Furthermore, even when age differences in the capacity of working memory are found, it is not always the case that age differences in performance on memory and language tasks are attributable to the working-memory differences (e.g., Hartley, 1986, 1993; Light & Anderson, 1985; see Light, 1991, for a review of the relevant literature on both of these points). A further complication is that there is a lack of consensus as to the specific aspect of working memory (i.e., storage, processing, or coordination mechanisms) that is compromised (cf. Craik & Jennings, 1992; Salthouse, 1990).

In sum, the literature on age-related performance differences, our central interest, has lent mixed support to the reduced-capacity approach. Despite the kinds of conceptual and empirical problems mentioned above, some authors (such as Craik & Jennings, 1992; Salthouse, 1990) continue to hold this up as a good model for generating and understanding research. However, others (Hasher & Zacks, 1988; Light, 1991) have called for alternative accounts. In our view, capacity theories, although both intuitively appealing and intermittently successful in accounting for a broad range of findings (at least on the surface), are ultimately not as productive as approaches that seek to reveal underlying processes. These processes (which may or may not be capacity-limited) will vary in their efficiency across individuals and groups and affect processing in complex and interesting ways that are not necessarily predicted by capacity views. We have generally found capacity explanations for individual as well as group differences to be unsatisfying, because there could be multiple reasons for capacity reductions and multiple ways in which these capacity reductions produce performance differences. In fact, we (Hasher & Zacks, 1988; Zacks & Hasher, 1994) have argued that other problems may be the underlying cause of what appears to be decreased capacity in older adults.

An Alternative View to Capacity

The failure of the capacity model of working memory to account satisfactorily for differences between older and younger adults' performance led Hasher and Zacks in 1988 to turn their attention from views that emphasized the sheer *capacity* of working memory to a new view emphasizing the *contents* of a working memory that might or might not be limited in size. At the time, Hasher and Zacks offered their view as an alternative to limited capacity; this is because they considered the notion of limited resources to be a problematic and possibly unnecessary assumption. At the very least, they considered capacity views to offer an incomplete explanation for patterns of performance. The alternative view developed by Hasher and Zacks was based on the idea that it was not the size of a working memory that would determine performance but how well the contents of the working-memory (or activated-memory) set represented the current task goals. If the activated information in memory were closely tied to the goals of the ongoing task, then performance would be good. If, on the other hand, the set of activated information included thoughts that were irrelevant to the task at hand, then the simultaneously processed relevant and irrelevant trains of thought would create a situation analogous to a divided-attention task.

A consequence of creating such a divided-attention situation is that comprehension and memory performance would be likely to suffer through several avenues. First, divided attention could create difficulties at encoding. "Cross talk" between concurrent streams of information would be likely to occur, especially if attempts were made to integrate irrelevant ideas with ongoing discourse. Because of these encoding complications, comprehension and retrieval would be less successful, either because the information to be retrieved was not sufficiently encoded or because the association of relevant and irrelevant material at the time of encoding created competition at retrieval among the relevant and irrelevant aspects of information. Competition could also cause slowed retrieval during the immediate memory searches that would be necessary to maintain coherence in the discourse (for example, searching for the referent of a pronoun). In addition, yet more retrieval interference would be likely if, at the time of retrieval, any further distractions were either internally generated or externally presented.

The key to successful processing, then, from Hasher and Zacks's viewpoint, is to allow relevant information to enter working memory, but to keep irrelevant information out of working memory. Moreover, because the nature of on-line processing ensures that information once relevant will sometimes become irrelevant as processing proceeds, the comprehender must work to remove that currently activated information from working memory in a routine, quick, and efficient manner. Hasher and Zacks (1988), therefore, suggested that the functioning of working memory was intimately tied to mechanisms of attentional selection. In particular, they postulated inhibitory processes that could accomplish the dual tasks of screening access to working memory and suppressing previously relevant, but currently irrelevant, information from working memory.

As we previously noted, Hasher and Zacks's inhibition view of working-memory processes arose in the context of accounting for adult age differences in memory and comprehension performance. There is extensive documentation in the aging literature of increased distractibility and susceptibility to perceptual interference in elderly adults. Compared with younger adults, older adults show elevated response times and errors in visual search when distractors are present in a display and there are no spatial cues to help them to focus their search (Madden, 1983; Plude & Hoyer, 1985; Rabbitt, 1965). Older adults show large Stroop interference effects, possibly because they are less able than younger adults to suppress the familiar response of reading a color word when asked to name the word's color (Cohn, Dustman, & Bradford, 1984; Comalli, Wapner, & Werner, 1962). In some cases, older adults are also more distracted than younger adults in "flanker" tasks, in which irrelevant information is visually presented in close proximity to relevant information (e.g., Cremer & Zeef, 1987; Shaw, 1991). Such findings of increased interference and general susceptibility to "noise" in the environment (Layton, 1975; Welford, 1958) led some researchers to suggest that an inhibitory process was impaired in the elderly (e.g., McDowd, Oseas-Kreger, & Fillion, 1995; Rabbitt, 1965).

Recent work has confirmed that elderly adults are impaired in one particular task that is thought to be a direct indicator of the inhibitory processes of attention. The task requires a simple selection response, but on some trials the item that previously served as a distractor becomes the

current target. On these trials, younger adults show slower response times
and errors compared with trials on which successive targets and distractors are unrelated (e.g., Dalrymple-Alford & Budayr, 1966; Neill, 1977;
Tipper, 1985). This difference in responding has been attributed to the
suppression of distractors, which results in making them temporarily less
available as a response (Tipper, 1985). If elderly adults suffer from an
inhibitory deficit, they should not show the suppression effect demonstrated by young adults, and this is just the pattern that has been obtained in several studies (Hasher, Stoltzfus, Zacks, & Rypma, 1991; Kane,
Hasher, Stoltzfus, Zacks, & Connelly, in press; McDowd & Oseas-Kreger,
1991; Stoltzfus, Hasher, Zacks, Ulivi, & Goldstein, 1993; Tipper, 1991).[1]
Hasher and Zacks (1988) suggested that the failure of inhibitory selection
mechanisms might be pervasive in elderly adults' cognitive performance,
impairing not only attention and perception but also memory, thinking,
and language processing, by providing only a loose monitor of the contents of working memory. The ultimate consequence of poor inhibitory
processing in elderly adults would be an increase in irrelevant or marginally relevant ideas in working memory, thus dividing attention, producing
interference, and culminating in increased memory and comprehension
failures.

Although the inhibition theory was devised as an explicit alternative
to capacity theories, it is conceivable that it could be interpreted as a
capacity view, in the sense that, when irrelevant information gains access
to working memory, it leaves less "space" for the storage or processing of
relevant information. In fact, it may be difficult to distinguish empirically
between, on the one hand, performance limitations that result from a
reduced capacity for relevant information caused by the maintenance of
irrelevant information and, on the other hand, performance limitations
that are the consequence of "cross talk" between concurrently activated
relevant and irrelevant information in a working memory with no intrinsic
capacity limit. It has also been suggested that inhibition might itself be a
resource-limited process (e.g., Neumann & DeSchepper, 1992; and see
Chapter 4 in this volume by Randall Engle), introducing another form of
capacity limitation. The synthesis of inhibition and capacity views may
turn out to be useful, in part because capacity notions by themselves are
insufficient. We now turn to a summary of some of our recent work that
has been motivated by the reduced-inhibition view.

Although failures in memory and comprehension are predicted by
many theories of aging (including several resource theories), the inhibition framework makes unique predictions about age differences in performance. The major predictions are as follows:

1. *Greater breadth (or enrichment) of working-memory information.*
   Because suppression mechanisms are less effective in blocking entrance to working memory in older as opposed to younger adults,
   older adults should show evidence of *more* information becoming

active in working memory than younger adults. The additional active units might include irrelevant word meanings or associates, contextually inappropriate interpretations of sentences, daydreams, or personalistic items.

2. *Sustained activation (or maintenance) of thoughts.* Older adults should have difficulty eliminating information from working memory when it is activated but becomes irrelevant. Older adults should therefore show greater activation of previously relevant information, even, perhaps, when it is inconsistent with their current goals or other simultaneously active representations.

3. *Greater interference at encoding and retrieval.* The opportunity for competition among thoughts should be increased for older adults at the time of both encoding and retrieval because of the concurrent presence of irrelevant thoughts during both encoding and retrieval and also because of the linking of irrelevant thoughts to target information in memory.

We now review some recent evidence bearing on the above predictions. As will be seen, much of the evidence is consistent with the inhibition theory, although there are some limits to the findings and the theory. These will be discussed in the final section of this chapter.

Prediction 1: Greater Breadth or Enrichment of Working-Memory Information

Much indirect evidence exists for the prediction of greater enrichment of working memory through the inability to suppress extraneous information. For example, Connelly, Hasher, and Zacks (1991) presented passages with distracting text (in standard font) intermixed with the target text (in italics). As indicated by their reading times and their performance on comprehension items, older adults had greater difficulty reading the passages with distracting text. This suggests that older adults were having difficulty inhibiting the irrelevant text as they read the target text. But how exactly is this related to decrements in comprehension? A condition in which distracting text was semantically related to the target text is relevant here: Older adults showed particularly compromised speed and comprehension in this condition. In these circumstances, "irrelevant" information is actually marginally relevant information, and it appears to enter working memory and to interfere with target processing to a greater extent in older adults than in younger adults (who showed no performance difference between text-relevant and text-irrelevant passages). As the same distractors appeared repeatedly throughout a paragraph in this study, an additional source of difficulty might have arisen from the opportunity for distractors to become familiar to older adults and therefore to become very easily reactivated when they were encountered again.

Another finding indicating that older adults have difficulty suppressing nontarget information comes from research using the flanker task. In this task, subjects categorize a central word (or letter) that is flanked on either side by nominally irrelevant words (or letters). Consistent with the reduced-inhibition view, Shaw (1991) recently found that, although older adults showed the same amount of facilitation as did younger adults from flankers whose category membership was consistent with the target, they showed a greater degree of interference from flankers whose category membership was inconsistent with that of the target.

A more direct study of the enrichment of working memory explored the activation of information during sentence processing by examining the availability of various sentence endings. The study used materials and procedures similar to those employed by Schwanenflugel and colleagues (see Schwanenflugel & LaCount, 1988; Schwanenflugel & Shoben, 1985) to investigate the effects of sentence constraint on the number of sentence endings that were available to subjects. Stoltzfus (1992) presented younger and older adults with sentences that were missing their final word (for instance, "The landlord was faced with a strike by the _____"). The availability of sentence endings was tested using a lexical decision response for words that were highly expected according to production norms (e.g., *tenants*) or relatively unexpected but quite appropriate for the context (e.g., *residents*). Lexical-decision response times were then compared with those in a control condition where subjects saw target words after a neutral context (strings of the letter X). Although younger adults showed priming only for the highly expected words, thus demonstrating a relatively narrow range of availability of endings, older adults showed priming for both types of endings, suggesting that a broader range of endings was available to them while processing the sentences.

Several studies of speech production have suggested that older adults also enrich their speech with a broader range of information than do younger adults. For example, older adults tend to produce more personalistic information and off-track comments in their narratives (Arbuckle & Gold, 1993; Gold, Andres, Arbuckle, & Schwartzman, 1988; Obler, 1980). These ideas may occur to younger adults as well, but they do not produce them as often as do older adults, perhaps because older adults cannot easily suppress such thoughts once they come to mind.

Prediction 2: Sustained Activation or Maintenance of Thoughts

The second prediction, that older adults should have sustained maintenance of activated information, should result from the difficulty in eliminating activated information that becomes irrelevant: In other words, they would fail to update working memory to reflect their current goals. The reading of garden-path passages represents one situation in which this ability to update is important. These passages begin by misleading their reader into making an inference that turns out to be false. For example, the reader might be led to believe that a character is on a hunting safari, when in fact he or she is on a photographic safari. In one such study, Hamm and Hasher (1992) presented various passages to younger and older adults and measured the availability of critical inferences at two points during the passages. Although older and younger adults performed in a similar manner on non-garden-path control passages, they showed a very different pattern of availability during passages that had a garden-path manipulation. For these passages, older adults were much more likely than younger adults to show activation of two separate, competing interpretations of the passage, despite the presentation of disambiguating information.

In addition to "on-line" evidence for the maintenance of information that should be rejected, there is evidence concerning the later retention of such information. Hartman and Hasher (1991) presented subjects with single sentence frames that had highly predictable endings. Subjects were instructed to generate an ending after reading a sentence frame, but were then sometimes presented with another ending to remember instead of their own, self-generated ending. In a task that, to subjects, appeared unrelated to the sentence-generation task, subjects were given an implicit memory test that tested memory for both generated but disconfirmed endings, and for the target endings that subjects had actually been instructed to remember in place of their own endings. Both older and younger adults showed memory for the target endings, but only older adults demonstrated memory for the disconfirmed endings. Hartman and Hasher concluded that the better memory shown by the older adults was a result of a compromised ability to suppress the disconfirmed endings.

A similar result arose in several experiments on directed forgetting carried out by Zacks, Radvansky, and Hasher (1994). Here, subjects were presented with lists of words, some of which they were instructed to remember, as well as others that they were instructed to forget. In a final free-recall task in which subjects were asked to recall the "forget" items as did well as the "remember" items, older adults tended to recall at least as many "forget" items as did younger adults, while showing much poorer recall of the "remember" items. This pattern suggests that older adults were less able to follow "forget" cues at encoding. In some cases, older adults in this study also showed increased numbers of intrusions from the previous lists when they attempted to recall each list's "remember" words during the experiment. Such a result is not surprising in the performance of older adults, who have been reported to show increased intrusions in the free recall of sentences (Stine & Wingfield, 1987), increased productions of already-produced responses (Koriat, Ben-Zur, & Sheffer, 1988; Whitaker, 1992), increased false alarms for semantic associates of previously presented words (Rankin & Kausler, 1979; Smith, 1975), and increased difficulty in changing a highly practised response pattern (e.g., Dulaney & Rogers, 1992; Hess, 1982, Experiment 3).

The inability to inhibit information that is no longer relevant has been targeted in another theory, which has been proposed to account for differences in verbal ability among young adults. Gernsbacher's (1990) "structure-building" framework assumes that general-suppression processes help comprehenders to build and to maintain an accurate and coherent text representation, and she has been quite successful in linking suppression efficiency to performance on various memory and comprehension tasks. Gernsbacher has shown, for example, that poor comprehenders maintain the inappropriate meanings of homographs longer than do good comprehenders (see Gernsbacher & Faust, 1991). The poor comprehenders in her studies appear to have no difficulty activating correct interpretations, but they are less efficient in suppressing candidate interpretations that turn out to be inappropriate. This pattern parallels the findings we see with younger and older adults.

Prediction 3: Greater Interference at Encoding and Retrieval

Data relevant to the prediction that the memory performance of older adults will show an increased sensitivity to interference effects at both encoding and retrieval come from our research using the "fan-effect" paradigm developed by Anderson (1974, 1983). In fan-effect experiments, subjects first learn a set of target facts, such as the following examples taken from Gerard, Zacks, Hasher, and Radvansky (1991): "The doctor took the car for a short test drive"; "The judge cut the apple pie into six pieces." In a subsequent speeded recognition test, subjects are asked to distinguish between the target facts and unstudied foil facts constructed from re-pairings of the subject and predicate phrases of the targets (e.g., "The doctor cut the apple pie into six pieces"). The fundamental finding, the fan effect, is tied to "fan size": The more facts learned about a particular concept (such as the doctor), the longer it takes to retrieve any one of those facts and usually the more errors are made.

Consistent with our expectations, Gerard et al. (1991) found that older adults showed much larger fan effects than did young adults in terms of both reaction times and errors. We attribute this outcome to the effects of reduced inhibition that occur both at encoding and at retrieval. To be specific, we believe that, at encoding, older adults are less able than younger adults to suppress irrelevant thoughts activated by the experimental materials, and that they may have a harder time constraining rehearsal to a single experimental item. Consequently, each experimental fact is likely to be associatively elaborated with additional information. At retrieval, this additional information is reactivated, thus creating problems for the older person in searching for the target information. In addition, older adults are likely to suffer more than young adults from additional irrelevant thoughts that may be elicited by the memory probes.

It may also be noted that, although there are some negative findings (cf. Kausler, 1990), the results of studies involving more traditional interference procedures (that is, retroactive and proactive interference) are, under certain circumstances at least, supportive of the notion that older adults show an enhanced sensitivity to interference from nontarget materials. These circumstances include the use of sensitive measures such as error analyses and reaction times and also experimental procedures that give the opportunity for significant amounts of interference. Under these conditions, older adults tend to show enhanced proactive and retroactive interference. A particularly interesting recent finding comes from a study by Kliegl and Lindenberger (1993), who used a paradigm in which subjects learned a sequence of paired-associate lists involving the re-pairing of the same items (in other words, an "A-B, A-Br" paradigm), and found that, even when the overall performance was equated across age groups, older adults showed an increase in intrusion errors consisting of responses that had been correct on the preceding lists (see Gerard et al., 1991, and Kane & Hasher, in press, for other relevant evidence).

Further Considerations and Future Directions

Taken as a whole, the evidence for the inhibition view is encouraging. Older adults appear to have difficulty inhibiting irrelevant information whether it is internally generated (e.g., during speech) or externally presented (e.g., when visual distractions are present during reading). They further have difficulty rejecting activated information when, under a variety of circumstances, it later becomes irrelevant. These circumstances lead to increased levels of interference at both encoding and retrieval.

Our model-building approach shares with that of Baddeley (1992) the strategy of using new data to influence the model's development. To this end, several issues regarding current findings need to be considered. First, we will address an empirical problem of separating broad activation from the sustained maintenance of activation (Predictions 1 and 2 above). Second, we will consider the issue of memory for irrelevant information, and the conflicting data in the literature about whether older adults are more likely to remember irrelevant information. Next, we will consider a related problem, that of measuring performance in the case of "relevant" and "irrelevant" information, since the determination of relevance may be difficult, especially given the potentially different goals of younger and older adults. Finally, we will discuss the functions of inhibition and situations where inhibitory deficits might lead to performance advantages.

Empirical Separability of Predictions 1 and 2

Hasher and Zacks (1988) considered the enrichment of working memory and the sustained maintenance of activation to be two separate consequences of inhibitory failure, but these might be difficult to separate empirically. The root of the problem is that addressing this issue requires precise knowledge of the time course of activation and suppression for younger and older adults in each task. This sort of on-line testing is difficult to implement (in studies of text processing, for example), and hence we have little evidence to distinguish clearly between broader initial activation in older adults and the failure of older adults subsequently to suppress information that is initially activated for both younger and older adults.

It should also be noted that there is a body of evidence against the initial-breadth prediction. For example, using word-production measures and single-word priming measures, both the strength and the breadth of the associations produced by younger and older adults are generally found to be the same (e.g., Burke & Peters, 1986; Burke, White, & Diaz, 1987; Howard, 1980, 1983; Howard, McAndrews, & Lasaga, 1981). There is also some evidence that multiple senses of homographs are not differentially activated in older and younger adults (Burke & Harrold, 1988). Finally, studies that have used introspective methods for determining the number of task-unrelated thoughts generated by young and older adults have suggested that older adults actually experience fewer task-unrelated thoughts and daydreams than do younger adults (e.g., Giambra, 1989).

On the other hand, one new line of work that is consistent with the broad-activation prediction assesses semantic priming under strict and short deadlines (Laver, 1992, 1994). Even under these brief and demanding circumstances, older adults show more priming than do younger adults. It might be that the greater number of alternatives activated by older adults increases the likelihood of a match between the prime and the target, thus producing the larger priming effects seen in older adults. In summary, evidence for the breadth prediction is more controversial than evidence for the failure-to-suppress prediction. It might be premature, however, to conclude that there is substantial evidence against a broad-spread activation view without further research. It is increasingly clear that small differences in the experiment-wide composition of materials can alter the strategies of younger subjects (e.g., Stoltzfus & Hasher, 1990; Tweedy, Lapinski, & Schvaneveldt, 1977), and this may also hold true for older adults. In addition, further exploration of the time course of processing in each task will be useful for resolution of this issue.

Memory for Irrelevant Information

If older adults process more irrelevant information, or if they experience more sustained activation of this information, it follows that they should not only have decreased memory for target information but should also have better memory for irrelevant information (proportionately, at least) than younger adults. However, the empirical evaluation of this prediction is complicated by the fact that the increased retrieval interference predicted for older adults should affect memory for both relevant and irrelevant information. With respect to target information, the impact of an increased sensitivity to interference is demonstrated by the following pattern of data, for which there is ample evidence: Older adults remember less target information on explicit memory tasks (see Kausler, 1990, for an overview), but they show a smaller or nonexistent impairment on implicit tasks that may involve minimal retrieval interference (e.g., Howard, 1988; Light & Singh, 1987).

The findings regarding memory for irrelevant information are likewise dependent upon the type of test used to measure memory (see also Hartman & Dusek, 1994). To illustrate this point, we return to a study that we described earlier, in which Connelly et al. (1991) asked subjects to read stories presented amid distracting text printed in a different typeface. Older adults showed a greater slowdown in reading time than young adults when distraction was present during reading, which suggests that they were paying more attention to the distracting words. However, younger and older adults showed equal retention for distractor items from the reading task when those distractor items were used as foil answers in a series of multiple-choice questions. In fact, some studies have found that older adults remember *less* distracting information than do younger adults when explicit memory tests are used (e.g., Kausler, 1990; Kausler & Kleim, 1978).

On the other hand, Shaw, Rypma, and Toffle (1992) recently used a procedure similar to that employed in the study by Connelly et al. (1991), and they found that older adults actually showed better memory for distractors using a priming measure in an implicit memory task, suggesting that older adults will show better memory for irrelevant information than will younger adults under certain circumstances, including those that minimize retrieval interference.

Patterns of memory performance within tests of implicit memory and within tests of explicit memory throughout the aging literature are not entirely consistent across studies, perhaps reflecting the mix of direct and indirect retrieval processes that together determine performance on a particular task (e.g., Jacoby, 1991). Close examination of the retrieval demands involved in different memory tasks may help to resolve this issue (see Hartman & Dusek, 1994). Nevertheless, there certainly appears to be evidence that older people show relatively better memory on tests that do not require explicit retrieval, and further that they may even outperform younger adults when irrelevant information is the focus of retrieval (see Hartman & Dusek, 1994; Hartman & Hasher, 1991; Shaw et al., 1992).

What do these differing results on various memory tests suggest about the nature of retrieval processes or representations in working memory for younger as compared to older adults? It would be expected that irrelevant information, even when activated, should be less thoroughly processed and less likely to enter rehearsal cycles, since it is not strongly supported by the context. Therefore, irrelevant information should be less likely to be remembered than target information, at least in explicit tests. Implicit tests, especially perceptually driven ones, are less sensitive to interference or competition at retrieval (Graf & Schacter, 1987) and are less sensitive to semantic encoding manipulations (Blaxton, 1989) than are explicit tests, and thus they might be more likely to pick up activation of irrelevant information in elderly adults. It is important to note that, although irrelevant information might not be available for explicit retrieval in older adults because of inappropriate or inadequate encoding and rehearsal, it might still interfere with the explicit retrieval of other relevant information.

What Is "Irrelevant" Information?

Thus far in our discussion of performance on various memory and language tasks we have assumed that the goals of the experimenter are generally the goals of the experimental subjects. This assumption is important to note, because selection of information to be attended to (and therefore the contents of working memory) will be determined by the goals of the reader or listener. In a text-comprehension situation, for example, we generally assume that the reader's goal is to comprehend the passage being read. However, the reader might be concerned about how the current text relates to his or her youngest daughter or how the moral of a story applies to one's own life. The reader could also be maintaining thoughts that are important to that individual but have little or nothing to do with the text, such as whether he or she should make lasagna or pizza for dinner. In each case, the contents of working memory will be somewhat different, reflecting the goals of the reader, who is also, of course, a person with individual values and interests. In this sense, nothing in working memory is ever truly "irrelevant," because the goals of the reader will always be reflected in the reader's thoughts. Thus, for example, both depressed (Ellis & Ashbrook, 1988) and anxious individuals (Eysenck, 1992) may have many irrelevant thoughts in mind, but these thoughts are only irrelevant by the standards of those whose goals are uninfluenced by these concerns.

This acknowledgment of the individual goals of the reader was particularly important to the theory of Hasher and Zacks (1988), as the populations compared in aging research are likely to have different goals in many situations, such as psychological experiments (LaBouvie-Vief & Blanchard-Fields, 1982). This may, in turn, cause older adults to consider a wider range of information to be relevant to their task. If older adults are bringing different values and therefore broader goals to the reading situation, they will necessarily have different information (and perhaps, as we have argued, more information) activated in working memory. Thus, distinguishing between the performance patterns associated with aging per se and performance determined by age differences in goals becomes a concern. This can probably best be handled experimentally by using, for example, text materials that are of special interest to older adults, as well as by studying the impact of inhibitory mechanisms upon performance in nondiscourse tasks, where goals of the sort identified by LaBouvie-Vief and Blanchard-Fields (1982) may play less of a role.

Beyond particular sets of goals, several other factors might influence which information gains access to and is maintained in working memory. For example, the function of the presented information may be important: If the information is clearly irrelevant when presented, older adults might find it easier to reject such information, as opposed to situations in which information is initially thought to be relevant, and only later is identified as irrelevant (as is the case in many of the studies discussed here). The spatial separation of the relevant and irrelevant information (especially when that separation may be used as an early cue to determine allocation of attention) also appears to benefit older adults' selection of target information (e.g., Carlson, Hasher, Connelly, & Zacks, 1995; Madden, 1983; Plude & Hoyer, 1985) and therefore may also affect patterns of memory for irrelevant information in older adults. Recent data from our laboratory have suggested another variable that may moderate the ability to suppress previously activated information: synchrony between the time of day when a subject is tested, and the particular subject's optimal time-of-day tendency, as measured by the Morningness-Eveningness Questionnaire (Horne & Ostberg, 1976). When older adults are tested at their nonoptimal time of day (generally the late afternoon), they may have more difficulty suppressing irrelevant information than at their optimal time of day (generally the morning) (May, Hasher, & Bhatt, 1994).

Potential Functions of Reduced Inhibition

Although we have generally focused on the difficulties arising from reduced inhibitory abilities (and they seem substantial and pervasive), there could be benefits as well, which we have only begun to pursue. Actually, in several of the tasks described in this chapter, age differences occur in the form of *benefits* (or a lack of decrement) in performance in critical conditions. For example, the basic finding in "negative-priming" tasks used to tap inhibitory processes is a slowdown in response time when a current response has been suppressed on an earlier trial. Older adults show no such response-speed decrement, presumably because they have not previously suppressed the current response. Such findings are interpreted as a decrement in inhibitory processes, and they are used to explain many of the negative cognitive effects of aging, but in these particular instances the lack of inhibition actually leads to performance advantages.

Although the negative-priming task seems unlike real situations, the results suggest that situations in which "irrelevant" information becomes relevant are places to look for performance advantages for older adults. Such situations might include garden-path passages, where keeping active those interpretations that were previously selected against would be an advantage if they were to become relevant again. Decision making might also offer situations in which performance could be enhanced if subjects did not eliminate or inhibit alternative choices prematurely.

The enrichment of the working memories of elderly adults that results in interference and memory failure might be another source of benefits for older adults. Discourse (including, potentially, lectures) may be more interesting if personalistic anecdotes and other "extraneous" information are routinely included. In fact, evidence shows that older adults are judged to tell stories of higher quality than younger adults (see Kemper, Rash, Kynette, & Norman, 1990; Mergler, Faust, & Goldstein, 1985; Pratt & Robins, 1991). Older adults might also be more likely to take multiple perspectives or to see multiple interpretations of a problem or a social situation once they are activated, which can often be an advantage, and this may be related to what we commonly refer to as "wisdom" (Baltes & Staudinger, 1993). The routine maintenance of all sorts of enriched information from various sources may, under certain circumstances, lead to the increased integration of ideas. Indeed, evidence shows that older adults are more integrative in their interpretations of metaphors than are young adults (Boswell, 1979).

The idea that processing benefits may be accounted for by the same cognitive mechanisms that produce processing deficits is an appealing one. Inhibitory efficiency may be useful in exploring all types of performance differences, whether those related to aging or other group or individual differences. In fact, theories involving inhibitory mechanisms have been proposed to explain various aspects of the performance of young adults (Gernsbacher, Varner, & Faust, 1990; and see Chapter 4 in this volume by Randall Engle), schizophrenics (Beech, Powell, McWilliams, & Claridge, 1989; Cohen & Servan-Schreiber, 1992), patients with frontal-lobe damage (Dempster, 1992), and both normal and abnormal children (Bjorklund & Harnishfeger, 1990; Pennington, Groisser, & Welsh, 1993). Indeed, though the inhibition theory that we have described here was developed in the context of explaining age differences, it can be seen (and indeed was always intended) as a more general cognitive framework for understanding the role of working memory in determining performance across a broad range of cognitive tasks and subject populations.

Acknowledgments

We gratefully acknowledge the support of grant RO1 AGO4306 from the National Institute on Aging.

Note

1. We are focusing here on identity suppression tasks: That is, on tasks in which subjects must respond to the identity of a target (e.g., by naming it). Tasks that require subjects to respond to the location of a target show a different pattern. It has been suggested that this reflects the existence of separate visual processing systems concerned with object location and object identity, and that these systems show a differential decline with age (see Connelly & Hasher, 1993). There are, however, some circumstances under which older adults show significant negative priming of identity (May, Kane, & Hasher, 1995; Sullivan & Faust, 1993). These circumstances appear to involve situations in which basic inhibitory processes are

supplemented by other processes (such as backward retrieval) occurring during a multiply determined task (see May et al., 1995).

References

Allport, A. (1989). Visual attention. In M. I. Posner (Ed.), *Foundations of cognitive science* (pp. 631–682). Cambridge, MA: MIT Press.

Anderson, J. R. (1974). Retrieval of propositional information from long-term memory. *Cognitive Psychology, 6*, 451–474.

Anderson, J. R. (1983). A spreading activation theory of memory. *Journal of Verbal Learning and Verbal Behavior, 22*, 261–295.

Arbuckle, T. Y., & Gold, D. P. (1993). Aging, inhibition, and verbosity. *Journal of Gerontology: Psychological Sciences, 48*, P225–P232.

Baddeley, A. (1986). *Working memory*. Oxford: Oxford University Press.

Baddeley, A. (1992). Is working memory working? The fifteenth Bartlett lecture. *Quarterly Journal of Experimental Psychology, 44A*, 1–31.

Baddeley, A., Logie, R., Nimmo-Smith, I., & Brereton, N. (1985). Components of fluent reading. *Journal of Memory and Language, 24*, 119–131.

Baltes, P. B., & Staudinger, U. M. (1993). The search for a psychology of wisdom. *Current Directions in Psychological Science, 2*(3), 75–80.

Beech, A., Powell, T., McWilliams, J., & Claridge, G. (1989). Evidence of reduced "cognitive inhibition" in schizophrenia. *British Journal of Clinical Psychology, 28*, 109–116.

Bjorklund, D. F., & Harnishfeger, K. K. (1990). The resources construct in cognitive development: Diverse sources of evidence and a theory of inefficient inhibition. *Developmental Review, 10*, 48–71.

Blaxton, T. A. (1989). Investigating dissociations among memory measures: Support for a transfer-appropriate processing framework. *Journal of Experimental Psychology: Learning, Memory, and Cognition, 15*, 657–688.

Boswell, D. A. (1979). Metaphoric processing in the mature years. *Human Development, 22*, 373–384.

Burke, D. M., & Harrold, R. M. (1988). Automatic and effortful semantic processes in old age: Experimental and naturalistic approaches. In L. L. Light & D. M. Burke (Eds.), *Language, memory, and aging* (pp. 100–116). New York: Cambridge University Press.

Burke, D. M., & Peters, L. (1986). Word associations in old age: Evidence for consistency in semantic encoding during adulthood. *Psychology and Aging, 1*, 283–292.

Burke, D. M., White, H., & Diaz, D. L. (1987). Semantic priming in young and older adults: Evidence for age-constancy in automatic and attentional processes. *Journal of Experimental Psychology: Human Perception and Performance, 13*, 79–88.

Carlson, M. C., Hasher, L., Connelly, S. L., & Zacks, R. T. (1995). Aging, distraction, and the benefits of predictable location. *Psychology and Aging, 10*, 427–436.

Cohen, J. D., & Servan-Schreiber, D. (1992). Context, cortex, and dopamine: A connectionist approach to behavior and biology in schizophrenia. *Psychological Review, 99*, 45–77.

Cohn, N. B., Dustman, R. E., & Bradford, D. C. (1984). Age-related decrements in Stroop color test performance. *Journal of Clinical Psychology, 40*, 1244–1250.

Comalli, P. E., Jr., Wapner, S., & Werner, H. (1962). Interference effects of Stroop color-word test in childhood, adulthood, and aging. *Journal of Genetic Psychology, 100*, 47–53.

Connelly, S. L., & Hasher, L. (1993). Aging and the inhibition of spatial location. *Journal of Experimental Psychology: Human Perception and Performance, 19*, 1238–1250.

Connelly, S. L., Hasher, L., & Zacks, R. T. (1991). Age and reading: The impact of distraction. *Psychology and Aging, 6*, 533–541.

Cowan, N. (1988). Evolving conceptions of memory storage, selective attention, and their mutual constraints within the human information processing system. *Psychological Bulletin, 104*, 163–191.

Cowan, N. (1993). Activation, attention, and short-term memory. *Memory & Cognition, 21*, 162–167.

Craik, F.I.M., & Jennings, J. M. (1992). Human memory. In F. I. M. Craik & T. A. Salthouse (Eds.), *The handbook of aging and cognition* (pp. 51–110). Hillsdale, NJ: Erlbaum.

Cremer, R., & Zeef, E. J. (1987). What kind of noise increases with age? *Journal of Gerontology, 42*, 515–518.

Dalrymple-Alford, E. C., & Budayr, B. (1966). Examination of some aspects of the Stroop color-word test. *Perceptual and Motor Skills, 23*, 1211–1214.

Daneman, M., & Carpenter, P. A. (1980). Individual differences in working memory and reading. *Journal of Verbal Learning and Verbal Behavior, 19*, 450–466.

Daneman, M., & Carpenter, P. A. (1983). Individual differences in integrating information between and within sentences. *Journal of Experimental Psychology: Learning, Memory, and Cognition, 9*, 561–583.

Daneman, M., & Tardif, T. (1987). Working memory and reading skill re-examined. In M. Coltheart (Ed.), *Attention and performance XII: The psychology of reading* (pp. 491–508). Hove, UK: Erlbaum.

Dempster, F. (1992). The rise and fall of the inhibitory mechanism: Toward a unified theory of cognitive development and aging. *Developmental Review, 12*, 45–75.

Dulaney, C., & Rogers, W. (1992). *The effects of environmental support on age differences in ignoring distraction in reading.* Paper presented at the Cognitive Aging Conference, Atlanta, GA.

Ellis, H. C., & Ashbrook, P. W. (1988). Resource allocation model of the effects of depressed mood states on memory. In K. Fiedler & J. Forges (Eds.), *Affect, cognition, and social behavior* (pp. 25–43). Göttingen, Germany: Hogrefe.

Engle, R. W., Cantor, J., & Carullo, J. J. (1992). Individual differences in working memory and comprehension: A test of four hypotheses. *Journal of Experimental Psychology: Learning, Memory, and Cognition, 18*, 972–992.

Engle, R. W., Carullo, J. J., & Collins, K. W. (1991). Individual differences in working memory for comprehension and following directions. *Journal of Educational Research, 84*, 253–262.

Eysenck, M. W. (1992). *Anxiety: The cognitive perspective.* Hove, UK: Erlbaum.

Gerard, L., Zacks, R. T., Hasher, L., & Radvansky, G. A. (1991). Age deficits in retrieval: The fan effect. *Journal of Gerontology: Psychological Sciences, 46*, P131–P136.

Gernsbacher, M. A. (1990). *Language comprehension as structure building.* Hillsdale, NJ: Erlbaum.

Gernsbacher, M. A., & Faust, M. E. (1991). The mechanism of suppression: A component of general comprehension skill. *Journal of Experimental Psychology: Learning, Memory, and Cognition, 17*, 245–262.

Gernsbacher, M. A., Varner, K. R., & Faust, M. E. (1990). Investigating differences in general comprehension skill. *Journal of Experimental Psychology: Learning, Memory, and Cognition, 16*, 430–445.

Giambra, L. M. (1989). Task-unrelated-thought frequency as a function of age: A laboratory study. *Psychology and Aging, 4*, 136–143.

Gold, D., Andres, D., Arbuckle, T., & Schwartzman, A. (1988). Measurement and correlates of verbosity in elderly people. *Journal of Gerontology: Psychological Sciences, 43*, P27–P33.

Graf, P., & Schacter, D. (1987). Selective effects of interference on implicit and explicit memory for new associations. *Journal of Experimental Psychology: Learning, Memory, and Cognition, 13*, 45–53.

Hamm, V. P., & Hasher, L. (1992). Age and the availability of inferences. *Psychology and Aging, 7*, 56–64.

Hartley, J. T. (1986). Reader and text variables as determinants of discourse memory in adulthood. *Psychology and Aging, 2*, 150–158.

Hartley, J. T. (1993). Aging and prose memory: Tests of the resource-deficit hypothesis. *Psychology and Aging, 8*, 538–551.

Hartman, M., & Dusek, J. (1994). Direct and indirect memory tests—what they reveal about age-differences in interference. *Aging and Cognition, 1*, 292–309.

Hartman, M., & Hasher, L. (1991). Aging and suppression: Memory for previously relevant information. *Psychology and Aging, 6*, 587–594.

Hasher, L., Stoltzfus, E. R., Zacks, R. T., & Rypma, B. A. (1991). Age and inhibition. *Journal of Experimental Psychology: Learning, Memory, and Cognition, 17*, 163–169.

Hasher, L., & Zacks, R. T. (1988). Working memory, comprehension, and aging: A review and a new view. In G. H. Bower (Ed.), *The psychology of learning and motivation* (Vol. 22, pp. 193–225). San Diego, CA: Academic Press.

Hess, T. M. (1982). Visual abstraction processes in young and old adults. *Developmental Psychology, 18*, 68–81.

Horne, J., & Ostberg, O. (1976). A self-assessment questionnaire to determine morningness-eveningness in human circadian rhythms. *International Journal of Chronobiology, 4*, 97–110.

Howard, D. V. (1980). Category norms: A comparison of the Battig and Montague (1969) norms with the responses of adults between the ages of 20 and 80. *Journal of Gerontology, 35*, 225–231.

Howard, D. V. (1983). The effects of aging and degree of association on the semantic priming of lexical decisions. *Experimental Aging Research, 9*, 145–151.

Howard, D. V. (1988). Implicit and explicit assessment of cognitive aging. In M. L. Howe & C. J. Brainerd (Eds.), *Cognitive development and adulthood: Progress in cognitive development research* (pp. 3–37). New York: Springer-Verlag.

Howard, D. V., McAndrews, M. P., & Lasaga, M. I. (1981). Semantic priming of lexical decisions in young and old adults. *Journal of Gerontology, 36*, 707–714.

Jacoby, L. (1991). A process dissociation framework: Separating automatic from intentional uses of memory. *Journal of Memory and Language, 30*, 513–541.

Just, M. A., & Carpenter, P. A. (1992). A capacity theory of comprehension: Individual differences in working memory. *Psychological Review, 99*, 122–149.

Kane, M. J., & Hasher, L. (in press). Interference. In G. Maddox (Ed.), *Encyclopedia of Aging*, second edition. New York: Springer.

Kane, M. J., Hasher, L., Stoltzfus, E. R., Zacks, R. T., & Connelly, S. L. (1994). Inhibitory attentional mechanisms and aging. *Psychology and Aging, 9*, 103–112.

Kausler, D. H. (1990). *Experimental psychology, cognition, and human aging* (2nd ed.). New York: Springer-Verlag.

Kausler, D. H., & Kleim, D. M. (1978). Age differences in processing relevant versus irrelevant stimuli in multiple-item recognition learning. *Journal of Gerontology, 33*, 87–93.

Kemper, S., Rash, S. R., Kynette, D., & Norman, S. (1990). Telling stories: The structure of adults' narratives. *European Journal of Cognitive Psychology, 2*, 205–228.

Kliegl, R., & Lindenberger, U. (1993). Modeling intrusions and correct recall in episodic memory: Adult age differences in encoding of list context. *Journal of Experimental Psychology: Learning, Memory, and Cognition, 19*, 617–637.

Koriat, A., Ben-Zur, H., & Sheffer, D. (1988). Telling the same story twice: Output monitoring and age. *Journal of Memory and Language, 27*, 23–39.

Labouvie-Vief, G., & Blanchard-Fields, F. (1982). Cognitive ageing and psychological growth. *Ageing and Society, 2*, 183–209.

Laver, G. D. (1992). *A speed-accuracy analysis of semantic priming effects in young and older adults.* Paper presented at the Cognitive Aging Conference, Atlanta, GA.

Laver, G. D. (1994). *Vocabulary and short-term memory span as mediators of the speed of semantic priming in young and older adults.* Paper presented at the Cognitive Aging Conference, Atlanta, GA.

Layton, B. (1975). Perceptual noise and aging. *Psychological Bulletin, 82*, 875–883.

Light, L. L. (1991). Memory and aging: Four hypotheses in search of data. *Annual Review of Psychology, 42*, 333–376.

Light, L. L., & Anderson, P. A. (1985). Working-memory capacity, age, and memory for discourse. *Journal of Gerontology, 40*, 737–747.

Light, L. L., & Singh, A. (1987). Implicit and explicit memory in young and older adults. *Journal of Experimental Psychology: Learning, Memory, and Cognition, 13*, 531–541.

MacDonald, M. C., Just, M. A., & Carpenter, P. A. (1992). Working memory constraints on the processing of syntactic ambiguity. *Cognitive Psychology, 24*, 56–98.

MacDonald, M. C., & Perlmutter, N. J. (1993, November). *Probabilistic constraints and working memory capacity in syntactic ambiguity resolution.* Paper presented at the annual meeting of the Psychonomic Society, Washington, DC.

Madden, D. J. (1983). Aging and distraction by highly familiar stimuli during visual search. *Developmental Psychology, 19*, 499–507.

May, C. P., Hasher, L., & Bhatt, A. (1994). *Time of day affects susceptibility to misinformation in younger and older adults.* Paper presented at the North Carolina Cognition Conference, Winston-Salem, NC.

May, C. P., Kane, M. J., & Hasher, L. (1995). Determinants of negative priming. *Psychological Bulletin, 118*, 35–54.

McDowd, J. M., & Oseas-Kreger, D. M. (1991). Aging, inhibitory processes, and negative priming. *Journal of Gerontology: Psychological Sciences, 46*, P340–P345.

McDowd, J. M., Oseas-Kreger, D. M., & Fillion, D. L. (1995). Inhibitory processes in cognition and aging. In F. N. Dempster & C. J. Brainerd (Eds.), *Interference and inhibition in cognition* (pp. 363–400). San Diego, CA: Academic Press.

Mergler, N., Faust, M., & Goldstein, M. (1985). Storytelling as an age-dependent skill. *International Journal of Aging and Human Development, 20,* 205–228.

Navon, D. (1984). Resources—a theoretical soup stone? *Psychological Review, 91,* 216–234.

Neill, W. T. (1977). Inhibitory and facilitatory processes in selective attention. *Journal of Experimental Psychology: Human Perception and Performance, 3,* 444–450.

Neumann, E., & DeSchepper, B. G. (1992). An inhibition-based fan effect: Evidence for an active suppression mechanism in selective attention. *Canadian Journal of Psychology, 46,* 1–40.

Obler, L. (1980). Narrative discourse style in the elderly. In L. Obler & M. Albert (Eds.), *Language and communication in the elderly* (pp. 75–90). Lexington, MA: Heath.

Pennington, B. F., Groisser, D., & Welsh, M. C. (1993). Contrasting cognitive deficits in attention deficit hyperactivity disorder versus reading disability. *Developmental Psychology, 29,* 511–523.

Plude, D. J., & Hoyer, W. J. (1985). Attention and performance: Identifying and localizing age deficits. In N. Charness (Ed.), *Aging and human performance* (pp. 47–99). New York: Academic Press.

Pratt, M. W., & Robins, S. L. (1991). That's the way it was: Age differences in the structure and quality of adults' personal narratives. *Discourse Processes, 14,* 73–85.

Rabbitt, P.M.A. (1965). An age decrement in the ability to ignore irrelevant information. *Journal of Gerontology, 20,* 233–238.

Rankin, J. L., & Kausler, D. H. (1979). Adult age differences in false recognitions. *Journal of Gerontology, 34,* 58–65.

Salthouse, T. A. (1990). Working memory as a processing resource in cognitive aging. *Developmental Review, 10,* 101–124.

Schwanenflugel, P. J., & LaCount, K. (1988). Semantic relatedness and the scope of facilitation for upcoming words in sentences. *Journal of Experimental Psychology: Learning, Memory, and Cognition, 14,* 344–354.

Schwanenflugel, P. J., & Shoben, E. J. (1985). The influence of sentence constraint on the scope of facilitation for upcoming words. *Journal of Memory and Language, 24,* 232–252.

Shaw, R. J. (1991). Age-related increases in the effects of automatic semantic activation. *Psychology and Aging, 6,* 595–604.

Shaw, R. J., Rypma, B., & Toffle, C. (1992). *The effects of environmental support on age differences in ignoring distraction in reading.* Paper presented at the Cognitive Aging Conference, Atlanta, GA.

Smith, A. D. (1975). Partial learning and recognition memory in the aged. *International Journal of Aging and Human Development, 6,* 359–365.

Stine, E. L., & Wingfield, A. (1987). Process and strategy in memory for speech among younger and older adults. *Psychology and Aging, 2,* 272–279.

Stoltzfus, E. R., & Hasher, L. (1990). *Individual differences in breadth of facilitation for high-constraint sentence completions.* Paper presented at the meeting of the Psychonomic Society, New Orleans, LA.

Stoltzfus, E. R. (1992). *Aging and breadth of availability during language processing.*

Unpublished doctoral dissertation. Department of Psychology, Duke University.

Stoltzfus, E. R., Hasher, L., Zacks, R. T., Ulivi, M. S., & Goldstein, D. (1993). Investigations of inhibition and interference in younger and older adults. *Journal of Gerontology: Psychological Sciences, 48,* P179–P188.

Sullivan, M. P., & Faust, M. E. (1993). Evidence for identity inhibition and interference in younger and older adults. *Psychology and Aging, 8,* 589–598.

Tipper, S. P. (1985). The negative priming effect: Inhibitory priming by ignored objects. *Quarterly Journal of Experimental Psychology, 37A,* 571–590.

Tipper, S. P. (1991). Less attentional selectivity as a result of declining inhibition in older adults. *Bulletin of the Psychonomic Society, 29,* 45–47.

Tweedy, J. R., Lapinski, R. H., & Schvaneveldt, R. W. (1977). Semantic-context effects on word recognition: Influence of varying the proportion of items presented in an appropriate context. *Memory & Cognition, 5,* 84–89.

Welford, A. T. (1958). *Aging and human skill.* Oxford: Oxford University Press.

Whitaker, H. A. (1992). Early effects of normal aging on perseverative and non-perseverative prefrontal measures. *Developmental Neuropsychology, 8,* 99–114.

Zacks, R. T., & Hasher, L. (1994). Directed ignoring: Inhibitory regulation of working memory. In D. Dagenbach & T. H. Carr (Eds.), *Inhibitory mechanisms in attention, memory, and language* (pp. 241–264). San Diego, CA: Academic Press.

Zacks, R. T., Radvansky, G. A., & Hasher, L. (in press). Studies of directed forgetting in older adults. *Journal of Experimental Psychology: Learning, Memory, and Cognition.*

4

Working Memory and Retrieval: An Inhibition-Resource Approach

Randall W. Engle

The idea that attentional resources are limited and that this limitation is reflected in some measure of memory span dates back at least to the nineteenth century (Baldwin, 1894). However, digit span, the earliest and the most commonly used measure of memory span, does not consistently predict mainstays of everyday cognition such as reading comprehension (Perfetti & Lesgold, 1977) or the amount of information recalled from primary or secondary memory (Martin, 1978; see Chapter 2 in this volume by Robert Logie). Daneman and Carpenter (1980) developed the first task that seems to be a valid measure of the capacity of working memory. The reading-span task is really a dual task requiring the subject to read or listen to a series of sentences and separately to keep track of the final word in each sentence so that it can subsequently be recalled. The span score is the maximum number of words that can be recalled perfectly. A wide variety of complex dual-task measures have now been used to estimate working-memory capacity (Kyllonen & Christal, 1990; Salthouse, Mitchell, Skovronek, & Babcock, 1989; Turner & Engle, 1989; see Chapter 3 in this volume by Ellen Stoltzfus, Lynn Hasher, and Rose Zacks), and I have argued that they reflect a common mechanism (Cantor, Engle, & Hamilton, 1991).

That mechanism would appear to be an important component of general cognition, because these measures of working-memory (WM) capacity predict performance in a wide variety of real-world cognitive tasks. A selected list of such relationships includes the following:

Reading and Listening Comprehension. Daneman and Carpenter (1980, 1983) and many others have found relatively high correlations between various measures of reading and listening comprehension and WM capacity. Subjects with high WM capacity showed better global comprehension in terms of their verbal scores on the Scholastic Aptitude Test and their scores on the Nelson-Denny Reading Test and better memory for specific details such as pronominal reference.

Learning to Spell. Ormrod and Cochran (1988) showed that measures of WM capacity during the early stages of learning to spell predicted those children who would subsequently have difficulty learning to spell.

Following Directions. Engle, Carullo, and Collins (1991) found that subjects with high WM capacity were capable of following directions better than those with low WM capacity, and that this difference became greater as the directions became more complex.

Vocabulary Learning. Probably most of the words in our vocabulary are learned by hearing or reading them in a broader context that helps to define their meaning. Clearly, if you have more of the context elements in WM when a word occurs, you should be better at associating the word with the elements in working memory when it occurs. Daneman and Green (1986) showed that WM capacity predicted the ability of subjects to learn the meaning of a very low-frequency word presented in context better than did the subjects' existing vocabulary knowledge.

Notetaking. Kiewra and Benton (1988) demonstrated that a student's ability to take good notes and to benefit from those notes on a subsequent test was predicted better by WM capacity than by grade point average or by the score on the American College Test. The notes of students with larger WM capacity contained more complex propositions, more main ideas, and more words.

Writing. Benton, Kraft, Glover, and Plake (1984) argued that good writers could hold more information in working memory and simultaneously manipulate that information more effectively than poor writers. They demonstrated that WM capacity was significantly correlated with measures of good writing.

Language Comprehension. King and Just (1991) and MacDonald, Just, and Carpenter (1992) have shown that, in a quite specific manner, the ability of subjects to parse and disambiguate ambiguous narrative and to maintain multiple meanings of ambiguous words is a function of their WM capacity. Subjects with high WM capacity were found to be able to make use of the multiple meanings of ambiguous words and phrases for longer periods than those with low WM capacity.

Complex Learning. Shute (1991) gave 260 subjects a battery of tests, including tests of general knowledge, tests of specific knowledge about algebra, and a variety of WM tasks. The subjects then received a 40-hour computer-aided course on PASCAL programming. Performance on a subsequent test of programming skill was predicted better by the WM tasks than by either the tests of general knowledge or the test of algebra knowledge. Kyllonen and Stephens (1990) found similar results with subjects who were learning complex logic gates.

Thus, individual differences in WM capacity are apparently important to cognition in a large sample of real-life situations, at least in those involving the acquisition of new information. Another feature that should be noticed about the above list is that all of the criterion tasks involve verbal skills, at least to some extent. It remains to be seen whether the relationship between WM capacity and performance in higher-level cognitive tasks is specific at the level of verbal versus nonverbal domains or is domain-free. But what is responsible for these individual differences in WM capacity? Why would the number of words recalled in the reading-span task, for example, predict our ability to comprehend what we read or hear and how well we can learn to write a computer program? My colleagues and I proposed a set of ideas called the General Capacity Theory to try to specify the mechanisms that mediate the relationship between measures of WM capacity and higher-level cognitive tasks (see Cantor & Engle, 1993; Engle, Cantor, & Carullo, 1992). We made the following assumptions:

1. The contents of working memory consist of those temporary or permanent knowledge units in long-term memory that are currently active above some threshold. Thus, working memory is much more extensive than previous conceptions of short-term memory.
2. These knowledge units vary in their ambient level of activation, and the total amount of activation in the system is limited.
3. Individuals differ in the total amount of activation available to their systems. This is a relatively abiding characteristic of the system and does not vary with changes in the knowledge structure.
4. Spreading activation occurs quickly, automatically, and without conscious, controlled attention or intention (cf. Posner & Snyder, 1975). Thus, this version of the model assumed that individual differences in WM capacity were a result of the number of long-term memory units that would have their activation raised by the automatic spread of activation from initiating units.
5. Short-term memory consists of the information that is maintained at a surface level of coding within the grasp of immediate consciousness or the focus of attention. Thus, short-term memory is a subset of working memory, which is in turn a subset of long-term memory.
6. One important function of working memory is that it allows us to shift attention away from the current task (for example, as a result of an interruption or distraction) then back to the initial task, and

to recover the relevant task information and the status of task variables at the time of the interruption. The model proposed by Schneider and Detweiler (1987) is particularly adept at accounting for this function. They proposed that a set or chunk of information is coded in terms of the context in which it occurred. Thus, the context cue could be rapidly used to retrieve the set of information back to the focus of attention. This function of working memory is also important in animal models: For instance, Goldman-Rakic (1992) demonstrated that monkeys with parts of their prefrontal cortex removed showed a rapid loss of information represented in working memory after being distracted.

An important prediction of the General Capacity Theory was that individual differences in WM capacity should be important not merely in the acquisition of new information but also in the retrieval of well-learned information. If the total amount of activation available to the system is an abiding characteristic of that system, then we should observe effects of individual differences in WM capacity upon the retrieval of information even if the subjects have been equated in terms of how well they know that information.

Free Retrieval from Natural Categories

One procedure we have used to study the relationship between WM capacity and retrieval is that of giving subjects a category cue (e.g., "animals") and 10 minutes to recall as many exemplars of the category as possible. This task has a long history, with forms dating back to the measurement of what Thurstone (1938) called "word fluency" or "verbal fluency." This task has more recently become an important diagnostic tool for frontal-lobe damage (see Butler, Rorsman, Hill, & Tuma, 1993).

Baddeley, Lewis, Eldridge, and Thomson (1984) carried out a series of experiments to determine whether retrieval was a controlled and effortful endeavor or the result of automatic activation. The general strategy was to have subjects perform learning and retrieval either under a concurrent load or under no load. Most tasks (such as paired-associate learning or immediate free recall) showed an effect of load on learning but no effect on retrieval, which supported the thesis that in these tasks retrieval was the result of an automatic and effortless process. The one retrieval task that did show an effect of a concurrent load was that of free retrieval from natural categories, and this suggests that free retrieval is based on controlled, effortful search. Based on these findings and predictions of the General Capacity Theory, one might expect that individual differences in WM capacity would covary with retrieval in the category-exemplar task.

Rosen and Engle (1994) carried out an experiment in which we simply asked subjects to recall as many exemplars of the category "animal" as possible within a 10-minute period. Subjects were instructed to avoid repeating any animal names. Subjects were classified as high or low WM capacity on the basis of the operations-word span (Turner & Engle, 1989; see also Chapter 1 in this volume by John Richardson). We transcribed the specific words and the time at which each word occurred from audio- and videotapes. Our original version of General Capacity Theory had argued that high-span subjects should be able to spread memory activation to more units in each retrieval attempt than low-span subjects, and therefore the difference in performance should increase over time. Figure 4.1 shows the mean number of words recalled, cumulated over the 10-minute recall period. It is clear that the performance of high-span subjects was only slightly higher during the first minute, but that the level of disparity increased thereafter.

As mentioned above, Baddeley et al. (1984) had found that retrieval in this task was hampered by a concurrent load, suggesting that retrieval from natural categories was a controlled, effortful process. Therefore, a logical question is whether a load would differentially affect subjects of high and low WM capacity. One obvious possibility is that, since low-span

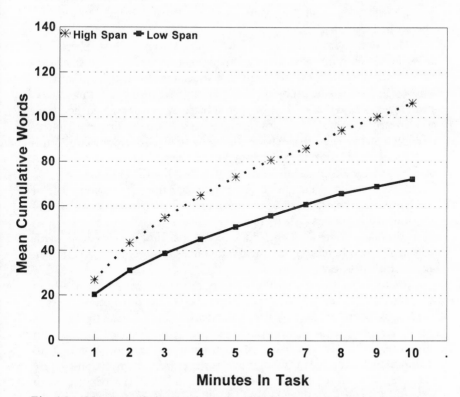

Fig. 4.1. Mean cumulative words produced in free retrieval from natural categories as a function of time for high-span and low-span subjects. (From Rosen & Engle, 1994.)

subjects have smaller resource capacities anyway, a load would hurt their performance, whereas high-span subjects would be able to use their greater resources to overcome the effect of such a load. If that were the case, differences between high-span and low-span subjects should be exaggerated under a concurrent load. Another possibility, however, is that high-span and low-span subjects rely upon different strategies to perform this task. It is possible that high-span subjects generate more words because they carry out the controlled, effortful search that Baddeley et al. (1984) attributed to their subjects. Low-span subjects, on the other hand, might use retrieval based upon automatic spreading activation, in which case they should be hurt less by a concurrent load than high-span subjects.

In our next study, Rosen and I asked high-span and low-span subjects to generate animal exemplars under one of two conditions. In one condition, the subject generated names of animals while reading aloud digits presented at a rate of one every 1.5 seconds in successive corners of a computer monitor. The subject was to press a key as quickly as possible whenever a third odd digit in a row occurred. This required the subject to keep a running set of between one and three digits in working memory and thus constituted a memory load. The no-load condition was identical to our first experiment and thus constituted a replication. Results are shown in Figure 4.2.

The control groups confirmed the findings from the first experiment, in showing superior generation of animal names among high-span subjects. Carrying out the concurrent digit-tracking task had no significant impact on the low-span subjects: Their cumulative recall performance was nearly identical to that of the low-span subjects who had no load, and both were nearly identical to the low-span subjects from the first experiment. The high-span group that retrieved under a load were significantly hampered in terms of the number of animals that they could generate, but even so they generated significantly more names than did the low-span subjects. Thus, the attention-demanding concurrent task hurt the performance of the high-span subjects but had no significant effect on the performance of the low-span subjects. These findings support the idea that high-span individuals use controlled, effortful search to perform retrieval from natural categories, whereas for low-span individuals retrieval is the result of an automatic, effortless process.

It should be noted that the subjects in these experiments had been instructed not to repeat any words. Thus, the task required the subjects to keep track of the items they had generated, and not to say those words again. Keeping track of previously recalled items is, itself, a drain on attentional resources. In our next experiment we wanted specifically to manipulate this feature by giving subjects a preload of items that they were *not* to recall. First, we asked subjects of high and low WM capacity to learn a list of 12 words until they could recall the list perfectly. Half of the subjects learned a list of high-frequency animal names (e.g., *bird*, *cat*, *cow*, and *dog*); this was the related condition. The other half of the subjects

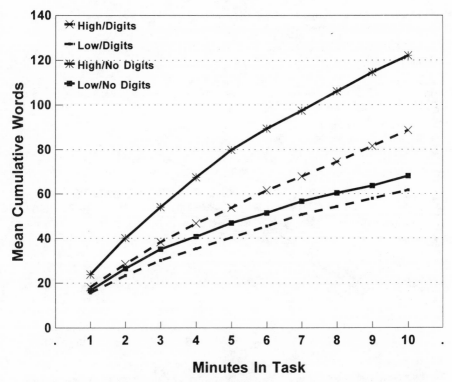

Fig. 4.2. Mean cumulative words produced in free retrieval from natural categories as a function of time and memory-load condition for high-span and low-span subjects. (From Rosen & Engle, 1994.)

learned a list of 12 high-frequency building parts (*wall, door, window*, etc.); this was the unrelated condition. After the relevant list had been learned, subjects were instructed to name as many animals as they could think of in 10 minutes but *not* to recall any of those words learned in the previous list and *not* to repeat any words.

We had anticipated that recall would be hurt most for the related condition and, after the findings of our second experiment, reasoned that the high-span subjects might be hurt more than the low-span subjects. We had also anticipated, however, that the unrelated condition would serve as a control group and be no different from the control group in our second experiment. After all, it made no sense to suppose that telling subjects not to recall building parts while they were trying to recall animal names should in any way interfere with their retrieval of animal names. Figure 4.3 shows the results of this experiment, along with the no-load control conditions from the previous experiment. Although recall was differentially hurt for the high-span subjects, the decrement was nearly as great for the unrelated condition as for the related condition. Both were significantly poorer than the control condition from the previous study. Being

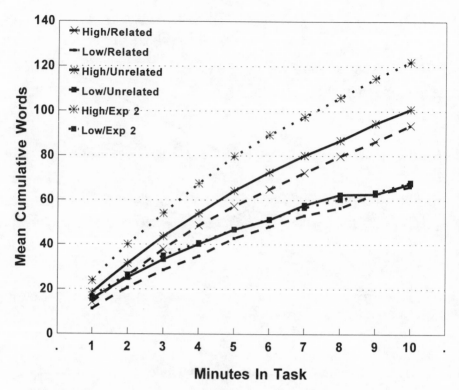

Fig. 4.3. Mean cumulative words produced in free retrieval from natural categories as a function of time and memory-load condition for high-span and low-span
subjects after prior exposure to related or unrelated words. The control data are
from the previous experiment. (Rosen & Engle, 1994.)

told not to recall items from the learned list hurt the retrieval of the high-
span subjects, regardless of whether or not the list was composed of items
from the animal category. As with the concurrent load condition, the low-
span subjects were unaffected by either preload condition. In fact, Figure 4.4 shows the low-span retrieval functions from all three experiments,
and it is clear that these are nearly coincident, regardless of load condition.

These studies show that individual differences on the working-
memory task correspond to individual differences in a free-recall task.
Further, either a concurrent memory load or a preload causes a decrement
in recall performance for high-span subjects, but it has no impact on
retrieval for low-span subjects. The category employed in these experiments was that of animals, and this category is sufficiently large that it is
unlikely that performance would be limited by differential knowledge
about animals or differential vocabulary knowledge for animal names. It
would nevertheless be useful to compare retrieval from memory when
there was more confidence that subjects did not differ in their level of
learning for the knowledge being retrieved. That was the purpose of the
next series of experiments.

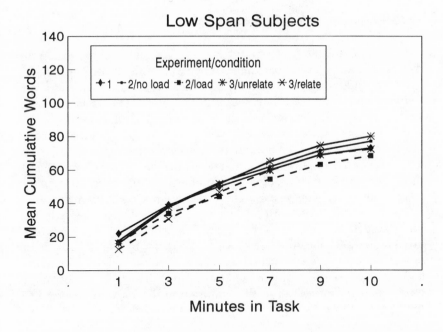

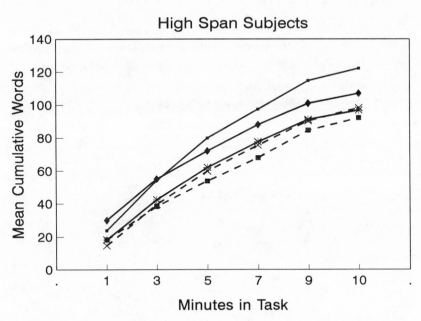

Fig. 4.4. Mean cumulative words produced in free retrieval from natural categories as a function of time and memory-load condition for high-span and low-span subjects in all three experiments. (Rosen & Engle, 1994.)

Speeded Recognition of Simple Facts

Cantor and Engle (1993) tested subjects of high and low WM capacity on
the speeded fact-retrieval paradigm known as the "fan procedure," developed by Anderson (1974). Subjects learned sets of facts such as "The
lawyer is in the boat," "The teacher is in the park," "The teacher is in the
boat," and so on. A complete set is represented in Figure 4.5. After
learning such sentences to a criterion of three perfect recall cycles, subjects
were shown the sentences along with appropriate foils and were asked to
make a speeded response to indicate whether the sentence was one of
those learned originally. The typical finding or "fan effect" is that sentences with a small fan, such as "The lawyer is in the boat," are recognized
much faster than those with a larger fan, such as "The teacher is in the
boat." Anderson (1983) hypothesized that the teacher sentence was recognized more slowly because *teacher* was associated with four different locations *(boat, church, bank,* and *park)*. Consequently, the activation in *teacher*
had to spread to four locations, and this divided the activation among the
four units. In contrast, all of the activation in the *lawyer* unit spread to
boat, and so this association was brought to threshold faster.

Cantor and I argued that, to the extent that the fan effect reflects a
division in the total activation available to the working-memory system,
and to the extent that individual differences in WM capacity are mediated
by differences in the total activation available to the system, subjects of
high and of low WM capacity should show differential effects of fan.
Specifically, subjects who perform poorly on tests of WM capacity should

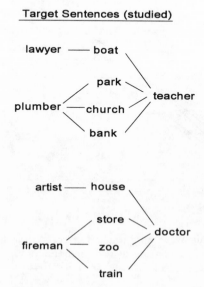

Target Sentences (studied)

Fig. 4.5. Propositional network from Cantor and Engle (1993). Copyright 1993
by the American Psychological Association. Reprinted with permission.

show a larger effect of fan size because they will have less activation to spread among the associated units than will subjects of high WM capacity. The verification times and errors for the target sentences are shown in Figure 4.6. Clearly, the prediction was confirmed. Even though the level of errors was very low and equivalent for the two groups of subjects, the low-span subjects were slowed substantially more with increasing fan size than were the high-span subjects. Thus, low-span span subjects were slow-

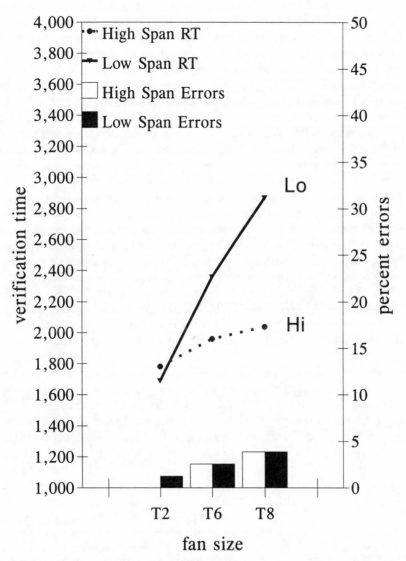

Fig. 4.6. Verification time and errors as a function of fan size for high-span and low-span subjects. (Cantor & Engle, 1993.) Copyright 1993 by the American Psychological Association. Reprinted with permission.

er to retrieve information than were high-span subjects, even though the level of learning for that information was indistinguishable for the two groups. Another important finding was that the correlation between performance on the tests of WM capacity and of reading comprehension was eliminated when the slope of the fan effect was partialed out. This suggests that the same mechanism might be responsible for individual differences on the two different tasks, even though one is a test of amount recalled whereas the other is a test of speed of recognition.

Results of this study raised an interesting question. I have talked about the different types of memory (short-term memory, working memory, and long-term memory) just as different levels of activation, and I have argued that people differ in the amount of activation available to the working-memory system at any given time. In the fan task, it is safe to assume that, just before the sentence is presented for recognition, it is relatively inactive, but that at presentation both the subject and the location of the target sentence must come to a higher state of activation for recognition to occur. The locus of the retrieval-time difference that Cantor and Engle (1993) found for high-span and low-span subjects could be specific to one of the levels of activation. On the one hand, it could be that these differences between high-span and low-span individuals occur in bringing the entire set of sentences associated with a given subject into the active portion of memory, in which case we could legitimately say that the difference was in retrieval from inactive or long-term memory. On the other hand, the two groups of subjects could be equivalent in the time to bring the set of information into the active state, but differ in the time taken to make the decision among the items in active memory. We probably cannot distinguish among the three levels of activation that we referred to above as STM, WM, and LTM, but we can certainly distinguish between two levels of activation. Thus, the question arises as to the locus of the retrieval-time differences between subjects of high and low WM capacity.

As Jones and Anderson (1987) pointed out, the fan task is, on the face of it, very much like the speeded-recognition task that was developed by Sternberg (1966). In this task, subjects take longer to recognize an item as being from a set if there are more items in that set. In fact, one explanation of the set-size effect in the Sternberg task is that there is a parallel spread of activation from the set-size cue to the members of the set (Anderson, 1983; Ratcliff, 1978); when the critical threshold is reached between the set-size cue and the item presented for recognition, a production fires, and this leads to a correct response. Obviously, the more items in the set, the less activation will accrue to each item from the set cue and the longer recognition will take. The set of information that is tested in the typical memory-search procedure can be presumed to be in a high state of activation, since the items are presented and then immediately tested. In the fan procedure, however, it may be that the set in question (for instance, locations associated with "teacher") is brought to a high state of activation before the recognition of the individual set-item association.

Conway and Engle (1994) modified the memory-search procedure to allow us to test whether subjects of high and low WM capacity differ in the time taken to bring a set of information into an activated state or in the time taken to activate the association between a set cue and any specific member of the set. We wanted to obtain a measure of retrieval time for knowledge that was already highly activated and another measure of retrieval time for knowledge that was relatively inactive. We had subjects learn sets of 2, 4, 6, and 8 letters, associated with a digit reflecting the set size (for instance, R and W associated with the digit 2). We could then test recognition of a digit–letter pair by varying the delay between the digit and the letter. For the letter set (R, W) as set size 2, we could present the "2" followed at some variable interval by the letter "R" for a test of speeded recognition. If we randomly presented the digit–letter pairs for recognition, we could then safely assume that, with no interval between the digit-set cue and the letter, the sets of letters would be minimally active. If we presented the digit-set cue and allowed sufficient time, the letters for that set would have been brought into an active state and would be maximally active when the target letter was presented. How long would it take to bring the sets into an active state?

In our first study, we asked subjects to learn sets of 2, 4, 6, and 8 letters, chosen such that no letter occurred in more than one set. After extensive learning, a recognition test was administered in which the subject was shown one of the digits 2, 4, 6, and 8, followed at a variable interval by a letter presented just below the digit. The subject was to press one key to indicate "Yes, the item was in the designated set" and another key for "No." The interval between the digit cue and the letter was 0, 200, 600, or 1000 ms. The question in this study was: When would increases in the interval between the digit cue and the letter lead to no further reduction in retrieval time? In other words, how long does it take to make a set of letters active? Response time as a function of set size and digit–letter onset interval is shown in Figure 4.7, together with the errors for each set size. Recognition takes the longest, for all set sizes, if the digit and the letter occur simultaneously. As the interval between digit and letter onset increases up to 600 ms, recognition time decreases, but there is no substantial benefit in increasing the interval between 600 and 1000 ms. Therefore, we can safely say that, by 1000 ms after the digit cue has been presented, the set information associated with that cue has been brought to a maximally useful level of activation.

Several other points should be noticed about these data. First, the standard set-size effect occurred for each interval, which suggests that the set-size effect is a result of the processing occurring after the set has been brought into a state of activation. Second, the slopes of the reaction-time functions for the various intervals were not significantly different from one another. This suggests that the time to retrieve a set into active memory (that is, the difference between the reaction times for the 0-ms and 1000-ms conditions) is the same regardless of whether the set contains two items or eight items, whereas recognition of set membership clearly

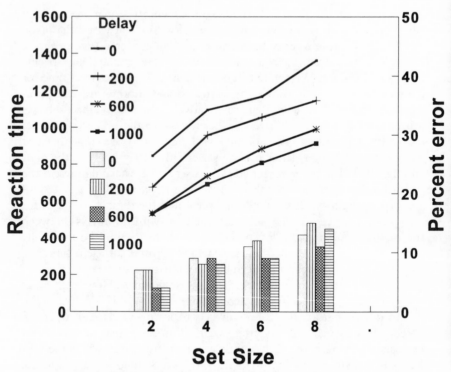

Fig. 4.7. Mean reaction time and errors in speeded recognition as a function of set size and delay between set cue and target. (Conway & Engle, 1994.) Copyright 1994 by the American Psychological Association. Reprinted with permission.

does depend on set size. In other words, the time to recognize an item as a member of a larger set is affected by the number of members in active memory, but not by the time to bring that set into active memory.

In our next study, we selected high-span and low-span span subjects and asked them to learn letters in sets of 2, 4, 6, and 8. We wanted to make this procedure as similar to the typical fan procedure as possible, and therefore each letter occurred in two sets. In the same way that the location *boat* was associated with both *lawyer* and *teacher*, the letter "R" might occur in both the set of size 2 and the set of size 6. After an extensive learning phase, subjects performed a speeded-recognition task in which they received a digit followed by a letter at either a 0-second delay or a 1-second delay. Subjects were instructed to respond as fast as possible but to be accurate. Given the logic of the methodology, we might expect the results from the targets to reflect one of the four patterns illustrated in Figure 4.8. (The predictions for the foils are less clear, and in fact the actual data from the foils were more variable.)

Figure 4.8a shows the results that we would expect if the high-span and the low-span subjects differed in terms of retrieval time from both active memory and inactive memory. Low-span subjects would have a

Hypothetical Results

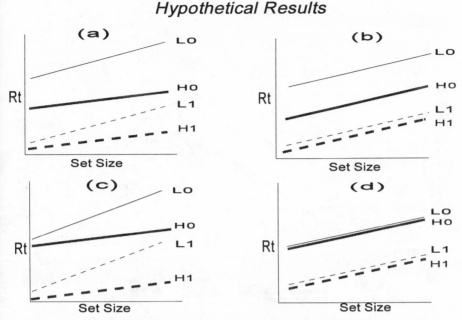

Fig. 4.8. Hypothetical patterns of results in speeded recognition with manipulation of set size and delay condition for high-span and low-span subjects. See text for further explanation. (Conway & Engle, 1994.) Copyright 1994 by the American Psychological Association. Reprinted with permission.

steeper slope than would high-span subjects in both of the delay conditions (representing the difference in retrieval from active memory). Furthermore, the difference between the two delay conditions (representing the time to bring the set into active memory) would be greater for the low-span subjects (L_0-L_1) than for the high-span subjects (H_0-H_1). If the high-span and low-span subjects differ in retrieval time from inactive memory but not from active memory, the results should look like those in Figure 4.8b. All four of the functions should be parallel over set size, whereas the intercepts should be equivalent for the high-span and the low-span subjects in the 1-second delay condition (representing retrieval from active memory) but would differ in the 0-second delay condition (since low-span subjects take longer to retrieve from inactive memory). Figure 4.8c shows the results that we would expect if WM capacity were reflected in retrieval from active memory but not in retrieval from inactive memory. The difference between 0-second and 1-second delay conditions (i.e., time to retrieve into active memory) would be the same for both high-span and low-span subjects, but the slopes would differ at each delay condition. If the high-span and the low-span subjects did not differ in retrieval time from either active or inactive memory, then the results would look like those in Figure 4.8d.

Figure 4.9 shows the actual results from this experiment. First, note

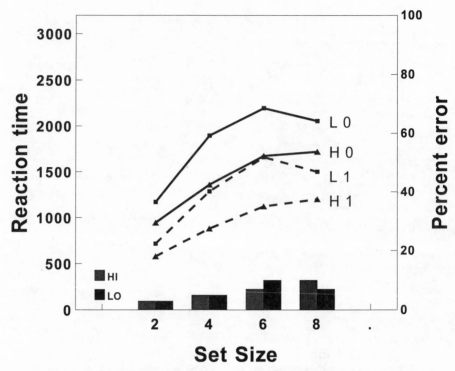

Fig. 4.9. Mean reaction time and errors in speeded recognition as a function of set size (with overlapping sets of letters) and delay between set cue and target for high-span and low-span subjects. (Conway & Engle, 1994.) Copyright 1994 by the American Psychological Association. Reprinted with permission.

from the bars at the bottom of the graph that the level of responding was fairly accurate and did not differ between the two groups of subjects. Second, notice that the response times look most like those in Figure 4.8c, a conclusion confirmed by statistical tests. The lower set of lines is from the 1-second delay conditions, representing the time taken to recognize an item as a member of a set of letters when the set was already in an active state. Low-span subjects showed a steeper slope against set size than did high-span subjects. The pattern is identical for the 0-second delay conditions, representing the time to bring the set to activation and then to recognize an item as a member of that set. This suggests that the time taken to bring the set into active memory did not differ between high-span and low-span subjects. Rather, WM capacity has its effect on the time to match the target letter with a letter in the set that is already active but has no effect on the time to bring the set into the active state.

One further point should be made about these results: The set-size functions have a curvilinear appearance that is more exaggerated in the case of the low-span subjects. The reader will note that this pattern is even more pronounced in the next experiment. We have no good explanation for this result, but we would simply point out that, in each of the groups, the two delay functions are virtually parallel, and the difference between them is essentially the same in both high-span and low-span subjects. Nevertheless, this is a puzzling result and one that merits inquiry in future research.

The next study attempted to establish the generalizability of these findings. We had high-span and low-span subjects learn high-frequency words in sets of 2, 4, 6, 8, 10, and 12, where each word occurred in two different sets. Otherwise, the procedure was identical to that of the previous study. The results, shown in Figure 4.10, again correspond most closely to those of Figure 4.8c and lead to the conclusion that the mechanisms responsible for individual differences in WM capacity are important in retrieval from active memory but are unimportant in retrieval from inactive memory. In both experiments, low-span subjects showed a steeper slope than did high-span subjects in both delay conditions, and the difference between the two delay conditions was about the same in both high-span and low-span subjects. These data also make a more general point beyond the WM capacity dimension. They support the notion that set size

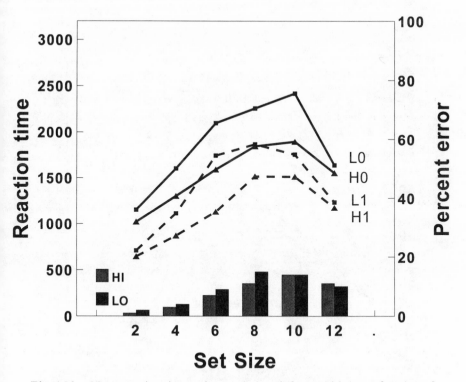

Fig. 4.10. Mean reaction time and errors in speeded recognition as a function of set size (with overlapping sets of words) and delay between set cue and target for high-span and low-span subjects. (Conway & Engle, 1994.) Copyright 1994 by the American Psychological Association. Reprinted with permission.

has its effect on retrieval from active or primary memory and not on retrieval from inactive or secondary memory. Both high-span and low-span subjects took no longer to activate a set of 10 or 12 words than they did to activate a set of 4 words. However, this relationship is not a simple one, because there was virtually no increase in retrieval time beyond set size 8, and in fact the time taken to retrieve items from a set of 12 was slightly less than the time taken to retrieve items from a set of 10.

These last two studies demonstrate that WM capacity is important in retrieval from primary memory but not in retrieval from secondary memory. The conclusions were the same regardless of whether the items were letters or words. Both studies were modeled after the fan procedure, in that each item was shared between two sets. This feature should not be important if differences between subjects of high and low WM capacity are the result of differences in the amount of activation available to spread to neighboring units. We therefore carried out two parallel studies that used sets whose membership was nonoverlapping. One study was identical to the experiment that had used letters as stimuli, except that no letter occurred in more than one set. Results are shown in Figure 4.11, and they are quite unlike those of the previous study, in that there was no interac-

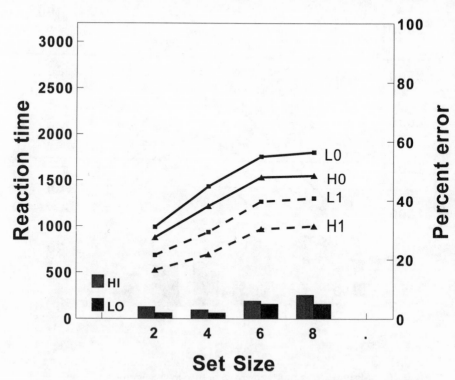

Fig. 4.11. Mean reaction time and errors in speeded recognition as a function of set size (with nonoverlapping sets of letters) and delay between set cue and target for high-span and low-span subjects. (Conway & Engle, 1994.) Copyright 1994 by the American Psychological Association. Reprinted with permission.

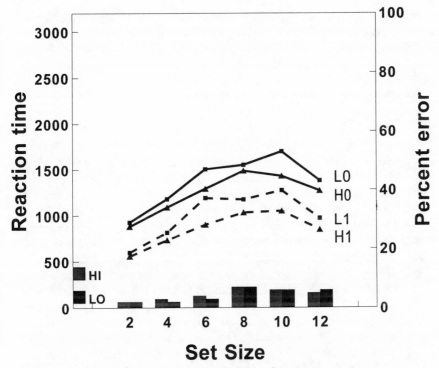

Fig. 4.12. Mean reaction time and errors in speeded recognition as a function of set size (with nonoverlapping sets of words) and delay between set cue and target for high-span and low-span subjects. (Conway & Engle, 1994.) Copyright 1994 by the American Psychological Association. Reprinted with permission.

tion between the effects of group and set size: Low-span subjects showed the same effect of set size as did high-span subjects. The second study used words as stimuli in sets of 2, 4, 6, 8, 10, and 12; again, no word was used in more than one set. The results, presented in Figure 4.12, also show no interaction between the effects of WM capacity (i.e., span group) and set size. There was a slight trend for low-span subjects to get slower with increasing set size, but this was not significant. Results of both studies conformed to Figure 4.8d, and this suggests that high-span and low-span subjects do not differ in retrieval from primary or secondary memory.

These memory-search studies suggest that working-memory capacity is important in retrieval from primary memory only when conditions of interference exist among the items being retrieved. Our original thoughts in the form of the General Capacity Theory viewed individual differences in working-memory capacity as being a result of differences in the amount of automatic spreading activation. However, a theory based upon individual differences in automatic activation does not predict the identical slopes obtained by high-span and low-span subjects in the last two experiments. This suggests that individual differences in reading span and operations span reflect differences not in memory representations but in controlled attention. It would therefore seem to be more appropriate to refer to the differences described here as differences in "working-attention" capacity than as differences in working-memory capacity.

Issues in Explaining Individual Differences in Working-Memory Capacity

Aside from the data presented here, there are several issues that we must consider when trying to explain why individual differences occur on tests of WM capacity and why performance on those tasks varies with performance on tests of higher-level cognition. I would like, first, to make a general point about the relationship between theories of individual differences in cognition and theories of developmental changes in cognition such as the account given by Ellen Stoltzfus, Lynn Hasher, and Rose Zacks in the previous chapter for changes in the second half of the life-span. Many theories of individual differences derive from theories of developmental changes; indeed, a common tendency is to assume that any explanation of developmental changes in some aspect of cognition automatically becomes a good candidate for a general theory of individual differences. This is an attractive strategy, and virtually every theory of individual differences to which I shall allude in this chapter has a counterpart in developmental psychology. Nevertheless, I believe it is important for us to understand that individual differences in working memory *may or may not* be mediated by the same factors that mediate the development of working memory. The reason I give this warning is that we must not rely on any given theory for explaining individual differences merely because it currently holds great support for explaining developmental changes.

One example of a factor that could mediate both developmental changes in cognition and individual differences in cognition is processing speed. Kail (1986, 1988) and Hale (1990) have presented evidence that there is an increase in general processing speed from birth to about 15 years of age. At some time in middle age, processing speed apparently starts to decline, and there is a corresponding decline in cognitive functions, particularly those that depend upon working memory. Salthouse (1991) has argued that the age-related decline in processing speed causes the decline in working memory. He obtained selected measures of general cognitive functioning, as well as measures of processing speed and WM capacity, in younger and older subjects. He found that the age-related differences on the general cognitive measures were accounted for by differences in the WM measures, but these in turn were accounted for almost completely by differences in the processing-speed measures. However, the processing-speed tasks that best account for the shared variance seem to have a heavy storage component as well.

For example, Salthouse often used a procedure described by Salthouse, Babcock, Mitchell, Palmon, and Skovronek (1990), in which subjects are timed while they compare lists of 3, 6, and 9 letters to see whether the lists match one another. Clearly, this places a heavy burden upon storage in working memory. Even mental rotation may involve central executive resources (see Chapter 2 in this volume by Robert Logie). Thus, it is difficult to separate processing speed from WM capacity in these tasks.

If we ignore the possible confounding of demands on WM in processing tasks and extrapolate from the developmental literature to that on individual differences, we might argue that individual differences in working memory simply reflect a more basic difference in processing speed. Indeed, some have argued that speed of information processing is a primal factor in intelligence (cf. Vernon, 1987). However, the study by Kyllonen and Stephens (1990) to which I alluded earlier included several tasks that they considered to be speed tasks; they found that these did not account for any variance in performance on the logic-learning task, whereas the WM tasks did. It might be that processing speed is important to developmental changes in cognition at both ends of the developmental continuum, but not to individual differences. Another possibility is that WM capacity and processing speed are independent determinants of intelligent behavior. It is too early to say. Again, I would caution that developmental changes and individual differences should be seen as mediated by different mechanisms until proven otherwise.

Another issue of concern when theorizing about individual differences in WM capacity is whether the resources of the central executive are unitary or modular. Baddeley (1986) described the central executive as a unitary source of attentional resources for the modular articulatory loop and the visuospatial scratchpad. I myself have written about working-memory capacity as a general capacity: in other words, as a unitary structure or resource. Nearly all the tasks that are described as measures of WM capacity are verbal tasks, so it is difficult to generalize very far from them. It is quite possible that the "central" executive really consists of independent multiple pools of resources, as Wickens (1984) proposed. However, even his theory has room for a central mechanism. Daneman and Tardif (1987) presented evidence against the idea of a unitary mechanism, but I have detailed the shortcomings of that study elsewhere (Engle et al., 1992; and see also Chapter 1 in this volume by John Richardson). Again, more research needs to be done on this question before we can provide an answer with any confidence. Support for the idea of a central mechanism comes from the study by Shute (1991) that I cited earlier. Shute used a wide variety of working-memory capacity tasks, including some that appear to be clearly spatial tasks, and found that the latter loaded on a WM factor as highly as other, more traditional, verbal tasks.

An Inhibition-Resource Hypothesis of Working-Memory Capacity

The data that I presented earlier appear to cause great difficulty for the notion that individual differences in working-memory capacity arise because of individual differences in the level of automatic activation available to the memory system. Results of the experiments by Conway and Engle (1994) using the memory-search task, in particular, seem to argue against an activation notion. Activation theory explains the set-size effect in this memory task by arguing that the limited amount of activation spreads simultaneously and in parallel from the set cue to the knowledge units that correspond to the items in the set (cf. Anderson, 1983). With larger sets, less activation is spread to each item, and thus each item will take longer to reach the threshold necessary for recognition. If individual differences in WM capacity reflect individual differences in the amount of activation that is available to each system, then we should see differences in the slope of the set-size function in the memory-search task, regardless of whether there is interference among the sets. That was not the case: Differences between high-span and low-span subjects in the slope of the set-size function were found only when items were shared by the different sets, thus creating interference or response competition. This suggests that our earlier version of the General Capacity Theory is wrong or at least inadequate to explain the results.

What then might account for individual differences in working-memory capacity and their relationship with performance in numerous tasks of real-world cognition? I propose an idea I call the Inhibition-Resource Hypothesis (to distinguish it from the Activation-Resource Hypothesis: Dempster, 1991). This is a hybrid that calls on concepts of individual differences in inhibition as resulting from differences in attentional resources. This approach seems to correspond with the description of the central executive (Baddeley, 1986; see also Chapter 2 in this volume by Robert Logie) but argues that limited attentional resources are necessary for the inhibition of distracting events or thoughts, as well as thoughts that are incompatible with the goals of the current task. Recent results from my laboratory support the notion that subjects defined as high or low in WM capacity on the basis of reading or operation span do not differ in terms of automatic aspects of memory but do differ in terms of controlled or intentional processes.

Natalie Oransky and I carried out an experiment using the process-dissociation procedure developed by Jacoby (1991), which allows one to determine whether a variable affects the automatic aspects of memory or the controlled, intentional aspects. We tested high-span and low-span subjects on a stem-completion task using this procedure and found that the two groups did not differ significantly on the contribution from automatic processing, but the contribution from controlled or intentional recollection was much greater for high-span than for low-span subjects. This indicates that whatever so-called working-memory tasks measure that is important to higher-level cognition reflects the attentional resources of the central executive but not differences in automatic activation.

Results of the experiments by Conway and Engle (1994) on memory search suggest that individual differences in central-executive resources might be most clearly revealed in tasks involving some level of either internally or externally generated interference. Recent papers by Bjork (1989), Dempster (1991), Hasher and Zacks (1988), and Stoltzfus and her colleagues (Chapter 3 in this volume) have encouraged cognitive psychologists to give more emphasis to inhibitory processes in developing explanations of cognitive processes. Hasher and Zacks (1988) argued that inhibitory processes were crucial to the efficient operation of working memory. These mechanisms serve to restrict the contents of WM to information that is relevant to the task being carried out at the time. They argued that the reason that WM capacity apparently declines with age is a decline in the inhibitory mechanisms. As a result, in older subjects working memory contains irrelevant information that would be inhibited or filtered out by younger subjects. That means that, because WM is limited in terms of the amount of information that it can hold, there is less task-relevant information available when needed. Hasher and Zacks and their colleagues (e.g., Hasher, Stoltzfus, Zacks, & Rypma, 1991) have provided a broad range of evidence that older subjects show a diminished role of inhibition in attention.

At the risk of contradicting the advice that I gave earlier about the gratuitous mixing of explanations of developmental changes and individual differences, I suggest that individual differences in the capacity of the central executive may lead to differences in vulnerability to the effects of interference. High-span subjects might be better able to inhibit or to suppress irrelevant information and to prevent it entering working memory. However, I argue that these differences in ability to inhibit are a result of the additional attentional resources available to high-span subjects. One could in fact extend this argument to say that the differences between young and old subjects that have been attributed to inhibition mechanisms (see Chapter 3 in this volume by Ellen Stoltzfus and her colleagues) might be the result of a decline in the capacity of the central executive. That would, however, be to fall into the trap that I outlined above, and I will try to avoid that trap.

As Bjork (1989) and Anderson and Bjork (1994) have pointed out, the term *inhibition* is used in a variety of ways in the literature. One way is simply to describe an experimental effect opposite to facilitation (in other words, a slowing of response time). Another use is more theoretical but nevertheless has a passive connotation. The retrieval of an item may be blocked by the increased activation of a different item. For example, suppose I retrieve item A and that item achieves full activation and then begins a normal course of decay. I am then cued to retrieve and activate item B, which then also begins a normal course of decay. If I now perform an act of retrieval from a context cue appropriate to both A and B, I will retrieve B simply because its level of activation is higher than A. Even if I try to retrieve to a cue that is more appropriate to A than to B, I may still retrieve B because its level of activation is higher (Raaijmakers & Shiffrin, 1981). We can say that B has inhibited A, but the real effect is caused by the activation of *B* being raised relative to *A* rather than by true inhibition or the suppression of *A* by *B*. Bjork (1989) refers to this mechanism as "blocking." He argues for the existence of inhibition in a stronger sense, that of an active, directed, and effortful suppression of an item or set of items, and he states that the response-set suppression demonstrated by Postman, Stark, and Fraser (1968) is an example of this.

I submit that this type of inhibition is the result of controlled or effortful processing and hence is resource demanding. Thus, individuals with more attentional resources would be better able to inhibit irrelevant information. I would further argue that any memory effects resulting from automatic activation would not show differences between subjects of high and low WM capacity, but that effects resulting from controlled processing would, if sufficiently taxing of resources, show differences reflecting WM capacity. (See Posner & Snyder, 1975, and Jacoby, 1991, for the sense in which I use "automatic" and "controlled" processing.) How would this sort of theory explain the results presented above for the role of WM capacity in the free generation of category exemplars and speeded-item recognition? Rosen and Engle (1994) suggested that at least two factors important to retrieval from natural categories were potentially relevant to differences between high-span and low-span subjects: One is the ability to perform a controlled, effortful, and systematic search of a category; another is the ability to inhibit or block the retrieval of previously retrieved items.

Retrieval in many situations can certainly be based upon automatic activation without recourse to controlled search (Baddeley et al., 1984). We would argue that the low-span subjects in our studies used just such a strategy in the exemplar-retrieval task, but that high-span subjects used a resource-demanding controlled search. It is likely that the effortful aspects of retrieval are represented in getting access to the label or cue for a given cluster, but, once that cluster label has been accessed, the items within that cluster become activated automatically. For example, we found in our experiment that the difference between high-span and low-span subjects occurred almost totally in the number of clusters recalled. The number of items per cluster differed only slightly between high-span and low-span subjects. The time between clusters was shorter for high-span subjects, but, once the recall of a cluster had begun, the interitem time was nearly the same for both high-span and low-span subjects.

When either a preload or concurrent load was imposed, then the recall function for high-span subjects was sharply diminished, whereas that for the low-span subjects was virtually unchanged. In other words, the low-span subjects were unaffected by the load conditions: Their recall functions were statistically the same in the three different load conditions as in the two control conditions. It is possible that the recall functions for the low-span subjects reflected the level of recall that was contributed by automatic processes (cf. Jacoby & Kelly, 1992). When the resources of high-span subjects were taken up by a load, the retrieval function was diminished because subjects had difficulty combining the attention-demanding concurrent task with controlled search.

Rosen and Engle (1994) instructed their subjects to retrieve as many exemplars as possible from the animal category but to avoid repeating any exemplars. According to the Inhibition-Resource Hypothesis, high-span and low-span subjects should differ in their ability to block the recall of previously retrieved exemplars. There are two stages at which this could occur: The item could be blocked at retrieval; or else the subject could retrieve a previously retrieved item but recognize it as one that had been previously reported and block the reporting of that item. We have no way of knowing whether high-span and low-span subjects differ in terms of the number of repetitions that occur at the first of these stages. However, we do know that low-span subjects made significantly more repetitions in their public reports. We would argue that their additional central-executive capacity allowed the high-span subjects to prevent the damaging effect of previous retrieval, but that low-span subjects did not have sufficient attentional resources to block these repetitions.

Conway and Engle (1994) argued that in speeded-item–recognition tasks with no overlap in set membership, performance was based upon the automatic aspects of memory. As no controlled search was involved, there were no differences in performance between high-span and low-span subjects. When the set cue and a target letter or word appeared on the screen, we argued that there was automatic addressing of the set, followed by an automatic, parallel spread of activation to all the members of that set. Presumably, the set-size effect occurred because of the spreading of a limited amount of activation over more items. Because retrieval was based upon automatic activation, high-span and low-span subjects did not differ either in the time to bring the set of items to activation or in the time for the link between the set cue and the target to reach threshold.

However, recognition of a target-cue relationship is different when there is overlap in set membership. Let us carry out a specific analysis of how recognition would occur in such a situation. Suppose that the letter *B* is a member both of a set of size 2 and of a set of size 6. On a verification trial the subject is shown 2 and *B*. There would be automatic activation of the association for 2 and *B* that would increase the tendency to make a "Yes" response, but there would also be automatic activation of the association between *B* and 6. The high-span subjects could inhibit the irrelevant association, in which case their performance would be much like that found in conditions with no overlap in set membership. We anticipate that low-span subjects are less able to inhibit the irrelevant association, and that this creates a condition of interference and possible confusion. One possibility is that, at this point, the low-span subjects are forced into an additional stage of processing, an effortful serial search to verify that *B* is indeed a member of the set of size 2.

In other words, in the overlap studies the high-span subjects perform on much the same basis as they do in the nonoverlap studies; low-span subjects, however, are forced into the slow, effortful, serial comparison that Sternberg (1966) originally proposed. This argument is supported by a comparison of the overlap and nonoverlap studies. The performance of the high-span subjects was nearly identical in both of the letter studies and in both of the two-word studies. Overlap in set membership appeared to have no effect on the high-span subjects. Low-span subjects were the ones affected by the overlap in set membership; performance was slowed considerably when the items belonged to two different sets.

To those readers who are averse to allowing any remnant of resource theory, I offer the appeal of a personal example. Imagine you and I are having a conversation about a psychological theory, and you are having to attend closely in order to follow the content of the conversation. If suddenly some other conversation strikes up near us in which one of the speakers has a voice similar to mine, you will feel as if you have to work harder and use more mental effort to block out the irrelevant speech. At an intuitive level, the inhibition of irrelevant information can require mental effort if the stimulus we are attempting to process is similar on some dimension to the stimulus we are attempting to block out.

Engle, Conway, Tuholski, and Shisler (1995) obtained evidence to support this intuition in a recent experiment, which tested the importance of central-executive resources in the negative-priming effect. One might show a subject a display consisting of a red letter and a green letter, somewhat superimposed, and the task is to name the red letter as accurately and as rapidly as possible. Tipper and Cranston (1985) argued that, on any given trial in this procedure, the subject attends to the red letter by inhibiting some representation of the green letter. If that is the case, then, if the rejected green letter becomes the named letter on the next trial, it should be named more slowly. That is exactly what Tipper and Cranston found, a phenomenon they referred to as "negative priming." The Inhibition-Resource Hypothesis asserts that the act of inhibition requires central-executive attentional resources. If that is so, then the negative-priming effect should be diminished under a mental workload. Between every other pair of letters for the naming task, we interspersed a word to be read silently. After four such words, the subject was cued to recall these words in the correct order. We assumed that, on the letter-naming trial just after the words had been recalled, naming would be performed in the absence of a workload since no words were to be remembered at that time. As each word was added to the list to be recalled, however, the load increased, culminating in a load of four. We found that with no load there was a significant negative-priming effect. However, as the load increased, the size of the negative-priming effect decreased and was positive but nonsignificant by a load of three words.

This experiment demonstrates that the processes leading to the negative-priming effect are sensitive to a mental load. Other evidence that inhibitory processes of this sort are resource-dependent comes from a study by Roberts, Hager, and Heron (1994), who used the antisaccade task; here, subjects fixate on a central cue, and a flashed cue to either side means that an object which had to be rapidly identified will be flashed to the opposite side of fixation. Efficient performance on this task requires that subjects inhibit their natural tendency to move their eyes toward the cue and instead move their eyes contrary to these natural saccades. Roberts et al. (1994) observed that, although subjects can inhibit the saccade to the flashed cue under normal circumstances, they have great difficulty inhibiting their natural saccades if they are also performing an attention-demanding shadowing task. This confirms the idea that inhibition, at least in this task, requires attentional resources.

Support for this idea can be also found in research by Nakagawa (1991), who found that inhibition in a lexical-decision task only occurred when the target was presented directly to the left cerebral hemisphere. Even more importantly, when the subject performed a concurrent shadowing task, inhibition did not occur at all. These findings converge on the idea that many phenomena attributed to inhibition depend upon attentional resources, and that, when these attentional resources are unavailable because of a concurrent load, the so-called inhibition phenomena may not be observed.

Certain questions still remain unanswered by the Inhibition-Resource Hypothesis as an explanation of individual differences in working memory. One problem is the apparent contradiction between the conclusions of the research by Carpenter, Just, and their colleagues and by Whitney and his colleagues, on the one hand, and the conclusions of work by Gernsbacher and her colleagues, on the other. MacDonald et al. (1992), King and Just (1991), and Whitney, Ritchie, and Clark (1991) have all found evidence that, when processing ambiguous or misleading words or phrases, those subjects identified as having high working-memory capacity were able to retain more irrelevant and unneeded meanings and for a longer period of time than did low WM subjects.

However, Gernsbacher and Faust (1991) found that those subjects identified as having high comprehension ability inhibited or dropped irrelevant and unneeded meanings faster than did low-comprehension subjects. Because of the reasonably high correlation between measures of WM capacity and of reading comprehension (Daneman & Carpenter, 1980), it is probably safe to assume that a group of subjects identified as high comprehension would have considerable overlap with a group identified as having high WM capacity.

Numerous procedural differences exist between these two groups of studies, but this contradiction would seem to be at the heart of the issue of whether individual differences in working-memory capacity reflect inhibitory or activation mechanisms. One advantage of the way I have conceptualized the resources of the central executive here is that it would presumably enable a high-capacity subject to keep multiple meanings available if the task encouraged such a strategy but to inhibit the irrelevant meanings if the task encouraged that strategy. In short, one could confirm the conclusion of either group of studies depending on the specific demands of the task.

A second concern about a theory based upon inhibitory mechanisms is that individual differences in WM correspond to performance differences across a variety of general cognitive tasks. However, most of the evidence for inhibition shows it to be quite specific and possibly confined to response mechanisms (see Neill, 1989). The evidence for true inhibition (that is, the actual dampening of the activation of one unit by the activity of another stronger unit) at the cognitive level is sketchy at best (Tipper & Driver, 1988). If the Inhibition-Resource Hypothesis is to have any credibility, one must demonstrate, first, that inhibition, at least of the type that Bjork (1989) calls "suppression," is controlled and resource dependent and, second, that individual differences in mechanisms of this sort are more general than is currently suspected. One possible solution to this problem is that generality may come from the limitations in the resources necessary to implement inhibition, rather than from the inhibition itself.

Conclusion

In summary, I have presented evidence that individual differences in the capacity of working memory predict performance across a wide variety of real-world tasks, at least tasks based on acquisition. Several new sets of experiments show that individual differences in performance on tasks presumed to reflect WM capacity correspond also to differences in performance on retrieval tasks. However, these differences seem to appear only under conditions that encourage controlled, effortful search. I have made the case that these individual differences do not reflect differences in the level of automatic activation as we once thought (see Engle et al., 1992), but that they reflect differences in attentional resources that seem to correspond to the component of working memory that is referred to as the central executive. I have further made the case that the resources of this central executive are necessary to inhibit distracting information and information or thoughts that are irrelevant to the goals of the current task.

References

Anderson, J. R. (1974). Retrieval of propositional information from long-term memory. *Cognitive Psychology, 6,* 451–474.

Anderson, J. R. (1983). A spreading activation theory of memory. *Journal of Verbal Learning and Verbal Behavior, 22,* 261–295.

Anderson, M. C., & Bjork, R. A. (1994). Mechanisms of inhibition in long-term memory: A new taxonomy. In D. Dagenbach & T. H. Carr (Eds.), *Inhibitory processes in attention, memory, and language* (pp. 265–325). New York: Academic Press.

Baddeley, A. (1986). *Working memory.* New York: Oxford University Press.

Baddeley, A., Lewis, V., Eldridge, M., & Thomson, N. (1984). Attention and retrieval from long term memory. *Journal of Experimental Psychology: General*, *113*, 518–540.

Baldwin, J. M. (1894). *Mental development in the child and the race*. New York: Macmillan.

Benton, S. L., Kraft, R. G., Glover, J. A., & Plake, B. S. (1984). Cognitive capacity differences among writers. *Journal of Educational Psychology*, *76*, 820–834.

Bjork, R. A. (1989). Retrieval inhibition as an adaptive mechanism in human memory. In H. L. Roediger III & F.I.M. Craik (Eds.), *Varieties of memory and consciousness* (pp. 309–330). Hillsdale, NJ: Erlbaum.

Butler, R. W., Rorsman, I., Hill, J. M., & Tuma, R. (1993). The effects of frontal brain impairment on fluency: Simple and complex paradigms. *Neuropsychology*, *7*, 519–529.

Cantor, J., & Engle, R. W. (1993). Working-memory capacity as long-term memory activation: An individual-differences approach. *Journal of Experimental Psychology: Learning, Memory, and Cognition*, *19*, 1101–1114.

Cantor, J., Engle, R. W., & Hamilton, G. (1991). Short-term memory, working memory, and verbal abilities: How do they relate? *Intelligence*, *15*, 229–246.

Conway, A.R.A., & Engle, R. W. (1994). Working memory and retrieval: A resource-dependent inhibition model. *Journal of Experimental Psychology: General*, *123*, 354–373.

Daneman, M., & Carpenter, P. A. (1980). Individual differences in working memory and reading. *Journal of Verbal Learning and Verbal Behavior*, *19*, 450–466.

Daneman, M., & Carpenter, P. A. (1983). Individual differences in integrating information between and within sentences. *Journal of Experimental Psychology: Learning, Memory and Cognition*, *9*, 561–583.

Daneman, M., & Green, I. (1986). Individual differences in comprehending and producing words in context. *Journal of Memory and Language*, *25*, 1–18.

Daneman, M., & Tardif, T. (1987). Working memory and reading skill re-examined. In M. Coltheart (Ed.), *Attention and performance XII: The psychology of reading* (pp. 491–508). Hove, UK: Erlbaum.

Dempster, F. N. (1991). Inhibitory processes: A neglected dimension of intelligence. *Intelligence*, *15*, 157–174.

Engle, R. W., Cantor, J., & Carullo, J. J. (1992). Individual differences in working memory and comprehension: A test of four hypotheses. *Journal of Experimental Psychology: Learning, Memory, and Cognition*, *18*, 972–992.

Engle, R. W., Carullo, J. J., & Collins, K. W. (1991). Individual differences in the role of working memory in comprehension and following directions in children. *Journal of Educational Research*, *84*, 253–262.

Engle, R. W., Conway, A.R.A., Tuholski, S. W., & Shisler, R. J. (1995). A resource account of inhibition. *Psychological Science*, *6*, 122–125.

Gernsbacher, M. A., & Faust, M. E. (1991). The mechanism of suppression: A component of general comprehension skill. *Journal of Experimental Psychology: Learning, Memory, and Cognition*, *17*, 245–262.

Goldman-Rakic, P. S. (1992). Working memory and the mind. *Scientific American*, *267*(3), 72–79.

Hale, S. (1990). A global developmental trend in cognitive processing speed. *Child Development*, *61*, 653–663.

Hasher, L., Stoltzfus, E. R., Zacks, R. T., & Rypma, B. (1991). Age and inhibition. *Journal of Experimental Psychology: Learning, Memory, and Cognition, 17,* 163–169.

Hasher, L., & Zacks, R. T. (1988). Working memory, comprehension, and aging: A review and a new view. In G. H. Bower (Ed.), *The psychology of learning and motivation: Advances in research and theory* (Vol. 22, pp. 193–225). San Diego, CA: Academic Press.

Jacoby, L. L. (1991). A process-dissociation framework: Separating automatic from intentional uses of memory. *Journal of Memory and Language, 30,* 513–541.

Jacoby, L. L., & Kelly, C. M. (1992). A process-dissociation framework for investigating unconscious influences: Freudian slips, projective tests, subliminal perception, and signal detection theory. *Current Directions in Psychological Science, 1,* 174–178.

Jones, W. P., & Anderson, J. R. (1987). Short- and long-term memory retrieval: A comparison of the effects of information load and relatedness. *Journal of Experimental Psychology: General, 116,* 137–153.

Kail, R. V. (1986). Sources of age differences in speed of processing. *Child Development, 57,* 969–987.

Kail, R. V. (1988). Developmental functions for speeds of cognitive processes. *Journal of Experimental Child Psychology, 45,* 339–364.

Kiewra, K. A., & Benton, S. L. (1988). The relationship between information-processing ability and notetaking. *Contemporary Educational Psychology, 13,* 33–44.

King, J., & Just, M. A. (1991). Individual differences in syntactic processing: The role of working memory. *Journal of Memory and Language, 30,* 580–602.

Kyllonen, P. C., & Christal, R. E. (1990). Reasoning ability is (little more than) working-memory capacity?! *Intelligence, 14,* 389–433.

Kyllonen, P. C., & Stephens, D. L. (1990). Cognitive abilities as determinants of success in acquiring logic skill. *Learning and individual differences, 2,* 129–160.

MacDonald, M. C., Just, M. A., & Carpenter, P. A. (1992). Working memory constraints on the processing of syntactic ambiguity. *Cognitive Psychology, 24,* 56–98.

Martin, M. (1978). Memory span as a measure of individual differences in memory capacity. *Memory & Cognition, 6,* 194–198.

Nakagawa, A. (1991). Role of anterior and posterior attention networks in hemispheric asymmetries during lexical decisions. *Journal of Cognitive Neuroscience, 3,* 313–321.

Neill, W. T. (1989). Lexical ambiguity and context: An activation-suppression model. In D. S. Gorfein (Ed.), *Resolving semantic ambiguity* (pp. 63–83). New York: Springer-Verlag.

Ormrod, J. E., & Cochran, K. F. (1988). Relationship of verbal ability and working memory to spelling achievement and learning to spell. *Reading Research and Instruction, 28,* 33–43.

Perfetti, C. A., & Lesgold, A. M. (1977). Discourse comprehension and sources of individual differences. In M. A. Just & P. A. Carpenter (Eds.), *Cognitive processes in comprehension* (pp. 141–183). Hillsdale, NJ: Erlbaum.

Posner, M. I., & Snyder, C. R. (1975). Attention and cognitive control. In

R. Solso (Ed.), *Information processing and cognition: The Loyola Symposium* (pp 55–85). Hillsdale, NJ: Erlbaum.

Postman, L., Stark, K., & Fraser, L. (1968). Temporal changes in interference. *Journal of Verbal Learning and Verbal Behavior, 7,* 672–694.

Raaijmakers, J. G., & Shiffrin, R. M. (1981). Search of associative memory. *Psychological Review, 88,* 93–134.

Ratcliff, R. (1978). A theory of memory retrieval. *Psychological Review, 85,* 59–108.

Roberts, R. J., Hager, L. D., & Heron, C. (1994). Prefrontal cognitive processes: Working memory and inhibition in the antisaccade task. *Journal of Experimental Psychology: General, 123,* 374–393.

Rosen, V., & Engle, R. W. (1994). *Working memory capacity and retrieval from long-term memory.* Unpublished manuscript.

Salthouse, T. A. (1991). Mediation of adult age differences in cognition by reductions in working memory and speed of processing. *Psychological Science, 2,* 179–183.

Salthouse, T. A., Babcock, R. L., Mitchell, D.R.D., Palmon, R., & Skovronek, E. (1990). Sources of individual differences in spatial visualization ability. *Intelligence, 14,* 187–230.

Salthouse, T. A., Mitchell, D.R.D., Skovronek, E., & Babcock, R. L. (1989). Effects of adult age and working memory on reasoning and spatial abilities. *Journal of Experimental Psychology: Learning, Memory, and Cognition, 15,* 507–516.

Schneider, W., & Detweiler, M. (1987). A connectionist/control architecture for working memory. In G. H. Bower (Ed.), *The psychology of learning and motivation: Advances in research and theory* (Vol. 21, pp. 53–119). San Diego, CA: Academic Press.

Shute, V. J. (1991). Who is likely to acquire programming skills? *Journal of Educational Computing Research, 7,* 1–24.

Sternberg, S. (1966). High-speed scanning in human memory. *Science, 153,* 652–654.

Thurstone, L. L. (1938). *Primary mental abilities.* Chicago: University of Chicago Press.

Tipper, S. P., & Cranston, M. (1985). Selective attention and priming: Inhibitory and facilitatory effects of ignored primes. *Quarterly Journal of Experimental Psychology, 37A,* 591–611.

Tipper, S. P., & Driver, J., (1988). Negative priming between pictures and words in selective attention task: Evidence for semantic processing of ignored stimuli. *Memory & Cognition, 16,* 64–70.

Turner, M. L., & Engle, R. W. (1989). Is working memory capacity task dependent? *Journal of Memory and Language, 28,* 127–154.

Vernon, P. A. (1987). *Speed of information-processing and intelligence.* Norwood, NJ: Ablex.

Whitney, P., Ritchie, B. G., & Clark, M. B. (1991). Working memory capacity and the use of elaborative inferences in text comprehension. *Discourse Processes, 14,* 133–145.

Wickens, C. D. (1984). Processing resources in attention. In R. Parasuraman & R. Davies (Eds.), *Varieties of attention* (pp. 63–102). New York: Academic Press.

5

Evolving Issues
in Working Memory

John T. E. Richardson

The previous chapters have described a wide variety of research paradigms through which psychologists have endeavored to investigate the nature and function of "working memory," defined very broadly as the mechanism responsible for the temporary storage and processing of information. Thirty-five years after this idea was first proposed by Miller, Galanter, and Pribram (1960), these different lines of argument and experimentation are gradually converging upon a loose consensus among psychologists as to the basic properties of this mechanism. To conclude this volume, I shall give an integrated statement of what we have learned about working memory as the result of research carried out in the intervening period by identifying the key issues that have divided researchers in this field.

Working Memory and Long-Term Memory

The original account that was given by Miller et al. (1960) interpreted working memory as a distinct component of the human information-processing system from the long-term store (or "dead storage": p. 65), and they went so far as to locate its anatomical substrate within the frontal lobes (pp. 200, 207). In the account provided by Atkinson and Shiffrin (1968), it is equally clear that the distinction between a short-term store, which served as the subject's working memory, and a relatively permanent long-term store was supposed to represent a basic structural feature of the memory system. Indeed, by the late 1960s, the notion that short-term memory and long-term memory reflected distinct structural components had become widely accepted among cognitive psychologists. Perhaps unsurprisingly, this notion was duly incorporated into many early textbook accounts of working memory.

However, it would appear to have been Norman (1968) who first pointed out that short-term memory and long-term memory might constitute different aspects of a single storage mechanism rather than two physically different systems. He proposed in particular that short-term storage might consist in the temporary activation of traces within the storage system, and that long-term storage would consist in permanent structural changes within the same system. Subsequently, Atkinson and Shiffrin (1971) were agnostic as to the status of their hypothetical working memory and its relationship to their long-term store, observing: "Our account . . . does not require that the two stores necessarily be in different parts of the brain or involve different physiological structures. One might consider the short-term store simply as being a temporary activation of some portion of the long-term store" (p. 83). As mentioned in Chapter 1, Anderson and Bower (1973) were adamant that "working memory is not structurally separate from long-term memory, but rather it is a *currently active partition* of long-term memory" (p. 216, italics in original).

Contemporary researchers are still very much divided over this basic question of whether working memory should be characterized as a distinct structural component or simply the region of declarative long-term memory that is currently activated. Three different answers are apparent in the previous contributions to this volume. First, the account originally put forward by Baddeley and Hitch (1974) has evolved considerably in the last two decades in a manner that was described in both Chapters 1 and 2, but Baddeley and his colleagues have consistently represented working memory as a complex system whose components are structurally distinct both from one another and from the long-term store. On this view, as Robert Logie made clear in Chapter 2, the precise nature of the relationship between working memory and long-term memory is a matter that is to be settled by empirical research rather than to be taken as axiomatic.

Nevertheless, on the basis of further arguments and evidence, Logie himself comes to the conclusion that the contents of working memory are based on the activation of representations in long-term memory (see also Logie, 1995, p. 126). This comes fairly close to the position originally advanced by Anderson (1972) and by Lindsay and Norman (1972, p. 426), and which is also adopted in Chapter 3 by Ellen Stoltzfus, Lynn Hasher, and Rose Zacks. On this account, the short-term store or working memory is a distinct structural component of the cognitive system, but its contents are identified with the set of items or nodes that are currently being activated by interpretative processes within long-term memory.

The third, more radical position is that the very concept of working memory is itself to be identified with the area or partition of long-term memory that is currently being activated, so that it is not a structurally separate component of the human information-processing system. Originally proposed by Anderson and Bower (1973), this conception of working memory has been adopted by Randall Engle and his colleagues. In Chapter 4, Engle suggested that within the activated region of long-term memory one should also distinguish the area that constituted the current focus of attention (see also La Pointe & Engle, 1990). A very similar account was given by Cowan (1988, 1993), and this was discussed by Robert Logie in Chapter 2.

The Capacity of Working Memory

These different positions concerning the fundamental architecture of the human cognitive system have a number of theoretical implications. Perhaps most important, they lead to quite distinct conceptions of the capacity of working memory. Following the work of Miller (1956), traditional theories of short-term memory interpreted the immediate memory span as evidence for the notion that its storage capacity was defined in terms of a particular number of items or "chunks." This idea was incorporated into some of the earlier accounts of working memory that regarded its limited capacity as a determinate feature of the mechanisms responsible for short-term storage. For example, as noted in Chapter 1, simple production-system models of working memory included a fixed number of "slots," each capable of holding a single stimulus element. Research carried out by Baddeley, Thomson, and Buchanan (1975) was explicitly intended to test Miller's account, and the effects of word length that they obtained were taken to be conclusive evidence against the idea that memory span was a constant number of items.

Instead, more recent accounts of working memory have interpreted its limited capacity as an emergent feature of the mechanisms responsible for cognitive processing in general. In the theory developed by Baddeley and his colleagues, working memory consists of a number of distinct cognitive structures that are specialized for the temporary storage and processing of information, and limitations in its capacity are due to the controlled mechanisms responsible for the allocation of attentional resources. These mechanisms are exhibited in particular in performance in cognitively demanding tasks requiring the concurrent processing and storage of information. From this viewpoint, the capacity of the central executive determines the rate of information processing, whereas the immediate memory span reflects the storage capacity of the phonological loop, and the effects of word length are to be attributed to the role of articulatory rehearsal in maintaining the contents of the phonological store (see Baddeley, 1990, pp. 74–79).

However, if working memory is instead taken to consist in the set of nodes or links in long-term memory that are currently in an active state, then limitations in its capacity will be due primarily to those automatic processes involved in the spread and decay of activation within long-term memory. These processes are exhibited most especially in priming effects obtained in simple tasks requiring lexical or semantic judgments and also in "fan" effects obtained in tasks requiring the storage and retrieval of simple facts. From this viewpoint, the rate of information processing is controlled by the current level of activation. The immediate memory span measures the sustained capacity of working memory rather than the amount of information that is momentarily active, which may in principle be much greater. The effects of word length are to be attributed to the role of articulatory rehearsal in maintaining a distribution of activation within long-term memory (see Anderson, 1983a, pp. 28–29, 86–89, 118–119; 1983b).

These are conceptually distinct notions of working memory and hence are logically incompatible if they are regarded as competing accounts of the same hypothetical component of the human cognitive system. However, they can also be regarded as characterizing different constraints upon cognitive processes and therefore as mutually consistent accounts of the limits on performance in particular tasks. One situation in which both types of constraint might well be involved is the learning of new skills. Indeed, in his general theory of cognitive architecture, Anderson (1983a) devoted considerable attention to procedural learning, which he described in terms of the acquisition of new productions through the compilation of relevant declarative knowledge that was held in working memory (chap. 6; see also Anderson, 1987). However, it should be noted that this account of procedural learning is formally independent of Anderson's assumptions about the nature and the capacity of working memory.

On the basis of this account, Woltz (1988) inferred that the limits of controlled attention processes would constrain the initial acquisition and interpretation of declarative knowledge concerning the relevant skill, but that the limits of automatic activation processes would influence the reorganization of individual condition-action rules into a single complex production. Woltz showed, as expected, that a composite index of controlled attention predicted performance in the early stages of skill acquisition, whereas a composite index of automatic activation predicted performance in the later stages. Woltz argued that both types of test were necessary to predict the rate at which subjects acquired new skills and that both types of limitation constrained the mechanisms of procedural skill acquisition. He also found that the two composite indices were essentially uncorrelated with each other. In subsequent work, Woltz (1990) obtained correlations between similar measures that were statistically significant but reflected a shared variance of less than 20 percent, and he concluded that "activation and attention processes that are central to popular working memory models seem to represent largely independent cognitive processing limits" (p. 400). Woltz and Shute (1993) demonstrated analogous phenomena in the acquisition of declarative knowledge (viz., the learning of paired associates and of basic mathematical concepts) through repetitive practice.

In principle, then, the contribution of working memory is constrained by both controlled attention processes and automatic activation processes. In practice, it is an empirical matter which type of constraint is of more importance in determining the level of performance in any particular task, though the evidence described by Randall Engle in Chapter 4 tends to point to the former. However, it should be reiterated that in both accounts the effective capacity of working memory is not a determinate quantity but an emergent feature of the underlying mechanisms. As Anderson (1993, p. 52) himself noted, it might sometimes be convenient to refer to this capacity in terms of a specific number of items, but this is only an approximation for expository purposes. However, it is consistent with both accounts of working memory that individuals might differ from one another in terms of their effective working-memory capacity. In Chapter 1, I noted that these individual differences have been studied quite extensively in the context of reading comprehension, often using variants of the "reading-span" test (in which subjects read aloud a series of unrelated sentences and attempt to recall the last word from each sentence in the order of presentation).

Perfetti and Lesgold (1977) argued that good readers and poor readers differed not in their total working-memory capacity, but in the efficiency of their encoding processes and consequently in the residual capacity that could be devoted to storing the results of those encoding processes during reading. Daneman and Carpenter (1980) argued similarly that good and poor readers would differ in terms of their residual working-memory capacity in the reading-span test, and they and other researchers produced findings in agreement with this prediction. However, Turner and Engle (1989) obtained evidence indicating that the residual capacity of working memory according to different variants of the reading-span test was essentially independent of the specific demands of the concurrent processing task. They concluded that individual differences in reading comprehension depended on the total capacity of working memory. One finding consistent with this idea is that subjects judged to have larger working-memory capacities appear to be more likely to maintain both alternative interpretations of ambiguous sentences (MacDonald, Just, & Carpenter, 1992). This position has subsequently been elaborated in terms of the total amount of activation available in working memory by Engle, Cantor, and Carullo (1992) and Just and Carpenter (1992). Consistent with such an interpretation, Cantor and Engle (1993) found that fan effects obtained in the retrieval of simple facts were more pronounced in subjects who were judged to have less working-memory capacity.

Inhibitory Processes in Working Memory

Many accounts of working memory based upon the spread of activation also postulate the existence of inhibitory mechanisms between competing items. These serve to prevent information that is irrelevant to the task at hand from gaining access to working memory and therefore from reducing the residual capacity available for processing task-relevant information. The latter was claimed by Eysenck (1982, pp. 99–100) to be the main factor in determining the effects of anxiety upon cognitive functioning, insofar as the task-irrelevant information involved in worry and self-concern should compete with task-relevant information for space in working memory. This theory is supported by the fact that both situational stress and state anxiety have a specific effect upon performance in tests of memory span (Eysenck, 1979; Hodges & Spielberger, 1969). Richardson and Snape (1984) similarly found that the stress induced by involvement in a serious accident led to impaired performance in immediate recall but not in delayed recall.

In the case of anxiety and stress, such effects are likely to result from changes in the goals and values of the subjects being tested, rather than from any deficits in the inhibitory mechanisms themselves. However, it is obvious that a reduction in the efficiency of these mechanisms will give rise to effects on cognitive performance by allowing task-irrelevant information to enter working memory and also by allowing information that has proved not to be relevant to the task at hand to be maintained within working memory. Hamm and Hasher (1992) found that older people were more likely to maintain two different interpretations of an ambiguous passage, even though one of the interpretations was implied by the subsequent text. Hasher and Zacks (1988) noted that this finding was inconsistent with the position that older people had reduced storage capacity in working memory, and they argued instead that there was an age-related decline in terms of the efficiency of inhibitory processes. In Chapter 3, Ellen Stoltzfus, Lynn Hasher, and Rose Zacks presented additional evidence to support this account. However, Hasher and Zacks (1988) described possible strategies that would enable older people to compensate for inhibitory deficits, and Stoltzfus and her colleagues pointed out that there were situations in which these "deficits" might actually prove advantageous for older people.

Conversely, any enhancement in the efficiency of these processes may give rise to an increase in cognitive performance by excluding irrelevant information. Pascual-Leone (1987) developed his neo-Piagetian account of intellectual development to incorporate four basic constructs:

M, the subject's capacity to activate task-relevant information structures stored in long-term memory;

I, the subject's capacity to inhibit or interrupt the activation of task-irrelevant structures that could interfere with relevant ones;

F, the subject's capacity to perform an action as a single, integrated whole; and

E, the subject's repertoire of executive schemes or plans.

Pascual-Leone regarded M and I as two capacities or resources whose power developed with age in intellectually normal subjects, thus explaining the emergence of Piaget's stages of cognitive development. Pascual-Leone claimed that a serious deficiency of earlier developmental theories of working memory was the failure to appreciate the need for an inhibitory mechanism to explain how a child was able to override its habitual but incorrect responses when faced with irrelevant or misleading cues in problem-solving tasks.

Inhibitory phenomena have been investigated in a variety of paradigms including negative priming, the priming of ambiguous words, negative error priming, directed forgetting, and stop-signal tests (see Arbuthnott, 1995, for an extensive review). In Chapter 4, Randall Engle pointed out that, simply because inhibitory processes seem to explain individual differences along one particular dimension or in one particular task, it should not be assumed that they will readily account for individual differences on other dimensions or in other tasks. However, the various contributors to this volume provide some basis for thinking that such mechanisms are of general significance in understanding variations in cognitive performance. Both Randall Engle and Ellen Stoltzfus and her colleagues refer to the work of Gernsbacher in this connection, and it will be useful to describe this in a little more detail.

Gernsbacher (1989) demonstrated that during the reading of sentences the activation (or enhancement) of previously mentioned concepts and the inhibition (or suppression) of other concepts were triggered by anaphors (for instance, "Ann predicted that Pam would lose the track race, but *she* came in first very easily"). The amount of suppression depended upon the explicitness of the anaphoric reference. In other research (Gernsbacher & Faust, 1991; Gernsbacher, Varner, & Faust, 1990), she showed that people who were less skilled in comprehension were less efficient in rejecting the inappropriate meanings of ambiguous words, the inappropriate forms of homophones, the highly typical but absent components of scenic arrays, and irrelevant pictures or words. These results indicated that less skilled comprehenders were less efficient at suppressing contextually irrelevant or inappropriate information that was activated during the comprehension of linguistic or nonlinguistic material (see also Gernsbacher, 1993).

Nevertheless, Gernsbacher and Faust (1991) proceeded to consider the alternative explanation that less skilled comprehenders had difficulty in rejecting this inappropriate information because they had less efficient enhancement mechanisms and consequently were less able to appreciate what information was contextually appropriate. They showed that less skilled comprehenders tended if anything to show more facilitation as the result of contexts that biased the appropriate meanings of ambiguous words and as the result of scenic arrays in which the test object was both typical and present. Gernsbacher (1993) concluded that less skilled readers were able to activate contextually appropriate information at least as well as more skilled readers. A fortiori, these results seem to be inconsistent with the idea that individual differences in reading comprehension depend simply on the total amount of activation available within working memory (cf. Cantor & Engle, 1993; Engle et al., 1992; Just & Carpenter, 1992).

On the basis of these and other studies, Gernsbacher and Faust (1995) put forward three general principles. First, suppression consists in the active dampening of activation rather than the passive decay of activation or compensatory inhibition (the idea that some memory nodes must decrease in activation simply because others have increased). Second, suppression takes the form of processing signals transmitted by activated nodes. This proposal contradicts the suggestion made by Just and Carpenter (1992) that lateral inhibition occurs because production rules serve to increment the activation of certain nodes while simultaneously reducing the activation of other, collateral nodes. It also contradicts a suggestion by Anderson (1993, p. 13) that inhibition takes the form of competition between these production rules rather than a process of direct transmission between the declarative structures to which they apply. Third, Gernsbacher and Faust argued that suppression is a general cognitive mechanism that is involved in the comprehension of both linguistic and non-linguistic material.

Gernsbacher and Faust also presented data to suggest that suppression varies with the demands of the experimental context, which implies that it is to a large extent under strategic control and is not a purely automatic and obligatory process. This is a conclusion with which the contributors to this volume would certainly agree, and additional evidence was reviewed by Ellen Stoltzfus and her colleagues in Chapter 3 and by Randall Engle in Chapter 4. Arbuthnott (1995) criticized contemporary models of inhibitory function for failing to specify precisely how such strategic control might operate to maintain task-relevant information and exclude task-irrelevant information from working memory. She suggested an effect upon either the lateral inhibition or the self-inhibition of activated nodes, but Randall Engle noted in Chapter 4 that the empirical evidence for such a mechanism is relatively sketchy.

The Gateway Hypothesis

Nevertheless, one consideration that appears to be directly pertinent to the issue of whether working memory is a distinct structural component or simply the region or partition of long-term memory that is currently being activated is the interpretation of working memory as some sort of gateway for information between sensory input and long-term storage, an idea discussed by Robert Logie in Chapter 2.

If working memory is taken to be a distinct structural component of the human information-processing system, it then remains an entirely open question whether it serves as the gateway to and from long-term storage. However, if working memory is taken to be the currently activated region of declarative long-term memory, this seems to commit one to the gateway hypothesis. For instance, Norman (1968) stated that "permanent changes in storage occur when there has been prior activation of temporary (primary) traces" (p. 525). Moreover, the theory of associative memory enunciated by Anderson and Bower (1973) and the family of theories advanced by Anderson (1983a, pp. 19–20) made the explicit assumption that information was permanently stored within declarative long-term memory as the result of processes that operated on the contents of working memory. Indeed, as Anderson (1983b) himself commented, "The basic encoding assumption of the ACT theory is that there is a probability that a transient working memory structure will be turned into a permanent long-term memory *trace*" (p. 262, italics in original).

In Chapter 2, Robert Logie pointed out findings contradicting the gateway hypothesis. He provided evidence and arguments to show that information can (indeed, must) gain access to long-term storage before being processed within working memory, and this was taken to imply that the contents of working memory were derived from currently activated representations in long-term memory. Nevertheless, these representations relate to general semantic knowledge concerning objects and language, not to specific episodic memories for past events. For example, the encoding of stimuli within the phonological loop depends upon knowledge concerning the phonology and pronunciation of the subject's native language, whereas the encoding of stimuli within the visuospatial scratchpad depends upon knowledge concerning the physical appearance of concrete objects.

It is, however, possible to go further and to argue that information concerning specific episodic memories for prior events can be represented in long-term memory without first having been held within working memory. This argument rests on evidence that it is possible to disrupt short-term storage without disrupting long-term storage. This was first demonstrated experimentally by Kintsch and Buschke (1969) in an analysis of performance in tests of probed recall using lists of unrelated words. They found that phonemic similarity among the items impaired performance in the last few serial positions, whereas semantic similarity among the items impaired performance in the early and middle serial positions. This was taken to mean that performance overall reflected the contribution of a short-term phonological store and a long-term semantic store, but the fact that these two components could be manipulated independently was taken as evidence against the idea that the former was a gateway to the latter.

Further evidence has come from research with brain-damaged patients, including some key studies briefly mentioned by Robert Logie in Chapter 2. Warrington and Shallice (1969) described a patient with closed head injury whose verbal learning and long-term retention appeared essentially normal, but whose verbal short-term memory was severely reduced. On the basis of further testing of this patient, Shallice and Warrington (1970) concluded that an impairment in short-term memory tasks did not necessarily lead to an impairment in verbal-learning tasks, and that the systems responsible for short-term and long-term storage must be functionally independent. Other cases have been described with similar selective deficits in verbal short-term memory (Basso, Spinnler, Vallar, & Zanobio, 1982; De Renzi & Nichelli, 1975; Warrington, Logue, & Pratt, 1971). Nevertheless, although there seems to be a broad dissociation between short-term memory and long-term memory within the verbal domain, this does not rule out the possibility that there are certain forms of verbal learning (for example, vocabulary acquisition) which depend on a judicious coordination between long-term and short-term storage and are therefore disrupted in patients with a deficit of short-term memory (Baddeley, Papagno, & Vallar, 1988).

De Renzi and Nichelli (1975) also described patients whose long-term spatial memory (as evidenced from informal observation as well as their performance on a test of maze learning) was essentially normal but whose short-term spatial memory (as evidenced from a spatial analog of the test of digit span) was severely impaired. De Renzi (1982, p. 226) commented that these findings confirmed the dissociation between long-term memory and short-term memory within the spatial domain and undermined the notion that information had to be held in a short-term store before it could be processed by long-term memory mechanisms. A similar case reported in the literature did appear to have problems in the use of imagery mnemonics and in spatial learning (Hanley, Young, & Pearson, 1991). However, this might have been because the subject's brain damage (resulting from the rupture and repair of an intracranial aneurysm that had caused a subarachnoid hematoma) had encroached upon a relatively large area. In fact, the brain regions that are responsible for spatial short-term memory and for spatial learning seem to be entirely distinct from each other (Ratcliff & Newcombe, 1973).

A Single Component or a Complex System?

Taken together, these findings indicate that the mechanisms involved in the encoding and retrieval of information in long-term declarative memory are functionally independent of the mechanisms involved in the storage of information in short-term memory. More specifically, they contradict the notion of working memory as one unitary component of cognitive processing that not only provides temporary storage but is also responsible for the creation of permanent records in declarative memory. One way of handling these findings would be to retain the idea of working memory as a unitary device, but to abandon the hypothesis that it serves as a form of gateway to long-term memory, possibly citing the arguments and evidence presented by Robert Logie in Chapter 2 that information can gain access to long-term storage before being processed in working memory. However, this strategy would radically undermine the entire notion of working memory as a general device responsible for all forms of executive function, including the encoding and retrieval of episodic traces in long-term memory.

The alternative solution is to retain the gateway hypothesis but to abandon the assumption that working memory is a unitary component of the human information-processing system. The latter assumption was virtually taken for granted in many early accounts of working memory: For instance, it was an explicit feature of the family of theories developed by Anderson (1976, 1983a). Nevertheless, research findings exist that tend to cast doubt upon the idea that a single cognitive mechanism is responsible both for executive processing and for the short-term retention of information. For instance, the main conclusion of Miller's (1956) classic paper, "The magical number seven, plus or minus two," was that the limited processing capacity of human beings (as evidenced by performance in tests of absolute judgment) was determined by the amount of information in the test stimuli, whereas the limited capacity of immediate memory was largely unrelated to the information content of the items to be remembered. This conclusion is not undermined by the finding of word-length effects in short-term recall.

Further evidence comes again from research on brain-damaged patients. The patients described by Shallice and Warrington (1970) and by Warrington et al. (1971) exhibited a selective impairment of verbal short-term memory and did not show a generalized disruption of their cognitive capabilities. Baddeley and Hitch (1974) commented that it was difficult to reconcile the existence of these patients with the hypothesis that the short-term store functioned as a crucially important working memory. In the case of normal individuals, Baddeley and Hitch found that a concurrent memory load, which approached the span of immediate memory, impaired performance in a range of tasks, but the degree of disruption was far from massive. They concluded that, "although the digit span and working memory overlap, there appears to be a considerable component of working memory which is not taken up by the digit-span task" (p. 75). Klapp, Marshburn, and Lester (1983) pointed out that, within the normal population, performance on the digit-span test was correlated with full-scale intelligence, but that this correlation was smaller than the correlations between most other subscales and full-scale intelligence. Finally, Klapp et al. (1983) remarked that individual differences in reading comprehension were largely unrelated to performance in tests of short-term serial recall, as I mentioned in Chapter 1.

These findings seem to imply that there exists a component of working memory which is responsible for short-term verbal recall, but which is not involved in cognitive processing more generally. Conversely, they seem to imply that there exists a component of working memory which is responsible for executive functioning but is not (primarily, at least) responsible for short-term recall. In fact, the latter view has quietly become adopted in research on working memory on both sides of the Atlantic. It is, of course, central to Baddeley and Hitch's (1974) multicomponent model that immediate serial recall is based upon components of working memory that are distinct from but subsidiary to the central executive. However, virtually all the main North American researchers in this field have explicitly acknowledged that their conceptions of working memory are tantamount to Baddeley's idea of the central executive (see, for instance, Cantor, Engle, & Hamilton, 1991; Conway & Engle, 1994; Daneman & Tardif, 1987; Hasher & Zacks, 1988; Just & Carpenter, 1992; and see also Chapters 3 and 4 in this volume). This then leaves open the possibility that other, subsidiary components such as the phonological loop and the visuospatial scratchpad are responsible for the performance obtained in tests of short-term recall.

Reading Span and Memory Span

This reconciliation of the multicomponent model with more general models of working memory might also help to resolve certain otherwise problematic findings obtained using variants of the test of "reading span" devised by Daneman and Carpenter (1980). It will be remembered that, in the original version of this test, subjects read aloud a series of unrelated sentences and attempted to recall the final words from the sentences in the order in which they had occurred. Daneman and Carpenter found that performance on this test was highly correlated with measures of reading comprehension but that a conventional measure of memory span for sequences of words was not. This pattern of findings was subsequently replicated by Masson and Miller (1983) and by Turner and Engle (1989), but it is somewhat problematic if both reading span and word span are supposed to be indices of the capacity of working memory. In fact, the two types of span seem to be essentially independent of one another, and this implies that they measure distinct components of a working-memory system (Masson & Miller, 1983; cf. Cantor et al., 1991). A possible explanation is that reading span measures the processing efficiency of the central executive in retrieving temporarily activated representations from long-term memory, but that conventional measures of memory span measure the storage capacity of the phonological loop (e.g., Baddeley, in press; Just & Carpenter, 1992).

It is consistent with this analysis that the validity of reading span as a predictor of reading comprehension does not depend upon whether it is scored to take serial-order information into account. In repeating their original experiment, Daneman and Carpenter (1980) asked subjects to decide whether the sentences were true or false (rather than reading them aloud) before trying to recall the final words. This version of the task proved to be so difficult that subjects were given credit for recalling any set of words without regard to the order of recall, but this did not appear to affect the pattern of results. Reading span was measured from item recall rather than serial recall in many subsequent studies (Daneman & Carpenter, 1983; Daneman & Green, 1986; Masson & Miller, 1983; Turner & Engle, 1989). Nevertheless, there is evidence that the phonological loop contributes to performance only in tasks requiring the retention of order information.

The most obvious source of information is experiments on free recall. First, Craik (1968) found that word length had no effect on performance in this task, whereas Glanzer and Razel (1974) actually found a slight tendency for disyllabic words to be better remembered than monosyllabic words that had been matched for frequency. Second, Craik and Levy (1970) found that phonemic similarity among the items to be remembered had a positive effect on recall, which they attributed to its use as an organizational principle in long-term memory. Third, Baddeley and Hitch (1974, 1977) found that a memory load impaired performance in free recall only when it exceeded the presumed capacity of the phonological store and so required the support of general-purpose workspace within the central executive. Conversely, Richardson (1984) found that a concurrent free-recall task impaired performance in serial recall, but did not attenuate the phonemic similarity effect in the latter task. In the same study, Richardson also found that unattended speech had no effect on performance in free recall, a finding subsequently confirmed by Salamé and Baddeley (1990). Finally, Richardson and Baddeley (1975) found that articulatory suppression had only a slight effect upon performance in free recall; this occurred with both auditory and visual presentation and with both immediate and delayed testing, and can once again be ascribed to the demands placed upon the central executive rather than to any contribution from the phonological loop.

Further evidence comes from the "missing scan" procedure devised by Buschke (1963). In this task, the subject is presented with eight of the nine nonzero decimal digits in a random order and is asked to determine which digit has been omitted. Klapp et al. (1983) found that articulatory suppression had no effect on performance in this task. This implied that, whereas the recall of a series of items in the order of presentation might be mediated by the sort of phonemic response buffer postulated by Baddeley and Hitch (1974), the recall of the same series of items in any order was not mediated by such a store and would therefore depend exclusively on the other components of working memory. Similarly, Jones and Macken (1993) found that a stream of varying auditory tones disrupted performance in the immediate serial recall of digits but not in the missing-scan task, which confirms that the recall of a series of items in any order is not based on the phonological loop. The finding that reading span is correlated with reading comprehension regardless of whether it is scored to encompass serial-order information therefore indicates that its predictive validity does not depend upon any contribution from the phonological loop.

This picture was complicated by evidence obtained by La Pointe and

Engle (1990), who evaluated both simple memory span and reading span using short and long items sampled without replacement from large sets of words. When tested by either free recall or serial recall, effects of word length were obtained with both indices, regardless of whether the background task used in measuring reading span involved sentences or arithmetic equations. Moreover, both indices predicted reading comprehension, a finding that was subsequently replicated (Cantor et al., 1991; Engle, Carullo, & Collins, 1991; Engle, Nations, & Cantor, 1990). These word-length effects were not eliminated by articulatory suppression, although the simple span no longer predicted reading comprehension. Nevertheless, the effects of word length on both the simple memory span and the reading span were abolished by articulatory suppression when the testing procedure required the serial recall of sequences drawn by repeated sampling from small word sets that the subjects had previously memorized.

These results suggest that word length may have two different effects on memory performance. The first effect is apparent in the serial recall of sequences drawn from known word sets. In this case, word length has an effect on the retention of order information, and this can be abolished by articulatory suppression. This is most naturally ascribed to the working of the phonological loop. The evidence tends to suggest that under these circumstances performance does not predict reading comprehension (Cantor et al., 1991; Masson & Miller, 1983). The second effect is apparent in the free recall and the serial recall of sequences drawn from indefinite word sets. In this case, word length has an effect on the retention of item information, which is not eliminated by articulatory suppression, and hence it is implausible to ascribe this effect to the phonological loop. Under these circumstances, however, performance undoubtedly does predict reading comprehension. Unfortunately, La Pointe and Engle did not refer to the study by Craik (1968), which had failed to find a word-length effect in the free recall of previously unknown lists of words, nor to the study by Glanzer and Razel (1974), which had found a slight tendency for longer words to be better recalled than short words. This raises the possibility that the effects on item recall found by La Pointe and Engle (1990) may have been due to some variable that was confounded with word length, although they were able to rule out both word frequency and concreteness in this regard.

Turner and Engle (1989) suggested a different proposal, that simple memory-span tasks allowed the subjects to make use of grouping and other rehearsal strategies that were strictly irrelevant to reading in order to circumvent the capacity limitations of short-term memory; conversely, in complex reading-span tasks, the background task "makes it more difficult to use these strategies and thus gives a clearer picture of the 'true' capacity of short-term memory" (p. 151). In Chapter 2, Robert Logie suggested that conventional tests of serial recall (and, by implication, tests of memory span, too) may not give an accurate indication of the capacity of working memory because they have a clear semantic component. The idea that memory span involves both a short-term component and a long-term component was first put forward by Craik (1968), but it needs to be given careful scrutiny.

In tests of serial recall following visual presentation, Besner and Davelaar (1982) found that nonwords which sounded like words (e.g., *phood*) were recalled more easily than were nonwords that did not (e.g., *thude*); this effect was not abolished by articulatory suppression. Similarly, Hulme, Maughan, and Brown (1991) found that memory span was greater for words than for nonwords, and that memory span for words in an unfamiliar foreign language was increased by learning the translations of those words into the subjects' native tongue. Nevertheless, this study confounded the meaningfulness of the stimuli with their familiarity and pronounceability. Crowder (1976) found that sequences of phonemically similar words were recalled better than were sequences of phonemically similar nonwords that were structurally derived from the words. However, this effect was abolished when subjects were told the items to be remembered, which places the locus of the effect at the level of item information rather than at the level of order information, and at the retrieval stage rather than at the encoding stage.

Similarly, Richardson (1979) found no overall difference in the serial recall of auditory stimuli between subjects who were told that the items in question were the letters of the alphabet *B*, *C*, *D*, *P*, and *T*, and subjects who were told that they were the words *bee*, *sea*, *Dee* (a river in Wales), *pea*, and *tea*. In short, if subjects are tested on a known set of familiar stimuli (words or nonwords), there appear to be no lexical or semantic effects on performance in serial recall, and therefore there is no reason to believe that the resulting level of performance fails to give an accurate indication of the capacity of working memory.

A General Resource or a Domain-Specific Resource?

A further question has to do with the organization of the resources that working memory is able to contribute to the performance of a particular cognitive task. If working memory is a unitary component, its resources simply constitute a general (though finite) pool that is available for the performance of the task at hand. However, if it is a complex system, then its resources might constitute a number of distinct pools that operate in a relatively independent manner with little or no scope for any virement or redistribution.

This issue has been addressed in a number of studies of reading span and analogous tasks. Daneman and Carpenter (1980) found that both reading comprehension and listening comprehension were highly correlated with both reading span and a "listening-span" task in which subjects decided whether each of a series of spoken sentences was true or false. They concluded that individual differences in reading comprehension resulted from general comprehension processes rather than from processes peculiar to reading. Turner and Engle (1989) similarly found that reading comprehension was predicted both by reading span and by performance in an "operations-word" task in which subjects judged whether each of a series of arithmetic equations was correct and attempted to recall unrelated words that had been presented in combination with the equations. They concluded that the residual capacity of working memory as measured by the primary task of remembering the words was independent of the particular skills involved in the secondary task. (As I mentioned in Chapter 1, this ignores the fact that linguistic skills may well be used in the parsing and encoding of arithmetic equations.)

However, various investigations have produced somewhat different results. First, Baddeley, Logie, Nimmo-Smith, and Brereton (1985) found that reading comprehension was highly correlated with reading span but was much less strongly associated with performance in a task in which subjects counted and subsequently recalled the number of dots in each of a sequence of visual displays. Daneman and Green (1986) similarly found that reading comprehension was highly correlated with reading span but was less highly correlated with performance in a task in which subjects had to generate aloud a different sentence containing each of a series of unrelated words. Finally, Daneman and Tardif (1987) found that reading comprehension was highly correlated with reading span but was less highly correlated with performance in a task in which subjects were required to recombine the digits in successive numbers or in a task in which subjects were required to evaluate a three-dimensional tic-tac-toe game. In each of these three studies, the correlation between reading comprehension and performance in the supposedly analogous task was reduced to a nonsignificant level when individual variations in reading span had been statistically controlled.

On the face of it, these findings are inconsistent with the notion of working memory as a pool of general-purpose resources, since on this view correlations with a criterion variable should remain constant, regardless of the task used to measure the available processing capacity. To retain this view, Baddeley et al. (1985) suggested that their alternate span task was not a good measure of working-memory capacity, but this is implausible in the case of the other two studies mentioned. Daneman and Green (1986) found that their "speaking span" was correlated with performance in a task in which subjects had to generate synonyms of target words appropriate to specific sentence contexts. Similarly, Daneman and Tardif (1987) claimed that their "mathematical span" was correlated with mathematical ability, whereas their "spatial span" was correlated with spatial ability. They did not present data to support these claims; nevertheless, they concluded that working memory consisted of at least two separate processors, one for representing and manipulating verbal-symbolic information, and another for representing and manipulating spatial information. Equivalently, Just and Carpenter (1992) suggested that working memory consisted of a large set of processing resources, only a subset of which was used for a given domain.

Nonetheless, findings of this nature can always be attributed to the existence of a single processing component that has access to a number of domain-specific representational systems. Consequently, the efficiency of working memory (and therefore its functional capacity) would depend on the processing characteristics of the specific task being performed. In fact, Daneman and Green (1986) offered exactly this interpretation of their own findings, thus enabling them to abandon the assumption that working memory had a unitary capacity but to retain the idea that it was a single system. It follows that correlational research using the reading-span paradigm can provide only weak evidence as to the structure and organization of working memory. More convincing evidence comes from the research on brain-damaged patients mentioned earlier. In particular, De Renzi and Nichelli (1975) described two cases with selective impairment of verbal short-term memory but with intact spatial short-term memory, and two cases with the opposite pattern of performance. This implies that the mechanisms responsible for verbal and spatial short-term memory are functionally dissociable.

Verbal and Visuospatial Working Memory

Within the framework originally put forward by Baddeley and Hitch (1974), of course, such findings can be accommodated by positing a general-purpose central executive supported by various domain-specific subsidiary systems. I suggested above that the latter systems were not in fact involved in the reading-span task, and Daneman and Tardif (1987) argued that their results could not be readily accommodated within Baddeley and Hitch's account. In particular, the absence of a correlation between spatial span and reading comprehension appeared to be inconsistent with the notion that one single executive processor was implicated both in reading and in other forms of cognitive functioning. As I mentioned in Chapter 1, however, Engle et al. (1992) questioned the validity of Daneman and Tardif's results. Moreover, other researchers have carried out experiments in line with the framework devised by Baddeley and Hitch to try to confirm the postulated functional independence of the phonological loop and the visuospatial scratchpad.

Farmer, Berman, and Fletcher (1986) studied the effects of concurrent tasks on performance in a "verbal-reasoning" task in which subjects judged whether a statement described the order of two letters (for example, "A is not followed by B—BA") and on performance in a "spatial-reasoning" task in which subjects identified which hand of a manikin figure held a target stimulus. Concurrent articulatory suppression impaired performance on the verbal task (especially on more difficult negative statements), but it had no effect upon performance in the spatial task. Conversely, a concurrent task involving guided hand movements had no effect upon performance in the verbal task, but it produced slower responses in the spatial task when the manikin was presented in an inverted orientation. These results were held to be consistent with the framework proposed by Baddeley and Hitch (1974), although the magnitude of the effects that had been obtained indicated that the role of the postulated slave systems in this task was rather limited.

Morris (1987) showed that the short-term recall of a visual pattern was disrupted by a task requiring irrelevant guided hand movements without any visual feedback and also by a concurrent verbal memory load, but not by articulatory suppression. (These findings were recently replicated by Toms, Morris, & Ward, 1993.) Morris also found that the short-term recall of auditory sequences of letters was disrupted by guided movements and by articulatory suppression. This suggested that the movement task had made demands upon the visuospatial scratchpad and the central executive, while articulatory suppression had only affected the phonological loop. Morris (1989) subsequently showed that irrelevant guided hand movements impaired the short-term recall of visual sequences of letters, but mainly when they were presented at unpredictable locations within a display. He concluded that spatial monitoring depleted the attentional resources used to encode visually presented items.

Smyth and Pelky (1992) similarly found that the short-term recall of sequences of locations was impaired by a brief retention interval in which the subjects were required either to carry out irrelevant guided movements with visual feedback or to count backwards from a three-digit number. In contrast, the short-term recall of sequences of digits was affected by backwards counting but not by guided movements. A more detailed analysis of the results suggested that the verbal task could be carried out with the sole support of the phonological loop. However, because the spatial task required the retention of serial-order information, Smyth and Pelky argued that it made demands both upon the representational capacity of the visuospatial scratchpad and also upon the place-keeping functions of the central executive.

These findings are all consistent with the idea of a general-purpose central executive supported by at least two modality-specific subsystems. Nevertheless, Baddeley (in press) recently acknowledged that the results were by no means decisive, and that whether this all-important component of working memory will eventually prove to be "a single coordinated system that serves multiple functions, a true executive, or a cluster of largely autonomous control processes, an executive committee, remains to be seen."

The Phonological Loop

It will be remembered from Chapter 1 that Baddeley and Hitch (1974) had originally proffered the idea of a speech-based subsystem to explain why subjects were able to hold a concurrent memory load of up to three items with essentially no effect upon their performance in tests of reasoning, comprehension, or free recall. They described it as "a phonemic response buffer which is able to store a limited amount of speech-like material in the appropriate serial order" (p. 77). Nevertheless, subsequent research indicated that this subsystem was intimately linked to the mechanisms that underlie speech production, and so it was referred to as an "articulatory rehearsal loop," an "articulatory loop system," or simply "an articulatory loop" (Baddeley, 1986; Baddeley, Lewis, & Vallar, 1984; Baddeley et al., 1975).

The evidence obtained to date suggests that this subsystem consists of two components. The first is a short-term phonological store that is operationally defined by the effect of phonemic similarity and the effect of unattended speech. The material that it contains is represented in an abstract phonological code, and it is subject either to interference from or displacement by irrelevant spoken stimuli. The second component is an articulatory control process that is operationally defined by the effect of word length and the effect of articulatory suppression. Although this mechanism can serve as a form of covert rehearsal, its use is prohibited when subjects engage in the concurrent vocalization of irrelevant sounds. With visual presentation, this control process is also needed to convert verbal stimuli into a phonological code.

Some years ago I pointed out that the effect of word length could in principle be attributed to phonological properties of the relevant words. For example, words with long vowels might happen to be more difficult to recall than words with short vowels (Richardson, 1984). In fact, Caplan, Rochon, and Waters (1992) found no difference in recall performance among words that varied in terms of the nature of their associated articulatory gestures when the number of syllables and phonemes was controlled. Because the relevant groups of words did appear to vary in terms of articulatory duration, Caplan et al. (1992) concluded (contrary to Baddeley et al., 1975) that the word-length effect should be attributed to the phonological structure of the words to be recalled rather than to their articulatory duration. This conclusion has been disputed by Baddeley and Andrade (1994), although Caplan and Waters (1994) have reiterated their original position. Nevertheless, the latter does not explain why immediate memory varies with articulation rate across different subjects when tested on the same stimulus material (Baddeley et al., 1975, Exp. VI).

Another possibility is that longer words take longer to say aloud or to write down, and so recalling them in a memory experiment might lead to forgetting of words that might otherwise have subsequently been recalled. In fact, Baddeley et al. (1984) recognized this possibility and permitted their subjects to write down long words in an abbreviated form. However, Longoni, Richardson, and Aiello (1993) found that this did not materially affect the level of performance. In the case of oral recall, Cowan, Day, Saults, Keller, Johnson, and Flores (1992) showed that there was in fact appreciable forgetting caused by the delay in articulating previous words.

This was confirmed by Avons, Wright, and Pammer (1994), who found that the word-length effect was much smaller when using probed recall for a single item in each sequence than when using full serial recall for all the items in a sequence. Nevertheless, Cowan et al. (1992) acknowledged that their account could not explain why the word-length effect disappears under conditions of articulatory suppression (nor, indeed, can it handle effects of word length obtained with written recall if the number of letters in long and short words is controlled: see, for example, Longoni et al., 1993).

I mentioned in Chapter 1 that studies of brain-damaged patients with acquired anarthria (who have lost a capacity to articulate speech sounds) have found that these patients may continue to demonstrate the effects of phonemic similarity and word length that are supposed to be diagnostic of the operation of the articulatory loop. More specifically, these findings seem to show a dissociation between deficits of articulatory rehearsal and deficits of articulatory translation (Cubelli & Nichelli, 1992). Waters, Rochon, and Caplan (1992) studied stroke patients with speech apraxia, who are impaired in speech planning or programming, but who are not anarthric. These patients showed no effect of phonemic similarity with visual stimuli and no effect of word length under either auditory or visual presentation. This pattern of results implies that acquired disorders of speech planning disrupt the articulatory translation of visual stimuli into phonological representations and the articulatory rehearsal of these representations in working memory. However, one or other of these functions may be preserved in patients with acquired disorders of speech output (i.e., anarthria).

Moreover, Bishop and Robson (1989) found that both functions seemed to be intact in children with congenital anarthria. They concluded:

> Rehearsal in short-term memory . . . must involve coding material in a phonological representation that is available to individuals who have never produced speech. We suggest that this is an abstract phonological representation, which, in normal individuals, would provide the input to a system that derives a speech motor program but does not itself contain an articulatory specification. (p. 139)

Baddeley (1990, p. 87) concluded that inner speech was not dependent upon outer speech for either its development or its operation and that the term "phonological loop" might be preferable to "articulatory loop" because the latter implied a direct involvement of articulation.

I have previously argued that this argument is unconvincing, for it flies in the face of the substantial evidence that (in normal individuals, at least) the word-length effect does indeed imply a direct involvement of articulation, not least because it is abolished when subjects are required to engage in articulatory suppression (Richardson, 1993). Instead, I put forward the view that the vocabulary of articulatory gestures was innate, based upon evidence that the phonological structure of all human languages was derived from a common set of distinctive articulatory features. This position had in fact been inferred by Liberman and Mattingly (1985) from an extensive body of evidence, although, as Bishop (1988) pointed out, it cannot readily account for the relatively restricted phonology that is observed in normal children when they first begin to speak.

On the face of it, the findings obtained with congenitally anarthric children can only be reconciled with the established evidence from normal individuals by assuming that articulatory rehearsal can be established in the absence of intelligible speech. Baddeley and Logie (1992) suggested that anarthric children had acquired the link between audition and speech automatically. I have argued that this is improbable, as they would have no information beyond heard sounds that might afford the establishment of such a link (Richardson, 1993). Nevertheless, in Chapter 2, Robert Logie spelled out how the effects of articulatory rehearsal and of articulatory suppression might represent the repeated activation of phonological traces in long-term memory, and how similar effects could be obtained in children who had failed to develop any coherent form of subvocal articulation.

Baddeley and Hitch's (1974) original account of the phonemic response buffer suggested a relatively unimportant mechanism that supplemented the storage capacity of the central executive processor when necessary but did not have a central role in cognitive functioning. As was mentioned above, subsequent work indicates that this system only contributes to performance in tasks requiring the accurate retention of serial-order information. Nevertheless, all human languages depend on sequential information to some extent, and a number of linguistic abilities seem to demand the resources of the phonological loop (see Baddeley, 1992; Logie, 1993). For instance, skilled readers take longer to read tongue-twisters (i.e., sentences where the same initial phonemes are repeated across different words) and also to decide immediately afterwards whether two words are presented in the order in which they had occurred in such a sentence; this suggests that phonemic information maintained in working memory is used in sentence comprehension (McCutchen, Dibble, & Blount, 1994). (For reasons discussed earlier, this may well not occur in tests of reading span, however.)

Moreover, the effects of unattended speech in serial recall indicate that the phonological store might have a crucial—although as yet largely uninvestigated—role in speech perception. Recent research has indicated that no disruption is generated by a single speech sound repeated either continuously or intermittently (Jones, Madden, & Miles, 1992), but that an effect of roughly the same magnitude as that produced by naturally occurring speech is generated by a continuous stream of vowel sounds and even by continuous random pitch glides if these are interrupted by short periods of silence (Jones, Macken, & Murray, 1993). This implies that the phonological store is accessed by a changing stream of irrelevant acoustic stimuli that are segmented either physically or categorically.

Macken and Jones (1995) found that the effects of articulatory suppression were enhanced both by changing state (i.e., repeating a single letter vs. repeating a sequence of different letters) and by vocalization of the speech sounds. This suggested that the memory codes from auditory, visual, and articulatory sources were functionally equivalent. However, with visual presentation the phonemic similarity effect is abolished by the vocalization of a single syllable (e.g., "the": Murray, 1967, 1968), which suggests that any additional effects of changing state must arise elsewhere than in the phonological store. Again, with visual presentation the phonemic similarity effect is abolished by silent mouthing of a series of syllables (Saito, 1993), which suggests that any additional effects of vocalization must also arise elsewhere than in the phonological store.

The final issue to be considered is the purpose of the relationship between the phonological store and the articulatory rehearsal process. As mentioned in Chapter 1, the contents of the phonological store are often assumed to be vulnerable to rapid decay within a period of 1 to 2 seconds, unless they can be refreshed by means of articulatory rehearsal (Baddeley, 1986, pp. 92–96; 1990, p. 72). In other words, an important function of either overt or covert articulation is supposedly to maintain the contents of the phonological store in the face of trace decay. Nevertheless, the evidence for any process of trace decay in verbal learning is actually indirect and rather weak (see Richardson, Longoni, & Di Masi, 1995, for discussion).

One of the anarthric patients tested by Cubelli and Nichelli (1992) did not show any effects of word length and was therefore viewed as having a selective impairment of the articulatory rehearsal mechanism. Although her digit span was slightly reduced (five items), she showed no evidence of forgetting when tested on the recall of consonant trigrams or the delayed matching of pairs of digits over unfilled intervals of up to 15 seconds. In Chapter 2, Robert Logie described an experiment by Longoni et al. (1993) using normal subjects; here, the phonemic similarity effect in serial recall persisted through a retention interval of 10 seconds in which subjects were required to engage in articulatory suppression. Indeed, Richardson et al. (1995) confirmed this with retention intervals of up to 20 seconds. We therefore concluded that the total duration of the phonological trace may well be longer than had been supposed by Baddeley and his colleagues, and that the importance of trace decay as a mechanism of forgetting in working memory may be very limited. The same conclusion would presumably apply pari passu to accounts of short-term forgetting based upon the decay of activation within long-term memory.

The Visuospatial Scratchpad

The possibility of a visual subsystem had been envisaged in Baddeley and Hitch's (1974) original theory of working memory, but the evidence on the nature and function of this subsystem has mainly been obtained during the last 10 to 15 years. It will be recalled from both Chapters 1 and 2 that different researchers have found that visual short-term memory can be disrupted by requiring subjects to engage in irrelevant movements, but also by presenting them with irrelevant visual material. The evidence has indeed tended to converge on a picture that is pleasingly symmetrical with current accounts of the phonological loop. As Robert Logie explained in Chapter 2, it appears likely that visual short-term memory is supported by a system that incorporates an "inner eye" (which has direct links with the processes that underlie visual perception) and an "inner scribe" (which enables visual material to be maintained by a form of spatial rehearsal that can be blocked or suppressed by irrelevant directed movements).

In the study by Morris (1987) that was mentioned earlier, irrelevant guided hand movements disrupted short-term memory for a visual pattern if they were performed during the stimulus presentation, but not if they were performed only during a subsequent 10-second retention interval. This would suggest that irrelevant movements disrupt the encoding of information, but do not themselves occupy storage capacity in the visuo-spatial scratchpad. However, Smyth and Pelky (1992) found that short-term memory for sequences of locations was disrupted by irrelevant hand movements performed during a retention interval of either 5 or 15 seconds. Taken together, these findings indicate that the maintenance of spatial sequences demands some form of spatial rehearsal that can be disrupted by irrelevant movements, but that the maintenance of a single integrated spatial pattern does not. However, this rehearsal process does not seem to be based upon some internal analog of overt movement, because the recall of sequences of spatial targets does not vary with the time taken to move between them (Smyth & Scholey, 1994).

Baddeley and Lieberman (1980) found that performance in visuospa-tial short-term memory was not significantly impaired by a concurrent task that involved judgments of the relative brightness of visual stimuli. How-ever, Beech (1984) observed that this finding had been based on a sample of only eight subjects, and he obtained a significant impairment in three separate experiments using exactly the same brightness-judgment task. In addition, Logie (1986) showed that concurrently presented visual pat-terns disrupted serial recall when subjects were using a mnemonic device based upon mental imagery. Toms, Morris, and Foley (1994) demon-strated that the exposure to irrelevant visual stimuli did have a specific effect on performance in the visuospatial memory task that had been em-ployed by Baddeley and Lieberman (1980). The level of disruption was roughly the same, whether the stimuli were presented concurrently with the material to be remembered or during a 20-second retention interval, and whether they consisted of a simple constant pattern or a changing complex display. These results tend to suggest that irrelevant visual stimuli gain obligatory access to a visuospatial memory and disrupt the storage and the maintenance of task-relevant information.

Nevertheless, there is evidence that movements directed to particular locations are represented in a different system from nondirected movements of different parts of the body (such as raising one's left leg or crossing one's arms). Smyth, Pearson, and Pendleton (1988) showed that the recall of sequences of familiar movements was impaired by concurrent body-related movements, but not by articulatory suppression or by concurrent movements directed to external spatial targets. Conversely, the recall of sequences of spatial locations was impaired by movements directed to spatial targets but not by articulatory suppression or concurrent body-related movements. Similar results were obtained by Smyth and Pendleton (1989), who suggested that the maintenance of representations in the visuospatial scratchpad employs the mechanisms responsible for movements directed toward external spatial targets, but that the retention of sequences of familiar movements of parts of the body involves a functionally distinct subsystem of working memory that is relatively specific to movement configurations.

The Central Executive

I mentioned in Chapter 1 that most early multicomponent models of working memory tended to assume that the central executive might itself function as an information store. I also mentioned earlier in the present chapter that North American researchers tend to equate their own interpretation of "working memory" with the notion of the central executive as a mechanism that has both processing and storage functions (even though some of these could be discharged to auxiliary subsystems). This idea was contradicted by the sort of account given by Baddeley (1986, 1990, 1993), in which the central executive was a general attentional resource that coordinated the contributions of the various storage subsystems but did not itself have storage capability.

If the major role of the central executive is to coordinate cognitive processes and their execution rather than to provide a memory substrate, Morris and Jones (1990) argued that it would be involved in the dynamic aspects of real-time processing in working memory and not in the passive maintenance of memory loads. They tested this prediction in the "running memory" task in which subjects are presented with sequences of items of an unknown length and then attempt to recall a specific number (six, say) of the most recent items. As expected, both irrelevant speech and articulatory suppression impaired performance in this task, but their effects were independent of the overall length of the sequence and hence of the number of occasions when the subjects had been required to update working memory. Morris and Jones inferred that memory updating was not carried out by the phonological loop but was a function of the central executive itself.

Further evidence about the function of the central executive has come from research into reasoning. Baddeley and Hitch (1974; Hitch & Baddeley, 1976) studied performance in the "verbal-reasoning" task mentioned earlier in which subjects decided whether a sentence correctly described the order of presentation of two letters of the alphabet. They found that subjects' response latencies were slower with a concurrent memory load of six items, although not with memory loads of one or two items, and only when subjects were specifically instructed to achieve correct recall of the memory load. The subjects' response latencies were also slower if they were required to engage in articulatory suppression or if the letters to be compared were phonemically similar to one another (e.g., BP or SF rather than SV or YX). The accuracy of responding was maintained at a high level throughout and showed no systematic variation with any of the experimental manipulations, but Farmer et al. (1986) subsequently found that articulatory suppression impaired both speed and accuracy in this task. The findings obtained by Baddeley and Hitch (1974) led them to conclude that their task depended upon a limited-capacity central executive and a peripheral articulatory system.

Nevertheless, one might question whether it was appropriate to refer to this sort of simple verification task as a test of "reasoning" at all. Kyllonen and Christal (1989) included it in a battery of tests that were assumed to measure the capacity of Baddeley and Hitch's working memory in that they required the simultaneous processing and storage of information. A factor analysis of data obtained from a large-scale correlational study showed that all of the relevant tests (including the sentence-verification task and both quantitative and verbal tests) had loadings of more than .6 on a single factor. Kyllonen and Christal regarded this as evidence that working-memory capacity was a unitary, domain-independent construct. They had also included a number of conventional reasoning tests, and these all had high loadings on a separate factor. However, this factor was highly correlated with the first and was defined by a letter-recoding task that had been included to measure the capacity of working memory. Kyllonen and Christal concluded that this second factor represented the executive skill that was needed for effective performance in reasoning and other cognitive tasks demanding attentional and learning capabilities.

In a much more extensive investigation, Kyllonen and Christal (1990) confirmed through four different studies that both working-memory capacity and reasoning ability were identified with two closely associated but separate factors. The sentence-verification task had been included as a "reasoning test" in three of these studies; it loaded on the working-memory factor in the first, but loaded on the reasoning factor in the second and third. This was partly because the reasoning tests seemed to define two different factors, depending on whether they were carried out using pencil and paper or using a computer, and the computerized version of the verification test that was used in this study loaded solely on the latter. The reasoning factors and the working-memory factor were differentiated by the fact that the former were correlated more with the subjects' breadth of general knowledge, whereas working-memory capacity was correlated more with subjects' speed of cognitive processing.

Kyllonen and Christal concluded that individual differences in human reasoning ability were due in part to the breadth of the general knowledge that each subject brought to a particular task, but mainly to the capacity of a domain-independent working memory. Indeed, using a much broader test battery, Kyllonen (1993) showed that the factor which could be identified with the capacity of working memory was essentially coextensive with the conventional psychometric concept of general ability. He concluded that these data were consistent with the assertion that "working memory is *the* general factor in cognition" (p. 401). Nevertheless, this latter factor was quite distinct from the breadth of the general declarative knowledge that the subject brought to a task, which was more closely related to the conventional psychometric concept of verbal ability.

The notion that the limited processing capacity of working memory is a cause of difficulty in human reasoning was put forward by Johnson-Laird (1983), and his account suggested that this should be most evident in the level of accuracy achieved with syllogisms or other varieties of deductive inference (see, e.g., chap. 5). As one indication of this, he mentioned a finding of his own that the accuracy of individual subjects in syllogistic reasoning was correlated with the processing capacity of working memory as measured by a subject's speed in carrying out a continuous letter-recoding task (p. 121). In contrast, in an investigation of conditional reasoning, Evans and Brooks (1981) found that neither articulatory suppression nor a memory load had a significant effect upon the accuracy of performance. A memory load produced significantly slower responses, but articulatory suppression actually led to significantly faster responses. Further experiments that were described by Evans (1982, pp. 245–248) suggested that any effects of these manipulations on conditional reasoning were weak and unreliable.

Evans and Brooks found that the magnitude of the effect of a memory load on response latencies did not vary with the difficulty of individual reasoning problems. This indicated that the items had not been directly competing with the task-relevant information for the limited resources of working memory. Evans and Brooks suggested that their subjects had simply committed these items to long-term memory before attempting the reasoning problems; this would have added a constant delay to their response times, but the items would not have constituted a concurrent load upon working memory itself. However, Halford, Bain, and Maybery (1984) pointed out that in this study, problem difficulty might have varied for reasons other than processing load. They found that the effects of a concurrent memory load did interact with the difficulty of mathematical-reasoning problems when the latter was explicitly defined in relation to processing demands and when the memory load was set at or just above memory span. Halford et al. (1984) concluded that competition between reasoning and short-term retention occurred only when the memory task entailed some form of active processing such as encoding or rehearsal that occurred simultaneously with reasoning.

Gilhooly, Logie, Wetherick, and Wynn (1993) found that performance in syllogistic reasoning was somewhat poorer when the premises were presented auditorily than when they were presented visually. They interpreted this finding to mean that reasoning was impaired if the premises themselves had to be maintained within working memory. In another study, performance in syllogistic reasoning was impaired (in terms of both speed and accuracy) when the subjects were simultaneously required to carry out random-number generation, but not when they carried out irrelevant guided hand movements or articulatory suppression. Moreover, the reasoning task gave rise to a substantial impairment in random-number generation and also a significant though slight slowing of concurrent articulation, but it had no effect on performance in the manual task. Gilhooly et al. (1993) argued that the central executive had a major role in the reasoning task, that the phonological loop had only a minor role, and that the visuospatial scratchpad was not involved in this task.

Similarly, Toms et al. (1993) noted that Evans and Brooks (1981) had employed a between-subjects design that might have been insensitive to the specific demands imposed by reasoning processes on working memory, and they argued that a more systematic investigation was needed. They found that a verbal memory load selectively reduced the likelihood that subjects would accept (valid) modus tollens inferences (denying the consequent), and that it also produced slower responses on all forms of conditional reasoning. However, neither irrelevant guided-hand movements nor articulatory suppression had any effect upon the accuracy or the latency of reasoning performance. This led Toms et al. (1993) to the view that the visuospatial scratchpad and the phonological loop were not implicated in conditional reasoning. They concluded instead that a memory load had interfered with the strategic deployment of memory constellations and had occupied some of the capacity of an abstract, general workspace required for accurate performance in conditional reasoning, which they identified with the central executive.

It may be noted that this conclusion is inconsistent with the notion that the central executive is simply a general attentional resource that does not itself possess storage capability. Nevertheless, on the basis of a variety of experimental and neuropsychological data, Baddeley (in press) recently suggested that the concept of the central executive should be elaborated in terms of a number of component functions: (a) the capacity to coordinate performance on separate tasks, which seems to be especially impaired in patients with Alzheimer's disease; (b) the capacity to switch retrieval plans or strategies, as reflected in the generation of random sequences of either letters or numbers; (c) the capacity to attend to one stimulus and inhibit the disrupting effect of others, which appears to be impaired in older individuals; and (d) the capacity to hold and manipulate temporarily activated information from long-term memory, as reflected in various measures of reading span. Baddeley was explicit that this was intended to converge with the account that had been developed by Ellen Stoltzfus, Lynn Hasher, and Rose Zacks, as described in Chapter 3 (see also Hasher

& Zacks, 1988), and also with the account that had been developed by Randall Engle, as described in Chapter 4.

Conclusion

The arguments and evidence that have been reviewed in this book can be summed up in the following theoretical statements:

1. Working memory is a complex system responsible for the temporary storage and processing of information. It can be studied using a variety of research paradigms, and important evidence has been obtained from the study of both intact individuals and brain-damaged patients.

2. Working memory is structurally and functionally distinct from the different forms of permanent or long-term memory. More specifically, there appears to be a basic dissociation between long-term memory and short-term memory in both the verbal domain and the visuospatial domain.

3. Nevertheless, the contents of working memory consist in the set of representations that are currently being activated by interpretative processes in long-term memory. This provides the mechanism by which semantic knowledge about objects and language can be brought to bear on uninterpreted phenomenal experiences.

4. The effective capacity of working memory is constrained (a) by the limited amount of activation that can be distributed across long-term memory and (b) by the limited attentional resources that are available to activate and maintain task-relevant information and to inhibit and remove task-irrelevant information.

5. The core of this system is a central processor that is involved in a wide variety of executive functions, including the coordination of performance in skilled tasks and the encoding of episodic information in long-term memory. Whether this is a single general-purpose component or several distinct and autonomous components is still an open question.

6. Some of the storage functions of this central executive can be discharged to auxiliary subsystems that are structurally and functionally distinct from one another but subsidiary to the central executive. These include the phonological loop, the visuospatial scratchpad, and perhaps a third subsystem involved in the representation of familiar body movements.

7. Given the theoretical properties attributed to working memory, it is likely to be fundamental in understanding intellectual performance, not just in the experimental laboratory but also in everyday situations in general. Equally, working memory is likely to be of crucial importance in explaining variations among individuals and

among groups of individuals in how they respond to the cognitive demands both of psychological experiments and of daily life. As a consequence, the concept of working memory can be expected to play a central role in the future development of cognitive psychology.

References

Anderson, J. R. (1972). FRAN: A simulation model of free recall. In G. H. Bower (Ed.), *The psychology of learning and motivation: Advances in research and theory* (Vol. 5, pp. 315–378). New York: Academic Press.

Anderson, J. R. (1976). *Language, memory, and thought.* Hillsdale, NJ: Erlbaum.

Anderson, J. R. (1983a). *The architecture of cognition.* Cambridge, MA: Harvard University Press.

Anderson, J. R. (1983b). A spreading activation theory of memory. *Journal of Verbal Learning and Verbal Behavior, 22,* 261–295.

Anderson, J. R. (1987). Skill acquisition: Compilation of weak-method problem solutions. *Psychological Review, 94,* 192–210.

Anderson, J. R. (1993). *Rules of the mind.* Hillsdale, NJ: Erlbaum.

Anderson, J. R., & Bower, G. H. (1973). *Human associative memory.* Washington, DC: Winston.

Arbuthnott, K. D. (1995). Inhibitory mechanisms in cognition: Phenomena and models. *Cahiers de Psychologie Cognitive, 14,* 3–45.

Atkinson, R. C., & Shiffrin, R. M. (1968). Human memory: A proposed system and its control processes. In K. W. Spence & J. T. Spence (Eds.), *The psychology of learning and motivation: Advances in research and theory* (Vol. 2, pp. 89–195). New York: Academic Press.

Atkinson, R. C., & Shiffrin, R. M. (1971). The control of short-term memory. *Scientific American, 225*(2), 82–90.

Avons, S. E., Wright, K. L., & Pammer, K. (1994). The word-length effect in probed and serial recall. *Quarterly Journal of Experimental Psychology, 47A,* 207–231.

Baddeley, A. (1986). *Working memory.* Oxford: Oxford University Press.

Baddeley, A. (1990). *Human memory: Theory and practice.* Hove, UK: Erlbaum.

Baddeley, A. (1992). Is working memory working? The fifteenth Bartlett Lecture. *Quarterly Journal of Experimental Psychology, 44A,* 1–31.

Baddeley, A. (1993). Working memory or working attention? In A. Baddeley & L. Weiskrantz (Eds.), *Attention: Selection, awareness, and control. A tribute to Donald Broadbent* (pp. 152–170). Oxford: Oxford University Press.

Baddeley, A. (in press). Exploring the central executive. *Quarterly Journal of Experimental Psychology.*

Baddeley, A., & Andrade, J. (1994). Reversing the word-length effect: A comment on Caplan, Rochon, and Waters. *Quarterly Journal of Experimental Psychology, 47A,* 1047–1054.

Baddeley, A. D., & Hitch, G. (1974). Working memory. In G. H. Bower (Ed.), *The psychology of learning and motivation: Advances in research and theory* (Vol. 8, pp. 47–89). New York: Academic Press.

Baddeley, A. D., & Hitch, G. J. (1977). Recency reexamined. In S. Dornic (Ed.), *Attention and performance VI* (pp. 647–667). Hillsdale, NJ: Erlbaum.

Baddeley, A., Lewis, V. J., & Vallar, G. (1984). Exploring the articulatory loop. *Quarterly Journal of Experimental Psychology, 36A,* 233–252.

Baddeley, A. D., & Lieberman, K. (1980). Spatial working memory. In R. S. Nickerson (Ed.), *Attention and performance VIII* (pp. 521–539). Hillsdale, NJ: Erlbaum.

Baddeley, A., & Logie, R. (1992). Auditory imagery and working memory. In D. Reisberg (Ed.), *Auditory imagery* (pp. 179–197). Hillsdale, NJ: Erlbaum.

Baddeley, A., Logie, R., Nimmo-Smith, I., & Brereton, N. (1985). Components of fluent reading. *Journal of Memory and Language, 24*, 119–131.

Baddeley, A., Papagno, C., & Vallar, G. (1988). When long-term learning depends on short-term storage. *Journal of Memory and Language, 27*, 586–595.

Baddeley, A. D., Thomson, N., & Buchanan, M. (1975). Word length and the structure of short-term memory. *Journal of Verbal Learning and Verbal Behavior, 14*, 575–589.

Basso, A., Spinnler, H., Vallar, G., & Zanobio, M. E. (1982). Left hemisphere damage and selective impairment of auditory verbal short-term memory: A case study. *Neuropsychologia, 20*, 263–274.

Beech, J. R. (1984). The effects of visual and spatial interference on spatial working memory. *Journal of General Psychology, 110*, 141–149.

Besner, D., & Davelaar, E. (1982). Basic processes in reading: Two phonological codes. *Canadian Journal of Psychology, 36*, 701–711.

Bishop, D. (1988). Language development in children with abnormal structure or function of the speech apparatus. In D. Bishop & K. Mogford (Eds.), *Language development in exceptional circumstances* (pp. 220–238). Edinburgh: Churchill Livingstone.

Bishop, D.V.M., & Robson, J. (1989). Unimpaired short-term memory and rhyme judgement in congenitally speechless individuals: Implications for the notion of "articulatory coding." *Quarterly Journal of Experimental Psychology, 41A*, 123–140.

Buschke, H. (1963). Relative retention in immediate memory determined by the missing scan method. *Nature, 212*, 1129–1130.

Cantor, J., & Engle, R. W. (1993). Working-memory capacity as long-term memory activation: An individual-differences approach. *Journal of Experimental Psychology: Learning, Memory, and Cognition, 19*, 1101–1114.

Cantor, J., Engle, R. W., & Hamilton, G. (1991). Short-term memory, working memory, and verbal abilities: How do they relate? *Intelligence, 15*, 229–246.

Caplan, D., Rochon, E., & Waters, G. S. (1992). Articulatory and phonological determinants of word length effects in span tasks. *Quarterly Journal of Experimental Psychology, 45A*, 177–192.

Caplan, D, & Waters, G. S. (1994). Articulatory length and phonological similarity in span tasks: A reply to Baddeley and Andrade. *Quarterly Journal of Experimental Psychology, 47A*, 1055–1062.

Conway, A.R.A., & Engle, R. W. (1994). Working memory and retrieval: A resource-dependent inhibition model. *Journal of Experimental Psychology: General, 123*, 354–373.

Cowan, N. (1988). Evolving conceptions of memory storage, selective attention, and their mutual constraints within the human information-processing system. *Psychological Review, 104*, 163–191.

Cowan, N. (1993). Activation, attention, and short-term memory. *Memory & Cognition, 21*, 162–167.

Cowan, N., Day, L., Saults, J. S., Keller, T. A., Johnson, T., & Flores, L. (1992).

The role of verbal output time in the effects of word length on immediate memory. *Journal of Memory and Language, 31,* 1–17.

Craik, F.I.M. (1968). Two components in free recall. *Journal of Verbal Learning and Verbal Behavior, 7,* 996–1004.

Craik, F.I.M., & Levy, B. A. (1970). Semantic and acoustic information in primary memory. *Journal of Experimental Psychology, 86,* 77–82.

Crowder, R. G. (1976). The locus of the lexicality effect in short-term memory for phonologically identical lists. *Bulletin of the Psychonomic Society, 7,* 361–363.

Cubelli, R., & Nichelli, P. (1992). Inner speech in anarthria: Neuropsychological evidence of differential effects of cerebral lesions on subvocal articulation. *Journal of Clinical and Experimental Neuropsychology, 14,* 499–517.

Daneman, M., & Carpenter, P. A. (1980). Individual differences in working memory and reading. *Journal of Verbal Learning and Verbal Behavior, 19,* 450–466.

Daneman, M., & Carpenter, P. A. (1983). Individual differences in integrating information between and within sentences. *Journal of Experimental Psychology: Learning, Memory, and Cognition, 9,* 561–584.

Daneman, M., & Green, I. (1986). Individual differences in comprehending and producing words in context. *Journal of Memory and Language, 25,* 1–18.

Daneman, M., & Tardif, T. (1987). Working memory and reading skill re-examined. In M. Coltheart (Ed.), *Attention and performance XII: The psychology of reading* (pp. 491–508). Hove, UK: Erlbaum.

De Renzi, E. (1982). *Disorders of space exploration and cognition.* Chichester, UK: Wiley.

De Renzi, E., & Nichelli, P. (1975). Verbal and non-verbal short-term memory impairment following hemispheric damage. *Cortex, 11,* 341–354.

Engle, R. W., Cantor, J., & Carullo, J. J. (1992). Individual differences in working memory and comprehension: A test of four hypotheses. *Journal of Experimental Psychology: Learning, Memory, and Cognition, 18,* 972–992.

Engle, R. W., Carullo, J. J., & Collins, K. W. (1991). Individual differences in working memory for comprehension and following directions. *Journal of Educational Research, 84,* 253–262.

Engle, R. W., Nations, J. K., & Cantor, J. (1990). Is "working memory capacity" just another name for word knowledge? *Journal of Educational Psychology, 82,* 799–804.

Evans, J. St. B. T. (1982). *The psychology of deductive reasoning.* London: Routledge & Kegan Paul.

Evans, J. St. B. T., & Brooks, P. G. (1981). Competing with reasoning: A test of the working memory hypothesis. *Current Psychological Research, 1,* 139–147.

Eysenck, M. W. (1979). Anxiety, learning, and memory: A reconceptualization. *Journal of Research in Personality, 13,* 365–385.

Eysenck, M. W. (1982). *Attention and arousal: Cognition and performance.* Berlin: Springer-Verlag.

Farmer, E. W., Berman, J.V.F., & Fletcher, Y. L. (1986). Evidence for a visuo-spatial scratch-pad in working memory. *Quarterly Journal of Experimental Psychology, 38A,* 675–688.

Gernsbacher, M. A. (1989). Mechanisms that improve referential access. *Cognition, 32,* 99–156.

Gernsbacher, M. A. (1993). Less skilled readers have less efficient suppression mechanisms. *Psychological Science, 4,* 294–298.

Gernsbacher, M. A., & Faust, M. E. (1991). The mechanism of suppression: A Component of general comprehension skill. *Journal of Experimental Psychology: Learning, Memory, and Cognition, 17,* 245–262.

Gernsbacher, M. A., & Faust, M. E. (1995). Skilled suppression. In F. N. Dempster & C. J. Brainerd (Eds.), *Interference and inhibition in cognition* (pp. 295–327). San Diego, CA: Academic Press.

Gernsbacher, M. A., Varner, K. R., & Faust, M. E. (1990). Investigating differences in general comprehension skill. *Journal of Experimental Psychology: Learning, Memory, and Cognition, 16,* 430–445.

Gilhooly, K. J., Logie, R. H., Wetherick, N. E., & Wynn, V. (1993). Working memory and strategies in syllogistic-reasoning tasks. *Memory & Cognition, 21,* 115–124.

Glanzer, M., & Razel, M. (1974). The size of the unit in short-term storage. *Journal of Verbal Learning and Verbal Behavior, 13,* 114–131.

Halford, G. S., Bain, J. D., & Maybery, M. T. (1984). Does a concurrent memory load interfere with reasoning? *Current Psychological Research and Reviews, 3*(2), 14–23.

Hamm, V. P., & Hasher, L. (1992). Age and the availability of inferences. *Psychology and Aging, 7,* 56–64.

Hanley, J. R., Young, A. W., & Pearson, N. A. (1991). Impairment of the visuospatial sketch pad. *Quarterly Journal of Experimental Psychology, 43A,* 101–125.

Hasher, L., & Zacks, R. T. (1988). Working memory, comprehension, and aging: A review and a new view. In G. H. Bower (Ed.), *The psychology of learning and motivation: Advances in research and theory* (Vol. 22, pp. 193–225). San Diego, CA: Academic Press.

Hitch, G. J., & Baddeley, A. D. (1976). Verbal reasoning and working memory. *Quarterly Journal of Experimental Psychology, 28,* 603–621.

Hodges, W. P., & Spielberger, C. D. (1969). Digit-span: An indicant of trait or state anxiety? *Journal of Consulting and Clinical Psychology, 33,* 430–434.

Hulme, C., Maughan, S., & Brown, G.D.A. (1991). Memory for familiar and unfamiliar words: Evidence for a long-term memory contribution to short-term memory span. *Journal of Memory and Language, 30,* 685–701.

Johnson-Laird, P. N. (1983). *Mental models.* Cambridge: Cambridge University Press.

Jones, D. M., & Macken, W. J. (1993). Irrelevant tones produce an irrelevant speech effect: Implications for phonological coding in working memory. *Journal of Experimental Psychology: Learning, Memory, and Cognition, 19,* 369–381.

Jones, D. M., Macken, W. J., & Murray, A. C. (1993). Disruption of visual short-term memory by changing-state auditory stimuli: The role of segmentation. *Memory & Cognition, 21,* 318–328.

Jones, D., Madden, C., & Miles, C. (1992). Privileged access by irrelevant speech to short-term memory: The role of changing state. *Quarterly Journal of Experimental Psychology, 44A,* 645–669.

Just, M. A., & Carpenter, P. A. (1992). A capacity theory of comprehension: Individual differences in working memory. *Psychological Review, 99,* 122–149.

Kintsch, W., & Buschke, H. (1969). Homophones and synonyms in short-term memory. *Journal of Experimental Psychology, 80,* 403–407.

Klapp, S. T., Marshburn, E. A., & Lester, P. T. (1983). Short-term memory does not involve the "working memory" of information processing: The demise of a common assumption. *Journal of Experimental Psychology: General, 112,* 240–264.

Kyllonen, P. C. (1993). Aptitude testing inspired by information processing: A test of the four-sources model. *Journal of General Psychology, 120,* 375–405.

Kyllonen, P. C., & Christal, R. E. (1989). Cognitive modeling of learning abilities: A status report of LAMP. In R. F. Dillon & J. W. Pellegrino (Eds.), *Testing: Theoretical and applied perspectives* (pp. 146–173). New York: Praeger.

Kyllonen, P. C., & Christal, R. E. (1990). Reasoning ability is (little more than) working-memory capacity?! *Intelligence, 14,* 389–433.

La Pointe, L. B., & Engle, R. W. (1990). Simple and complex word spans as measures of working memory capacity. *Journal of Experimental Psychology: Learning, Memory, and Cognition, 16,* 1118–1133.

Liberman, A. M., & Mattingly, I. G. (1985). The motor theory of speech perception revised. *Cognition, 21,* 1–36.

Lindsay, P. H., & Norman, D. A. (1972). *Human information processing: An introduction to psychology.* New York: Academic Press.

Logie, R. H. (1986). Visuo-spatial processes in working memory. *Quarterly Journal of Experimental Psychology, 38A,* 229–247.

Logie, R. H. (1993). Working memory in everyday cognition. In G. M. Davies & R. H. Logie (Eds.), *Memory in everyday life* (pp 173–218). Amsterdam: Elsevier.

Logie, R. H. (1995). *Visuo-spatial working memory.* Hove, UK: Erlbaum.

Longoni, A. M., Richardson, J.T.E., & Aiello, A. (1993). Articulatory rehearsal and phonological storage in working memory. *Memory & Cognition, 21,* 11–22.

MacDonald, M. C., Just, M. A., & Carpenter, P. A. (1992). Working memory constraints on the processing of syntactic ambiguity. *Cognitive Psychology, 24,* 56–98.

Macken, W. J., & Jones, D. M. (1995). Functional characteristics of the "inner voice" and the "inner ear": Single or double agency? *Journal of Experimental Psychology: Learning, Memory, and Cognition, 21,* 436–448.

Masson, M.E.J., & Miller, J. A. (1983). Working memory and individual differences in comprehension and memory of text. *Journal of Educational Psychology, 75,* 314–318.

McCutchen, D., Dibble, E., & Blount, M. M. (1994). Phonemic effects in reading comprehension and text memory. *Applied Cognitive Psychology, 8,* 597–611.

Miller, G. A. (1956). The magical number seven, plus or minus two: Some limits on our capacity for processing information. *Psychological Review, 63,* 81–97.

Miller, G. A., Galanter, E., & Pribram, K. H. (1960). *Plans and the structure of behavior.* New York: Holt.

Morris, N. (1987). Exploring the visuo-spatial scratch pad. *Quarterly Journal of Experimental Psychology, 39A,* 409–430.

Morris, N. (1989). Spatial monitoring in visual working memory. *British Journal of Psychology, 80,* 333–349.

Morris, N., & Jones, D. M. (1990). Memory updating in working memory: The role of the central executive. *British Journal of Psychology, 81,* 111–121.

Murray, D. J. (1967). The role of speech responses in short-term memory. *Canadian Journal of Psychology, 21,* 263–276.

Murray, D. J. (1968). Articulation and acoustic confusability in short-term memory. *Journal of Experimental Psychology, 78,* 679–684.

Norman, D. A. (1968). Toward a theory of memory and attention. *Psychological Review, 75,* 522–536.

Pascual-Leone, J. (1987). Organismic processes for neo-Piagetian theories: A dialectical causal account of cognitive development. *International Journal of Psychology, 22,* 531–570.

Perfetti, C. A., & Lesgold, A. M. (1977). Discourse comprehension and sources of individual differences. In M. A. Just & P. A. Carpenter (Eds.), *Cognitive processes in comprehension* (pp. 141–183). Hillsdale, NJ: Erlbaum.

Ratcliff, G., & Newcombe, F. (1973). Spatial orientation in man: Effects of left, right, and bilateral posterior cerebral lesions. *Journal of Neurology, Neurosurgery, and Psychiatry, 36,* 448–454.

Richardson, J.T.E. (1979). Precategorical acoustic storage and postcategorical lexical storage. *Cognitive Psychology, 11,* 265–286.

Richardson, J.T.E. (1984). Developing the theory of working memory. *Memory & Cognition, 12,* 71–83.

Richardson, J.T.E. (1993). Commentary: Developing the model of working memory. In G. M. Davies & R. H. Logie (Eds.), *Memory in everyday life* (pp. 219–230). Amsterdam: Elsevier.

Richardson, J.T.E., & Baddeley, A. D. (1975). The effects of articulatory suppression in free recall. *Journal of Verbal Learning and Verbal Behavior, 14,* 623–629.

Richardson, J.T.E., Longoni, A. M., & Di Masi, N. (1995). *Plotting the decay of the phonological trace.* Manuscript submitted for publication.

Richardson, J.T.E., & Snape, W. (1984). The effects of closed head injury upon human memory: An experimental analysis. *Cognitive Neuropsychology, 1,* 217–231.

Saito, S. (1993). Phonological similarity effect is abolished by a silent mouthing task. *Perceptual and Motor Skills, 76,* 427–431.

Salamé, P., & Baddeley, A. (1990). The effects of irrelevant speech on immediate free recall. *Bulletin of the Psychonomic Society, 28,* 540–542.

Shallice, T., & Warrington, E. K. (1970). Independent functioning of the verbal memory stores: A neuropsychological study. *Quarterly Journal of Experimental Psychology, 22,* 261–273.

Smyth, M. M., Pearson, N. A., & Pendleton, L. R. (1988). Movement and working memory: Patterns and positions in space. *Quarterly Journal of Experimental Psychology, 40A,* 497–514.

Smyth, M. M., & Pelky, P. L. (1992). Short-term retention of spatial information. *British Journal of Psychology, 83,* 359–374.

Smyth, M. M., & Pendleton, L. R. (1989). Working memory for movements. *Quarterly Journal of Experimental Psychology, 41A,* 235–250.

Smyth, M. M., & Scholey, K. A. (1994). Characteristics of spatial memory span: Is there an analogy to the word length effect, based on movement time? *Quarterly Journal of Experimental Psychology, 47A,* 91–117.

Toms, M., Morris, N., & Foley, P. (1994). Characteristics of visual interference with visuospatial working memory. *British Journal of Psychology, 85,* 131–144.

Toms, M., Morris, N., & Ward, D. (1993). Working memory and conditional reasoning. *Quarterly Journal of Experimental Psychology, 46A,* 679–699.

Turner, M. L., & Engle, R. W. (1989). Is working memory capacity task dependent? *Journal of Memory and Language, 28,* 127–154.

Warrington, E. K., Logue, V., & Pratt, R.T.C. (1971). The anatomical localisation of selective impairment of auditory verbal short-term memory. *Neuropsychologia, 9*, 377–387.

Warrington, E. K., & Shallice, T. (1969). The selective impairment of auditory verbal short-term memory. *Brain, 92*, 885–896.

Waters, G. S., Rochon, E., & Caplan, D. (1992). The role of high-level speech planning in rehearsal: Evidence from patients with apraxia of speech. *Journal of Memory and Language, 31*, 54–73.

Woltz, D. J. (1988). An investigation of the role of working memory in procedural skill acquisition. *Journal of Experimental Psychology: General, 117*, 319–331.

Woltz, D. J. (1990). Repetition of semantic comparisons: Temporary and persistent priming effects. *Journal of Experimental Psychology: Learning, Memory, and Cognition, 16*, 392–403.

Woltz, D. J., & Shute, V. J. (1993). Individual difference in repetition priming and its relationship to declarative knowledge acquisition. *Intelligence, 17*, 333–359.

Author Index

Aiello, A., 58–59, 64, 138, 152
Alexander, J., 38, 65
Allport, D. A., 41, 60, 67, 83
Anderson, J. R., 7–9, 24, 76, 83, 98, 100, 110, 116, 118, 121–24, 127–28, 130, 148
Anderson, M. C., 111, 116
Anderson, P. A., 68–69, 86
Andrade, J., 138, 148
Andres, D., 74, 85
Antonis, B., 41, 60
Arbuckle, T. Y., 74, 83, 85
Arbuthnott, K. D., 126–27, 148
Ashbrook, P. W., 80, 84
Atkinson, R. C., 4–6, 8–9, 24, 33–34, 40, 60, 120–21, 148
Attig, M. S., 16, 30
Avons, S. E., 139, 148

Babcock, R. L., 37, 65, 89, 108, 119
Baddeley, A. D., v, 5, 11–12, 17–27, 29–30, 33–34, 36, 41–42, 44–53, 57–58, 60–61, 63–64, 66, 68, 77, 83, 92–94, 109–10, 116–17, 121–22, 129–32, 135–44, 146–49, 151, 153
Bain, J. D., 145, 151
Baker, S., 52, 63
Baldwin, J. M., 89, 117

Baltes, P. B., 82–83
Basso, A., 129, 149
Beech, A., 82–83
Beech, J. R., 21, 25, 142, 149
Benton, S. L., 90, 117–18
Ben-Zur, H., 75, 86
Berman, J. V. F., 41, 62, 136–37, 150
Besner, D., 38, 50, 61, 134, 149
Bhatt, A., 81, 86
Bishop, D. V. M., 20, 25, 51, 61, 139–40, 149
Bisiach, E., 54, 61
Bjork, R. A., 111–12, 116–17
Bjorklund, D. F., 82–83
Blanchard-Fields, F., 80, 86
Blaxton, T. A., 80, 83
Blossom-Stach, C., 51, 64
Blount, M. M., 140, 152
Bobrow, D. G., 22, 28
Boswell, D. A., 82–83
Bower, G. H., 8, 24, 121–22, 128, 148
Bradford, D. C., 71, 83
Brereton, N., 11, 25, 36, 61, 68, 83, 135, 149
Bressi, S., 41–42, 61
Broadbent, C., 20, 27
Brooks, P. G., 145–46, 150

Brown, G. D. A., 38, 63, 134, 151
Bruce, V., 53, 65
Buchanan, M., 18, 25, 49, 61, 122, 149 Budayr, B., 72, 84
Burke, D. M., 78, 83
Buschke, H., 128, 132, 149, 151
Butler, R. W., 92, 117

Cantor, J., 8, 13, 15, 17, 25–26, 37, 62, 67, 84, 89, 91, 98–100, 117, 124, 127, 131, 133, 149–50
Caplan, D., 40, 61, 138–39, 149, 154
Cappa, S. F., 20, 30
Carlson, M. C., 81, 83
Carpenter, P. A., vi-vii, 7, 10–14, 23, 25–27, 35–37, 40–41, 43, 55, 62–63, 68–69, 84–86, 89–90, 115, 117–18, 124, 127, 131–32, 134–36, 150–52
Carullo, J. J., 13, 15, 26, 37, 62, 67–68, 84, 90–91, 117, 124, 133, 150
Case, R. D., 23, 25, 37, 61
Chalmers, P., 52, 63
Chapman, M., 23–25
Charness, N., 38, 61
Chase, W. G., 38, 62
Christal, R. E., 89, 118, 144–45, 152
Claridge, G., 82–83
Clark, M. B., 115, 119
Cochran, K. F., 90, 118
Cohen, J. D., 82–83
Cohn, N. B., 71, 83
Colle, H. A., 19, 26
Collins, A. M., 7, 26
Collins, K. W., 15, 26, 68, 84, 90, 117, 133, 150
Comalli, P. E., Jr., 71, 84
Connelly, S. L., 72–73, 79, 81, 82 *n.* 1, 83–84, 86
Conrad, R., 33, 49, 61
Conway, A. R. A., 17, 26, 101–7, 110, 113–14, 117, 131, 149
Cooper, L. A., 54, 61, 65
Cowan, N., 8, 26, 37–38, 41, 55, 61, 66, 84, 122, 138–39, 149–50
Craik, F. I. M., 34, 61–62, 70, 84, 132–34, 150
Cranston, M., 16, 30, 114, 119

Cremer, R., 71, 84
Crowder, R. G., 52, 62, 134, 150
Cubelli, R., 20, 26, 139, 141, 150
Cunitz, A. R., 33, 62

Dalrymple-Alford, E. C., 72, 84
Daneman, M., 10–14, 23, 26, 35–37, 62, 67–69, 84, 89, 90, 109, 115, 117, 124, 131–32, 134–36, 150
Davelaar, E., 38, 50, 61, 134, 149
Day, L., 138–39, 149
Decker, S., 39, 64
De Groot, A. D., 38, 62
Delaney, S. M., 54, 65
Della Sala, S., 41–42, 52, 59, 61–63
Dempster, F. N., 82, 84, 110–11, 117
De Renzi, E., 129, 136, 150
DeSchepper, B. G., 72, 87
Detweiler, M., 92, 119
Diaz, D. L., 78, 83
Dibble, E., 140, 152
Di Masi, N., 141, 153
Donchin, E., 41, 63
Doren, B., 16, 30
Driver, J., 116, 119
Dulaney, C., 75, 84
Dusek, J., 79, 85
Dustman, R. E., 71, 83

Eldridge, M., 49, 61
Ellis, H. C., 80, 84
Ellis, N. C., 51, 62
Engle, R. W., vi, 8, 13–15, 17, 23, 25–27, 30, 35, 37, 41, 62, 65, 67–69, 72, 82, 84, 89–107, 109–10, 112–14, 116–17, 119, 122, 124, 126–27, 131–33, 135–36, 147, 149–50, 152–53
Ericsson, K. A., 7, 26, 38–39, 62
Evans, J. St. B. T., 145–46, 150
Eysenck, M. W., 17, 26, 80, 84, 125, 150

Farmer, E. W., 41, 62, 136–37, 144, 150
Faust, M. E., 76, 82, 82 *n.* 1, 85, 87–88, 115, 117, 126–27, 151

Fillion, D. L., 71, 86–87
Fillmore, C. J., 8, 26
Findler, N. V., 7, 26
Finke, R. A., 53, 62
Fletcher, Y. L., 41, 62, 136–37, 150
Flores, L., 138–39, 149
Foley, P., 142, 153
Fraser, I. H., 53, 62
Fraser, L., 112, 119

Galanter, E., 3, 28, 120, 152
Gathercole, S. E., 24, 26
Gerard, L., 76–77, 84
Gernsbacher, M. A., 76, 82, 84–85, 115, 117, 126–27, 150–51
Giambra, L. M., 78, 85
Gilhooly, K. J., 49, 62–63, 145–46, 151
Glanzer, M., 33, 62, 132–33, 151
Glover, J. A., 90, 117
Gold, D. P., 74, 83, 85
Goldberg, J., 37, 61
Goldman, S. R., 10–11, 29
Goldman-Rakic, P. S., 92, 117
Goldstein, D., 72, 88
Goldstein, M., 82, 87
Gopher, D., 22, 28, 48, 64
Graf, P., 54, 62, 79, 85
Grant, S., 21, 25
Greaves, D. E., 20, 29
Green, I., 11–12, 26, 90, 117, 132, 135–36, 150
Groisser, D., 82, 87

Hager, L. D., 114–15, 119
Hale, S., 108, 117
Halford, G. S., 23–24, 27, 145, 151
Halliday, M. S., 52, 63
Halligan, P. W., 54, 63
Hamilton, G., 15, 25, 89, 117, 131, 149
Hamm, V. P., 16, 27, 30, 75, 85, 125, 151
Hanley, J. R., 20, 27, 129, 151
Harnishfeger, K. K., 82–83
Harrold, R. M., 78, 83
Hartley, J. T., 69, 85
Hartman, M., 75, 79, 85
Hasher, L., vi, 15–17, 27, 30, 37, 41, 55, 63, 67, 70–81, 82 *n.* 1,

83–88, 89, 108, 111, 118, 121, 125, 131, 146–47, 151
Hennelly, R. A., 51, 62
Heron, C., 114–15, 119
Hess, T. M., 75, 85
Hill, J. M., 92, 117
Hitch, G. J., v, 17–18, 20–22, 25, 27, 48, 52, 61, 63, 121, 130–32, 136–38, 140–41, 143–44, 148, 151
Hodges, W. P., 125, 151
Horne, J., 81, 85
Howard, D. V., 78–79, 85
Hoyer, W. J., 71, 81, 87
Hulme, C., 38–39, 59, 63, 134, 151
Hunt, E., 48, 65

Jackson, P., 6, 27
Jacoby, L. L., 79, 85, 110, 112, 118
James, W., 32–33, 63
Janowsky, J. S., 4, 30
Jennings, J. M., 70, 84
Johnson, T., 138–39, 149
Johnson-Laird, P. N., 145, 151
Jones, D. M., 24, 27, 60 *n.* 1, 63, 132, 140–41, 143, 151–52
Jones, W. P., 100, 118
Just, M. A., 7, 9–10, 15, 25, 27, 35–37, 40–41, 43, 55, 63, 69, 85–86, 90, 115, 118, 124, 127, 131, 135–36, 151–52

Kahneman, D., 15, 27
Kail, R. V., 108, 118
Kane, M. J., 72, 82 *n.* 1, 86
Kausler, D. H., 75–76, 79, 86–87
Keller, T. A., 138–39, 149
Kelly, C. M., 112, 118
Kemper, S., 82, 86
Kiewra, K. A., 90, 118
King, J., 35, 63, 90, 115, 118
Kintsch, W., 8–10, 27, 38, 62, 128, 151
Klahr, D., 6–7, 28
Klapp, S. T., 5, 27, 41, 63, 130, 132, 151–52
Kleim, D. M., 79, 86
Kliegl, R., 77, 86
Koriat, A., 75, 86
Kosslyn, S. M., 53, 63

Kraft, R. G., 90, 117
Kurland, D. M., 37, 61
Kyllonen, P. C., 89, 91, 109, 118,
    144–45, 152
Kynette, D., 82, 86

Labouvie-Vief, G., 80, 86
LaCount, K., 74, 87
Laiacona, M., 52, 63
Langley, P., 6–7, 28
Lapinski, R. H., 78, 88
La Pointe, L. B., 15, 27, 122,
    132–33, 152
Lasaga, M. I., 78, 85
Laver, G. D., 78, 86
Layton, B., 71, 86
Lesgold, A. M., 10–11, 29, 89, 118,
    124, 153
Lester, P. T., 5, 27, 130, 151–52
Lewis, V. J., 19, 25, 49, 51, 61, 138,
    148
Levy, B. A., 21, 27, 51, 63, 132, 150
Liberman, A. M., 140, 152
Lieberman, K., 21, 25, 53, 61, 142,
    149
Light, L. L., 68–70, 79, 86
Lindenberger, U., 77, 86
Lindsay, P. H., 8, 27, 29, 121, 152
Liu, Y., 41, 65
Locke, J., 32, 59, 63
Lockhart, R. S., 34, 61–62
Loftus, E. F., 7, 26
Logie, R. H., v-vi, 8, 11, 14, 17, 21,
    25, 28, 36, 39, 41–42, 45–53,
    61–64, 68, 83, 89, 109–10,
    121–22, 127–29, 133, 135,
    140–42, 145–46, 149, 151–52
Logue, V., 129, 153–54
Longoni, A. M., 58–59, 64, 138–39,
    141, 152–53

MacDonald, M. C., 69, 86, 90, 115,
    124, 152
Macken, W. J., 60 *n*. 1, 63, 132,
    140–41, 151–52
Madden, C., 140, 151
Madden, D. J., 71, 81, 86
Mane, A., 41, 63
Marcel, A. J., 54, 64
Marchetti, C., 52–53, 62–63

Marshall, J. C., 54, 63
Marshburn, E. A., 5, 27, 130,
    151–52
Martin, M., 89, 118
Martin, R. C., 51–52, 64
Masson, M. E. J., 11, 14, 28,
    131–33, 152
Mattingly, I. G., 140, 152
Maughan, S., 38, 63, 134, 151
May, C. P., 81, 82–83 *n*. 1, 86
Maybery, M. T., 145, 151
McAndrews, M. P., 78, 85
McCutchen, D., 140, 152
McDowd, J. M., 71–72, 86–87
McLaughlin, G. H., 23, 28
McWilliams, J., 82–83
Mergler, N., 82, 87
Miles, C., 140, 151
Miller, G. A., 3–7, 28, 31, 64, 120,
    122, 130, 152
Miller, J. A., 11, 14, 28, 131–33,
    152
Milner, B., 33, 64–65
Mitchell, D. R. D., 89, 108, 119
Moizo, C., 23, 28
Monsell, S., 20, 28
Morra, S., 23, 28
Morris, N., 21, 28, 137, 142–43,
    152–53
Morris, R. G., 44, 64
Murray, A. C., 140, 151
Murray, D. J., 51, 64, 141, 152

Nakagawa, A., 115, 118
Nations, J. K., 13, 26, 133, 150
Navon, D., 22, 28, 48, 64, 67, 87
Neches, R., 6–7, 28
Neill, W. T., 16, 28, 72, 87, 116,
    118
Nettick, A., 41, 63
Neumann, E., 72, 87
Newcombe, F., 129, 153
Newell, A., 6–7, 28
Nichelli, P., 20, 26, 129, 136, 139,
    141, 150
Nimmo-Smith, I., 11, 25, 36, 61, 68,
    83, 135, 149
Norman, D. A., 6, 8, 22, 27–29, 33,
    65, 121, 128, 152–53
Norman, S., 82, 86

Oakhill, J., 37, 65
Obler, L., 74, 87
Ohlsson, S., 6, 29
Oransky, N., 110
Ormrod, J. E., 90, 118
Oseas-Kreger, D. M., 71–72, 86–87
Ostberg, O., 81, 85

Paivio, A., 53, 64
Palmon, R., 108, 119
Pammer, K., 139, 148
Papagno, C., 129, 149
Parker, D. M., 58, 62
Parkin, A. J., 17, 29, 37, 65
Pascual-Leone, J., 23, 29, 125–26, 153
Pearson, N. A., 21, 30, 129, 143, 151, 153
Pelky, P. L., 137, 142, 153
Pellegrino, J. W., 48, 65
Pendleton, L. R., 21, 30, 53, 65, 143, 153
Pennington, B. F., 82, 87
Pennington, N., 7, 26, 38–39, 62
Perfetti, C. A., 10–11, 29, 89, 118, 124, 153
Perlmutter, N. J., 69, 86
Peters, L., 78, 83
Piaget, J., 23–24
Pitt, M. A., 52, 62
Plake, B. S., 90, 117
Plude, D. J., 71, 81, 87
Polson, P. G., 39, 62
Posner, M. I., 33, 64, 91, 112, 118
Postman, L., 112, 119
Powell, T., 82–83
Pratt, M. W., 82, 87
Pratt, R. T. C., 129, 153–54
Pribram, K. H., 3, 28, 120, 152
Purcell, D. G., 53, 64

Quig, M., 74, 87
Quillian, M. R., 7–8, 29
Quinn, J. G., 21, 29, 53, 64

Raaijmakers, J. G., 111, 119
Rabbitt, P. M. A., 71, 87
Radvansky, G. A., 75–76, 84, 88
Ralston, G. E., 21, 29, 53, 64
Rankin, J. L., 75, 87

Rash, S. R., 82, 86
Ratcliff, G., 129, 153
Ratcliff, R., 100, 119
Razel, M., 132–33, 151
Reisberg, D., 49, 53, 64
Reynolds, P., 41, 60
Richardson, J. T. E., 20, 22, 29, 35, 48, 58–59, 64, 68, 93, 109, 125, 132, 134, 138–41, 152–53
Ritchie, B. G., 115, 119
Roberts, R. J., 114–15, 119
Robins, S. L., 82, 87
Robson, J., 20, 25, 51, 61, 139, 149
Rochon, E., 138–39, 149, 154
Rogers, W., 75, 84
Rorsman, I., 92, 117
Rosen, V., 92–97, 112–13, 119
Rumelhart, D. E., 6, 8, 29
Rypma, B. A., 16, 27, 72, 79, 85, 87, 111, 118

Saariluoma, P., 38, 64
Saito, S., 141, 153
Salamé, P., 19, 29, 48, 50, 64, 132, 153
Salthouse, T. A., 37, 64–65, 70, 87, 89, 108, 119
Saults, J. S., 138–39, 149
Schaafstal, A. M., 52, 63
Schacter, D. L., 54, 62, 65, 79, 85
Schank, R. C., 8, 30
Schlosberg, H., 53–54, 65
Schneider, W., 92, 119
Scholey, K. A., 142, 153
Schraagen, J. M. C., 52, 63
Schvaneveldt, R. W., 78, 88
Schwanenflugel, P. J., 74, 87
Schwartzman, A., 74, 85
Scopesi, A., 23, 28
Servan-Schreiber, D., 82–83
Shallice, T., 4, 22, 28, 30, 40, 65, 128–30, 153–54
Shaw, R. J., 71, 74, 79, 87
Sheffer, D., 75, 86
Shell, P., 7, 25
Sheptak, R., 41, 63
Shiffrin, R. M., 4–6, 8–9, 24, 33–34, 40, 60, 111, 119, 120–21, 148
Shimamura, A. P., 4, 22, 30
Shisler, R. J., 114, 117

Shoben, E. J., 74, 87
Shute, V. J., 90, 109, 119, 123, 154
Simon, H. A., 6, 28
Singh, A., 79, 86
Skovronek, E., 89, 108, 119
Smith, A. D., 75, 87
Smith, M. M. C., 20, 29
Smyth, M. M., 21, 30, 53, 65, 137, 142–43, 153
Snape, W., 125, 153
Snyder, C. R., 91, 112, 118
Spielberger, C. D., 125, 151
Spinnler, H., 41–42, 61, 129, 149
Squire, L. R., 4, 30
Stark, K., 112, 119
Staudinger, U. M., 82–83
Stephens, D. L., 91, 109, 118
Sternberg, S., 100, 114, 119
Stewart, A. L., 53, 64
Stine, E. L., 75, 87
Stoltzfus, E. R., vi, 16, 27, 37, 41, 72, 74, 78, 85–88, 89, 108, 111, 118, 121, 125–27, 146
Sullivan, M. P., 82 *n.* 1, 88

Tardif, T., 12–13, 26, 36, 62, 67, 69, 84, 109, 117, 131, 135–36, 150
Terry, K. M., 16, 28
Teuber, H.-L., 33, 65
Thomson, N., 18, 21, 25, 49, 61, 122, 149
Thurstone, L. L., 92, 119
Tipper, S. P., 16, 30, 72, 88, 114, 116, 119
Toffle, C., 79, 87
Toms, M., 137, 142, 146, 153
Tuholski, S. W., 114, 117
Tulving, E., 54, 65
Tuma, R., 92, 117
Turner, M. L., 13–14, 30, 37, 65, 89, 93, 119, 124, 131–33, 135, 153
Tweedy, J. R., 78, 88

Ulivi, M. S., 72, 88

Valdes, L. A., 16, 28
Valentine, T., 53, 65
Vallar, G., 19–20, 25, 30, 51, 61, 129, 138, 148–49

Van Dijk, T. A., 9–10, 27
Varner, K. R., 82, 85, 126, 151
Vaughan, H. G., 33, 65
Vernon, P. A., 109, 119

Wapner, S., 71, 84
Ward, D., 137, 153
Warrington, E. K., 40, 65, 128–30, 153–54
Waters, G. S., 40, 61, 138–39, 149, 154
Waugh, N. C., 33, 65
Weingartner, A., 48, 65
Welford, A. T., 71, 88
Welsh, A., 19, 26
Welsh, M. C., 82, 87
Werner, H., 71, 84
Wetherick, N. E., 38–39, 49, 59, 62, 65, 145–46, 151
Wetzel, W. F., 51, 64
Whitaker, H. A., 75, 88
White, H., 78, 83
Whitney, P., 115, 119
Wickens, C. D., 41, 48, 65, 109, 119
Wight, E., 21, 25
Wilson, B., 20, 25
Wingfield, A., 75, 87
Woltz, D. J., 123, 154
Woodin, M. E., 52, 63
Woodworth, R. S., 53–54, 65
Wright, K. L., 139, 148
Wright, R., 39, 64
Wynn, V., 49, 52, 62–63, 145–46, 151

Yaffee, L. S., 51, 64
Yee, P. L., 48, 65
Young, A. W., 129, 151
Yuill, N., 37, 65

Zacks, R. T., vi, 15–17, 27, 30, 37, 41, 55, 63, 67, 70–73, 75–77, 80–81, 83–86, 88, 89, 108, 111, 118, 121, 125, 131, 146–47, 151
Zanobio, M. E., 129, 149
Zeef, E. J., 71, 84
Zucco, G., 45–47, 64

Subject Index

Activation, 37–39, 43–45, 47, 51, 54–55, 57–59, 66, 70, 72–76, 91–94, 98–101, 107, 110, 116, 121–23, 126–28, 147
  breadth, 72–74
  sustained, 74–76
Activation-Resource Hypothesis, 110
Adaptive Control of Thought, 9
Age differences, vi, 15–16, 69–82, 125
Alzheimer's disease, 42, 44–45, 146
Anarthria, 20, 51, 139–41
Antisaccade task, 114–15
Anxiety, 125
Articulatory loop, 19, 22, 48, 59, 138. *See also* Phonological loop
Articulatory rehearsal, 19, 33, 48–49, 51–52, 57–59, 122–23, 138–41
Articulatory suppression, 18, 19–20, 49, 51, 57–59, 132, 136–38, 140–41, 143–46
Articulatory translation, 20, 139
Associative networks, 7–9
Attention, 16, 37–38, 48, 71, 91, 107–8, 147
Attentional resources, 22–23, 89, 94–95, 109–10, 122–23
Auditory imagery, 52

Automatic activation, 123
Automatic processing, vi, 15

Brain damage. *See* Frontal lobes; Impairment of short-term memory; Neuropsychological evidence

Capacity of working memory, 31, 33, 35–48, 67–70, 122–24
Central executive, 21–23, 24, 43–47, 122, 131, 140, 146–47
Coding differences, 33–34, 59
Complex learning, 90–91
Complex span, 11–15, 133, 135–36. *See also* Counting span; Reading span; Spatial span
Components of working memory. *See* Multicomponent theories
Concurrent memory load, 18, 21–22, 92–96, 112, 132, 137, 144–46
Concurrent movements. *See* Irrelevant movements
Conditional reasoning, 146
Consciousness, 5
Contemplation, 31–32, 59–60
Contents of working memory, 70–73
Controlled attention, 107–8

161

Controlled processing, vi, 15, 110, 122–23
Counting span, 11–12, 37

Dementia. *See* Alzheimer's disease
Digit span, 10, 39–44, 69, 89, 130. *See also* Immediate memory span
Directed forgetting, 75
Directions, following, 90
Dual-task experiments, 22, 41–49
Dysexecutive syndrome, 22

Effortful processing. *See* Controlled processing
Executive processing, 4, 22
Expertise, 37–39, 52

Fan effect, 76, 98–100, 123
Field of attention, 23
Following directions, 90
Frontal lobes, 4, 92

Gateway hypothesis, 32, 34, 40–41, 50, 54–56, 127–29
General Capacity Theory, 15, 17, 91–93, 107, 110
General concept of working memory, 5, 23
Goals (of subjects), 70, 80

Immediate memory span, 17–18, 23, 89, 122–23, 130, 133–34. *See also* Digit span
Impairment of short-term memory, 19, 40, 50, 128–29, 136
Individual differences, 33, 35–36, 38–39, 52, 67–70, 90–92, 98, 105–10, 115–16
Inhibition, vi, 16–17, 71–78, 81–82, 89, 109–19, 124–27
    benefits of, 81–82
    criticisms of, 77–80
Inhibition-Resource Hypothesis, 110, 113–16
Intellectual development, 125–26
Intelligence, 130
Interference, 71, 76–77, 79–80, 107, 110, 114
Irrelevant information, memory for, 78–80

Irrelevant movements, 21, 43, 53, 136–37, 142–43, 146–47
Irrelevant pictures, 21
Irrelevant speech. *See* articulatory suppression; Unattended speech effect
Irrelevant visual stimuli, 21, 142

Learning to spell, 90
Levels of processing, 34
Listening comprehension, 89–90

"Magical number seven, plus or minus two," 6, 31, 39, 130
Mathematical span, 135
Memory load. *See* Concurrent memory load
Memory span. *See* Immediate memory span
Memory updating, 143
Mental arithmetic, 46–47
Missing scan, 132
Multicomponent theories, v–vi, 13–24, 40–41, 121, 129–31, 137

Negative priming, 16, 71–72, 114, 126
Nelson-Denney Reading Test, 90
Neo-Piagetian theories, 23–24, 125–26
Neuropsychological evidence, 40, 48, 51–52, 54
Newton's laws of motion, 39–40
Nonwords, memory for, 134
Notetaking, 90

Order information, 132–33

Phonemic response buffer, 18–19, 21–22, 138, 140
Phonemic similarity effect, 18–20, 48–49, 52, 58–59, 132, 134, 138–39
Phonological coding, 34, 48–53, 55–59
Phonological loop, 20, 24, 50–53, 55–58, 121, 122, 136, 137–41, 146–47
Phonological store, 19, 48–52, 58–59, 138–41

Plans, 3–4, 22
Primary memory, 31–34, 89, 106–7
Priming effects, 16, 54, 71–72, 78,
    126. *See also* Negative priming
Procedural learning, 123
Production systems, 6–7

Random generation (of letters or
    numbers), 22, 146
Reading comprehension, 9–15,
    34–37, 89–90, 100, 115, 136
Reading span, 11–13, 35–37, 68–69,
    89, 91, 131–36
Reasoning, 49, 143–47
Rehearsal, 34. *See also* Articulatory
    rehearsal
Rehearsal buffer, 5
Resources. *See* Attentional resources
Response competition, 110
Retrieval processes, 76–77, 79–80,
    92–96, 98, 100–7, 111–13, 116
Running memory task, 143

Scholastic Aptitude Test, 11, 90
Secondary memory, 33, 89, 106–7
Selective attention. *See* Attention
Semantic networks, 7
Set-size effect, 100–6, 110, 113
Seven ages of working memory, v,
    31–41
Short-term store, 5, 120–21
Simple span. *See* Digit span;
    Immediate memory span
Spatial neglect. *See* Visual neglect
Spatial span, 12–13, 135–36
Speeded recognition, 17, 98–108

Spelling, 90
Spreading activation, 7–8. *See also*
    Activation
Stress, 125
Suppression. *See* Articulatory
    suppression; Inhibition
Syllogistic reasoning, 145–46

Time of day, 81
Trace decay, 19, 141
Tracking (as secondary task), 41–46

Unattended speech effect, 19–20, 48,
    50, 57, 60 *n*. 1, 132, 138, 140,
    143

Verbal fluency, 92
Verbal versus visual tasks, 136–37
Visual neglect, 54–55
Visuospatial scratchpad, 21, 24,
    48–50, 53–57, 131, 141–43,
    136, 146–47
Vocabulary learning, 90

Word fluency, 92
Word-length effect, 18–19, 49,
    51–52, 59, 132–33, 138–39
Working memory
    as processor, 34, 55
    as short-term memory, 33. *See also*
        Short-term store
    as single flexible system, 33, 37,
        40–43, 46–48, 129–30
    as workspace, 22, 32, 39, 41, 50,
        56
Writing, 90